AN
INTRODUCTION
TO
AUGUSTINE

AN INTRODUCTION TO AUGUSTINE

Robert E. Meagher

New York • New York University Press • 1978

Library of Congress Cataloging in Publication Data

Meagher, Robert E
An introduction to Augustine.

Bibliography: p.
1. Augustinus, Aurelius, Saint, Bp. of Hippo—
Philosophy. 2. Augustinus, Aurelius, Saint, Bp. of
Hippo—Theology. I. Augustinus, Aurelius, Saint, Bp.
of Hippo. Selections. English. 1978. II. Title.
B655.Z7M385   230′.1′40924   77-99085
ISBN 0-8147-5423-6

Manufactured in the United States of America

To my mother,
Marjorie F. Meagher

PREFACE

These reflections on Augustine have emerged in their own way and time, unevenly and unpredictably, in the classroom. In them, I was always teaching and being taught, leading and being led. Inevitably, much of the excitement of insight and discussion fails to survive, as an event is labored into a thing. In the face of this reduction, and as the one most responsible for it, I urge the reader to bring this process to full circle and to speak with others, with Augustine, to learn, and to teach what may surely be learned and taught from the reenacted, rethought memory of his life of deeply personal, deeply human questioning, a life always passionately at peace.

As a teacher who would introduce students to the thought of Augustine, I must and do recognize the primacy of their direct encounter with his writings. And it is this recognition which has led me to place the selected readings at the head of each chapter. If these works are, indeed, primary and stand as the sources from which my commentary and all ensuing discussions appropriately proceed, then they ought to occupy the primary position in this text and in our reading of it. Admittedly, there is awkwardness and disorientation to be endured when one meets an ancient author straight on, without provision, without a program of expectations and interpretations. But surely this pain of not knowing quite what to think or to say, as well as the struggle to come to one's own first thoughts and words, are integral to the work of education, which this book is intended to serve. Ideally the reader's path will come full circle and return to the sources after having been offered whatever guidance my essays might provide.

In the writing of these essays, and in the translation of the texts, I have endeavored to avoid in all instances the use of "man" and of masculine pronouns to denote both men and women. I always before regarded the foreseeable violation of form called for by such an endeavor to exceed and to excuse the violation of human equality implied in conventional usage. But it would be tedious and self-important of me to trace the changing of my own mind in this matter. May it suffice to say that I am no longer able to persuade myself that when we say "man" we really include women. Our intentions here are largely beside the point.

In this and other matters I have frequently sought the counsel and criticism of many fine friends and scholars. I know that I have grown with their response to my work; and that growth is, to a degree, reflected in the final version of this text. Not so as to buttress decisions which in each case remain my responsibility, but rather so as to give grateful recognition to my colleagues and critics in the preparation of this text, I wish to name the following: William Barrett, R. Kenyon Bradt, John S. Dunne, Ernest L. Fortin, Jean Higgins, Hans Jonas, Robert J. O'Connell, William W. O'Grady, John J. O'Meara, and Eugene TeSelle. In addition, I have had two special companions in the preparation of this book: Rachel Kitzenger and Charles M. Sherover. So keen and congenial have been their insights that theirs is a particular presence in this book, which would not be as it is without them. I wish also to extend my appreciation to Malcolm C. Johnson, Jr., Despina Papazoglou, and Hugh van Dusen for their unremitting interest and care in the production of this volume. Finally, my thanks to those who, at various stages in the writing of this manuscript, have lent their skill to one who engraves faster than he types: Thelma

Alward, Barbara Greenspon, Susan Overstreet, and Lenore Platt.

Lastly, I must note my two children, who have consistently preferred my engaging in any other activity to my laboring on this book. Theirs has been a posture of seldom silent long-suffering, which I hope will not be the case for anyone else. Yet, whatever simple human perspective I may have sustained in and out of this book, I owe as much to their interruptions as to anything else, which I trust they know.

R.E.M.

Amherst, Massachusetts

CONTENTS

FOREWORD

Why has St. Augustine become so powerful and interesting a figure for us today? The "interest" I mean here does not have to do with any scholarly reviving of a dead or minor reputation. Augustine is a towering figure, and his major place in history has long since been recognized and fixed. Indeed, in the matter of intellectual influence he has to be reckoned as one of the three major thinkers, along with Plato and Aristotle, that the West has produced; and in point of his actual and direct influence on historical matters he is perhaps greater than these other two. Thus, virtually single-handed, he created Catholic Christianity for the Latin West and so shaped the intellectual and spiritual life of a thousand years of the Middle Ages that followed. He was the dominant authority invoked in the explosive theological controversies of the Protestant Reformation in the sixteenth and seventeenth centuries. And philosophically, he was a constant if uninvoked companion of Descartes throughout the latter's *Meditations*. Subsequently, as our civilization became more and more secular, the figure of Augustine naturally receded, though there was never any question of the diminution of his reputation. But now, in our time, he begins to come closer to us, and there is a certain urgency about this closeness. Why?

I am particularly led to raise this question again after reading Robert Meagher's admirable book, which has the unusual quality in a scholarly work of being thoroughly alive and quickened by its subject. The result is that we enter into the spirit of Augustine's text and become present with him in the particular historical situation he faced. He speaks to us from that unique position in history when a great era of civilization—a whole millennium of pagan classical civilization—is coming to an end and is about to be replaced by something new. And I think that is why, to come back to our opening question, Augustine begins to emerge as a figure peculiarly close and intimate to us now. For we live today with the uneasy feeling that a whole era of the civilization we have known may be coming to an end, indeed cannot escape coming to an end, and, even, must come to an end if human beings are to survive.

Are these apprehensions exaggerated? They are not invented by me; you will find them everywhere in the general consciousness of our times, on the popular as well as intellectual level, sometimes slumbering and unspoken, but at other times galvanized into the loud bark of the media. The rumblings of apocalypse are always with us: the civilization will blow itself up or collapse through internal conflicts. Meanwhile, the new Barbarians (like the ancient ones in Augustine's time) press at our gates. Internally, the human spirit seems to be corroded by self-doubt, as if the civilization had lost belief in its own values. If you doubt all this, look at the bulk of the literature of this century: despair, self-laceration, nihilism— in general, a mournful lament over ourselves as the victims of history. "In the destructive element immerse!" advised one great writer near the beginning of our century; and it is as if most of modern literature, art and music have sought to follow his injunction and sharpen their weapons of destruction and self-dissolution. The end of the novel! The end of the easel painting! The end of diatonic music! These cries have been so persistent that they are by now banal slogans for a culture that seems to find some of its greatest accomplishments exhausted and turns away from them in impotence. And we begin to sense the need of some kind of renewal, the precise nature of which we cannot yet guess.

Consequently, too, we begin to feel closer to a thinker like
Augustine, who was watching a whole world pass away, attempt-
ing to preserve what was of value in it, and at the same time
calling forth and creating the new thing that was to replace it.

That Mr. Meagher does help us to come closer to Augustine is
one of the many virtues of his book. He has not so much written
about Augustine as he has inserted himself into the latter's
thought, and even into his manner, risking a certain incantatory
style to lead us into the incantation of the Augustinian texts
themselves. The risk, in my judgment, succeeds admirably and
manages to convey some of that vast vitality of yearning and love
that is Augustine's. Mr. Meagher seems to me entirely correct in
placing emphasis upon Augustine's historical role in seeking to
preserve the two great heritages—Greek and Hebraic—of a
civilization that was crumbling. He is correct in his bold stroke, for
example, in translating as "blessedness" Aristotle's *eudaimonia,*
usually rendered as "happiness," in order to emphasize the
continuity between Augustine and Greek philosophy. "Happiness" suggests the later utilitarian calculation of the balance of
pleasures over pains. *Eudaimonia,* for the Greek of Aristotle's
time, was something different—the blessedness of a life favored by
the gods and fortune, as well as by a man's own wise management
of himself and his possibilities. Similarly, beatitude *(beatitudo)*
was Cicero's word for happiness, and the Roman of Augustine's
time would have heard this as a part—a part included in a greater
whole, but not rejected—of the latter's meaning. The saints, the
beati, are the richly endowed, but in goods that far surpass the
worldly riches and possessions of the affluent. Augustine intended
his Christian message to be the continuation and the consumma-
tion, not the destruction, of what was best in Greek wisdom.

But if this large framework—as the preserver and continuator of
the two great traditions that have shaped our culture—is the right
context in which to see Augustine, we cannot nevertheless close
our eyes to that other, and personal, dimension of this extraordinary saint. The unique power of Augustine's mind, his genius for
introspective imagination and analysis, at once intricate and
incisive, have never ceased to fascinate his readers. Imagine a
Dostoevski with the systematic intelligence of Kant! Mr. Meagher

does justice to this "existential" Augustine too. The concern of his
book, after all, is "the question to myself"—one of the many
imperishable Augustinian phrases. This "question to myself" is
not an adventitious interrogation that may flit through my mind
from time to time, but the core of my being. I who ask that
question am myself the question I ask. Each of us is the question
to himself or herself. Here was a philosophical insight into the
nature of human existence—into the peculiar kind of being that is
our being—that went far beyond any of the concepts of Plato or
Aristotle. It is not by chance that the most monumental philosophical analysis of human existence in our century—that by
Heidegger—should have been produced after long and reflective
study of Augustine. Indeed, Heidegger's *Being and Time,* which
analyzes our human reality as essentially one of care and self-
concern, is a thoroughly Augustinian work—up to a point. For if
we return to Augustine after reading Heidegger, we shall find the
latter lacking. Heidegger's *Dasein*—his incarnation of human
being—does not have Augustinian love at its center, and to that
degree is empty and falls short of full personal being.

Mr. Meagher is not personally known to me, so that these
remarks of mine have not been made out of any partisan feeling
of friendship. His book, in a thoroughly Augustinian spirit, is a
work of love, and thus kindles love in return. Courses in "the
philosophy of religion" are usual in our colleges; and if I were
now teaching such a course, I would certainly use this book. It has
a life and zest beyond the usual text; and if its special character
might pass some students by, these are not likely to be the saving
remnant anyway, whether in or out of class. But in so recommend-
ing it, I am not for a moment assigning it to the slot of the
classroom text. It could serve as a text only because it has a vitality
and appeal for a far wider audience. It will be valued by anyone
already interested in St. Augustine; and particularly valuable for
those who have not yet read him and wish to approach him from
that aspect in which he poses a question to us and our civilization
today. But more than this; more even than being a fresh and
imaginative scholarly interpretation, Mr. Meagher's book is a
brave adventure of the spirit on the part of a young man who has

survived the varied seductions of his generation in order to come
up with something very positive indeed. And that in itself is a
good reason why he will be of interest to all readers who are
concerned with the possibilities of the spirit in our time.

WILLIAM BARRETT
New York University

TRANSLATORS' NOTES

In preparing translations of the Augustine texts in this book, we have used the editions of his works available in the *Corpus Scriptorum Ecclesiasticorum Latinorum* (Vienna) and the *Patrologiae Cursus Completus, Series Latina*, ed. J.-B. Migne (Paris).

All Augustine texts enclosed within the commentaries of this book have been translated by Robert Meagher. The translations of the selected readings are, however, the collaborative work of both Rachel Kitzenger and Robert Meagher. In the list of Augustinian references, the translator of each specific work from which selections have been drawn is indicated by either the initials RK or RM. Although in translating these texts we have sought to avoid confusing inconsistencies, we have not worked toward a simply uniform translation. For it is important for the readers to be made aware, now and again, that they are reading translations which are always at best echoes of the author's words.

Certain decisions we have made are best conveyed, even if briefly, although the final case for such decisions must lie with the translations themselves. Mention has already been made of the attempt of the book to refrain from male designations for the generically human. Specifically, as a rule we have used the words "human being" to translate *homo* and *anthrōpos,* the Latin and Greek words, respectively, for man as opposed to beast or god. This word, in whatever language, is necessarily generic, substantive, or essential in reference; for individuals are always either male or female. In contemporary English, which barely recognizes a distinction between sex and gender, generic "human being" has, in our opinion, the neuter pronoun as its most appropriate grammatical accomplice. The neuter form here suggests abstraction from sexual identity and thus from individuality and nothing more. Likewise, in the light of their similarly substantive reference, person *(persona),* mind *(mens),* and nature *(natura)* are ordinarily referred to by neuter pronouns, without any depreciation of their spiritual status.

Two other conventions we have considered to be substantially distorting of Augustine's thought are the capitalization of divine predicates and the setting off of biblical citations either with italics or with quotation marks. In both cases the issues are complicated, and our own resolution of them is no better than a witting experiment. We wish to suggest that divine names are more likely to bear the emphasis which Augustine would consider appropriate if they are not capitalized, so routine has their capitalized form become. Also, Augustine would never see himself quoting scripture. The modern sense of quoting places the speaker at a safe remove from the words quoted, which is surely foreign to Augustine's relationship to his scriptural sources. Augustine wishes to speak scripture, not quote it. If the readers of this work could be expected to hear the words of scripture as such in Augustine's words, we would leave them altogether undesignated. Instead, we have merely identified them when it seemed important to do so, which is, we hope, a helpful compromise.

Finally, as a simply general and concluding consideration, we ask the reader to be aware that our effort throughout has been to provide an even, accurate, accessible translation of a wide range of Augustinian texts which are otherwise available only in distractingly diverse translations or not at all. With this aim in mind it seems not dishonest to keep to ourselves the multiple enigmas and abiding tangles which descend upon anyone who sets out to translate Augustine, the once and always rhetor. Those who are able to sympathize are appreciated, and everyone else is, in an introductory text of this sort, to be absolved to their own temporary good fortune.

M.R.K.
R.E.M.

Amherst, Massachusetts

ABBREVIATIONS FOR
THE BOOKS OF
THE BIBLE

Ac.	Acts	Hg	Haggai
Am	Amos	Ho	Hosea
Ba	Baruch	Is	Isaiah
1 Ch	1 Chronicles	Jb	Job
2 Ch	2 Chronicles	Jdt	Judith
1 Co	1 Corinthians	Jg	Judges
2 Co	2 Corinthians	Jl	Joel
Col	Colossians	Jm	James
Dn	Daniel	Jn	John
Dt	Deuteronomy	1 Jn	1 John
Ep	Ephesians	2 Jn	2 John
Est	Esther	3 Jn	3 John
Ex	Exodus	Jon	Jonah
Ezk	Ezekiel	Jos	Joshua
Ezr	Ezra	Jr	Jeremiah
Ga	Galatians	Ju	Jude
Gn	Genesis	1 K	1 Kings
Hab	Habakkuk	2 K	2 Kings
Heb	Hebrews	Lk	Luke

Lm	Lamentations	Ps	Psalms
Lv	Leviticus	Qo	Ecclesiastes
1 M	1 Maccabees	Rm	Romans
2 M	2 Maccabees	Rt	Ruth
Mi	Micah	Rv	Revelations
Mk	Mark	1 S	1 Samuel
Ml	Malachi	2 S	2 Samuel
Mt	Matthew	Sg	Song of Songs
Na	Nahum	Si	Ecclesiasticus
Nb	Numbers	Tb	Tobit
Ne	Nehemiah	1 Th	1 Thessalonians
Ob	Obadiah	2 Th	2 Thessalonians
1 P	1 Peter	1 Tm	1 Timothy
2 P	2 Peter	2 Tm	2 Timothy
Ph	Philippians	Tt	Titus
Phm	Philemon	Ws	Wisdom
Pr	Proverbs	Zc	Zechariah
		Zp	Zephaniah

ABBREVIATIONS FOR AUGUSTINE'S WRITINGS CITED IN THIS TEXT

Ad Simpl., De diversis quaestionibus ad Simplicianum (To Simplicianum, On Various Questions)
Conf., Confessiones (Confessions)
C. Acad., Contra Academicos (Against the Academics)
C. duas ep. Pel., Contra duas epistulas Pelagianorum (Against Two Letters of the Pelagians)
C. Fort., Contra Fortunatum disputatio (Argument against Fortunatus)
De beat. vit., De beata vita (On the Blessed Life)
De civ. Dei, De civitate Dei (The City of God)
De doct. chr., De doctrina christiana (On Christian Instruction)
De Gen. ad litt., De Genesi ad litteram (Literal Commentary on Genesis)
De Gen. c. Man., De Genesi contra Manichaeos (On Genesis against the Manichaeans)
De lib. arb., De libero arbitrio (On the Freedom of the Will)
De mor., De moribus ecclesiae catholicae, de moribus Manichaeorum (On the Ways of the Catholic Church and of the Manichaeans)

De mus., De musica (On Music)

De nat. boni, De natura boni (On the Nature of the Good)

De ord., De ordine (On Order)

De serm. Dom., De sermone Domini in monte (On the Lord's Sermon on the Mount)

De Trin., De Trinitate (On the Trinity)

De util. cred., De utilitate credendi (On the Usefulness of Believing)

De ver. rel., De vera religione (On True Religion)

En. in Ps., Ennarationes in Psalmos (Expositions on the Psalms)

Epist., Epistulae (Letters)

In Joann. ev., Tractatus in Joannis evangelium (Tracts on the Gospel of John)

Retr., Retractiones (Retractions)

Serm., Sermones (Sermons)

Solil., Soliloquiae (Soliloquies)

Tr. in Joann. ep., Tractatus in epistulam Joannis ad Parthos (Tracts on the First Epistle of John)

AN
INTRODUCTION
TO
AUGUSTINE

INTRODUCTION

Aurelius Augustinus was born in 354 in the Roman town of Thagaste in North Africa (now Souk Ahras, in Algeria). He was nine years old when the last pagan emperor, Julian, died and fifty-seven years old when Alaric and the Goths sacked Rome. As Roman society crumbled around him, Augustine emerged as the preeminent architect of the new Rome, a spiritual city, the City of God, which was to inherit and fulfull the wisdoms of Athens, Jerusalem, and pagan Rome. Augustine is the first great Christian philosopher. The elements of his vision are essential and their energy pure. His thinking is skeletal for the corpus of European civilization: its form, its movement, and its limits. Augustine died and was buried on August 28, 430, in the city of Hippo, which the Vandals set ablaze in the following year. The Augustine library, however, survived the destruction, a library which Augustine's only contemporary biographer, Possidius, bishop of Calama, thought too vast for anyone to read.

If we wish to know Augustine in some intelligent, heartfelt way, there is little point in our pursuing his myriad concerns with indiscriminate enthusiasm or dutifulness, however the case may be. The profile which emerges from a mere tracing of his treatises, by title and topic, is not the profile of a philosopher but rather that of a brilliant and beleaguered prelate. Augustine the philosopher was, to some real degree, lost to the world and to himself on the day of his ordination to the priesthood, over which loss he was said to have wept. Augustine the learned bishop, combining in his person the authority of his office and the wisdom of his intellect, soon became an oracle of sorts, consulted on every pressing issue, whether thological, political, or personal. The result of these demands from every corner and of the seriousness with which Augustine regarded his own duty to respond to them was quite predictable.

Augustine's writings unfolded, for the most part, as responses to the requirements of others and thus followed the illogic of the eventful and the urgent. Merely to outline Augustine's writings, with whatever care and comprehension, is to outline his times as they pressed upon him and compelled his attention. In short, Augustine's writings are mostly expressive of an active life, the active life of a would-be contemplative. Even if the reader should not accept in principle this tension described between the thoughts of an active life engaged by the timely and the thoughts of a contemplative life engaged by the timeless, Augustine knew it well and, for a time, experimented with its avoidance. In the end, however, Augustine lived both lives at once; and the free, speculative, passionately questioning mind of Augustine is nearly always discernible within the often rigid development of church dogma or teaching. Augustine the philosopher speaks in and through and most often beneath Augustine the theologian, lost only to the most literal and ecclesiastical of readings.

In fact, it has been a rather literal ecclesiastical reading which Augustine has mostly received. For it is a church, active and never far removed from the agony of attack and doubt, which has the longest history of poring over his writings. Thus, the Augustinian tradition has been an expressly theological and dogmatic tradition derived principally from Augustine's watershed controversies with the Manichaeans, the Pelagians, and the Donatists. That tradition, originally the clear creation of controversy, was still more sharply defined by the controversy of the Reformation when Augustinian doctrines spread like Greek fire over the face of Europe. It has indeed become commonplace to identify the Augustinian doctrines as those of sin, grace, free will, divine sovereignty, and predestination. As for the philosophy of Augustine, I might mention two readings of the Augustinian tradition which have come to predominate. On the one hand, Augustine has quite often been read and interpreted in Thomistic categories as precursor par excellence of Christian scholasticsm, however personalistic and unsystematic he is for such alleged lineage. Likewise, Augustine is claimed to have heralded and informed the essential roots of modern Continental philosophy, whose acrid secularity is nevertheless altogether incompatible with Augustine's devout faithfulness. However, it is no part of my purpose here to develop an intellectual history of the Augustinian tradition; and thus I must risk claiming, without arguing, that the philosopher Augustine cannot find full justice within the partial images or masks provided by the Lutheran or Calvinist Augustine, the Thomistic Augustine, or the Cartesian Augustine. Augustine the philosopher is neither dogmatic nor systematic nor secular. Rather, his thought is pervasively questioning, personal, and prayerful, as ours must be if we are to think with him, walk his way, even if only imaginatively, for a while, and with little conviction.

Any authentically open inquiry into the thinking of another person must at some point take the form of commentary, of "minding-with" that person. To mind with someone is to assume a common posture of mind with that person. Thus, any student of Augustine must become a companion to Augustine before becoming his critic. Indeed, unless we are willing to think Augustine's thoughts we cannot presume to think about them. In short, we must take his side, strain the limits of our sympathetic imagination, and manage to ignore the prevalent nonsenical claim that genuine understanding is neutral. Far closer to the truth of the matter is the quite ancient claim that like understands like and thus that all understanding is properly participatory. To seek to understand the vision of Augustine must involve our taking his part; and this is only secondarily, if at all, a matter of scholarly discipline, which has come to mean interpretation committed to current, usually historicist, critical methodology. Understanding is, instead, primarily a matter of spiritual discipline, the discipline of doubt and of wonder. We must somehow grant Augustine the full reality of his questions and his quest, letting our skepticism fall back upon us rather than upon him. If it comes to this, we must permit our most unquestionable foundations to fall into doubt, without our universalizing that doubt and smugly reassuring ourselves that, after all, every question and every quest is relative and thus self-contained and delusory. So too we must let ourselves wonder, when our minds and our hearts fall blank and cold upon what Augustine thrills to see, to hear, and to say—when, in short, we simply fail to follow him. In most obvious terms, historical study is a form of travel toward times and places which are undeniably human but often not at all familiar. As travelers in a foreign land, it is we who are strangers, we whose ways seem beyond imagining, we who must suffer the embarrassment of having to ask the most obvious question, without in the least knowing how to do so. Indeed, the most naive questions are the mark of the most willing foreigner and of the most willing student. While we pride ourselves as the most widely traveled and learned of ages, our studies amount all too often to sheer tourism, free of spiritual risk and growth.

It is a professional fact that within the academy today most philosophical and theological discussions, with undeniable self-restraint, seldom deviate from the curricular limits of linguistics and methodology. This dogmatic obsession of today's scholasticism with essentially prospective and retrospective concerns, always avoiding the center, the substance, of serious human thought is in the end a digression. At best it is a matter of waiting; at worst it appears to be a matter of stalling. In either case, this widely agreed upon recourse to the periphery of human spiritual life is grounded, whether knowingly or unknowingly, in the modern despair of prephilosophical experience, of commonsense knowledge and commonsense discourse. The particular form this despair takes in the study of thinking foreign to our own is the conviction that the substantive vision of the thinker, in this case Augustine, is inaccessible to us. That vision is commonly assumed to be so inseparably related to an unrepeatable historical moment that it necessarily suffers essential modification when the student endeavors again to see with that vision, to ask again its questions, and to consider again its responses.

The most readily available solution to this problem is to take a step back from participation and to study the texts of Augustine as texts, as objects in themselves, to study how they are arranged, how they put things. Soon we are not studying Augustine's faith but rather his concept of faith; we no longer think with Augustine about God but work, instead, at constructing an adequate representation of Augustine's concept or doctrine of God. The craft or skill in such work may be perfect; but its perfection is altogether different from the perfection which Augustine sought. For whatever reason, Augustine's own activity is abandoned and a derivative, meta-activity is undertaken in its stead. What I am calling a commentary, however, strives to resume and to continue the original activity. Thus, a commentary on the philosophy of Augustine strives itself to be philosophy as Augustine would have understood it. Commentary, as historical understanding, is the repetition or recurrence of a prior moment of understanding.

If authentic commentary upon historically remote thinking is not possible from a position of entrenched modernity, neither is it possible from a position of sheer bewildered openness. If we are to think with Augustine we must find common ground with him, we must come to share an intelligible context within which our participation in his questions and concerns makes genuine sense to us. Most often that common ground and context lie deepest, in the very center of our own thinking and of the thinking which we strive to follow and to understand. And it is surely the first task of any introduction to Augustine's thinking to stake out the ground and the context for the commentary which is then to follow, namely to strike the center, the source, from which his thinking and ours with him will then unfold.

The endeavor to discern and set forth the ground and source for a path of thinking may be quite variously understood and practiced, depending upon one's theories of language and history. The most common and self-evident inquiry into sources, known as *Quellenforschung*, seeks to establish textual parallels between what an author wrote and what an author must therefore have read. Such inquiries, together with occasional outright information from Augustine, provide a sketch of Augustine's context and sources in the sense of formal learning. Educated as a *rhetor*, or orator, in the Roman tradition, the preoccupation of Augustine's formal education fell far from substance upon the art of crafting words. He emerged a perfectionist, attentive to the details of speech, with an outstanding memory and an open heart, virtually ignorant of Greek, and knowing only a handful of Latin authors in any depth (Vergil, Terence, Cicero, and Sallust). His later studies brought him, most notably, to Plotinus and Porphyry in the Latin translations of Marius Vicorinius, to Varro, Seneca, Apuleius, Aristotle via Cicero, and to the Latin Bible of Africa, whose crudities were an offense to Augustine the stylist. However, it must be stressed that the voices and influences of the ancient world were for Augustine oftentimes so diffuse and oblique that any clarity regarding sources must be limited to texts and not to ideas, presuming a decisive difference between the two.

Illuminating as it is to read Augustine in the setting of his own reconstructed education, it does not go without saying that we find therein the most appropriate context for our own study of and with Augustine. After all, the meeting, the dialogue, the struggle in which works of thought or art shine forth most are quite often arranged in retrospect between unwitting participants. I am convinced that reflecting upon Aristotle and Plato opens for us a path of insight and understanding most appropriate to our study of Augustine, a path less derivative and syncretistic and more commonly accessible than Plotinus would provide, although he is a more literal, textual Augustinian source. Finally, however, the claim I am making is not methodological but substantive; and its merits will be either clear or not as we proceed in our commentary.

Two realities dwell in the center of Augustine's thinking: blessedness *(beatitudo)* and word *(verbum)*. It is commonly recognized in Augustinian scholarship and evident in Augustine's writings that blessedness is a, if not the, magisterial idea. But before blessedness is an idea thought or a word spoken it is the object of irresistible, universal human desire. Human spiritual life is at center, for Augustine, a matter of will; and will is first of all desire. And, finally, the willing or desiring of blessedness is so central and all-pervasive that it informs and drives every single act of willing or desiring. Whatever and whenever, according to Augustine, we desire, we seek blessedness. Human becoming is desiring; and all desiring, wittingly or unwittingly, is the desiring of blessedness, namely of human well-being. Desire, then, is equivalent with human activity in time, and both are defined by their inevitable and only appropriate object: blessedness. So, too, word is equivalent with human activity. Augustine imagines every human activity, which is to say, every human willing and desiring as the uttering of a word. Human becoming in all its moments and metamorphoses unfolds toward these two realities: blessedness and the word.

There is a text in book one of Aristotle's *Nicomachean Ethics* (with which Augustine was not likely familiar) which is quite illuminating of the relationship between "blessedness" and "word" in Augustine's thinking, and illuminating, as well, of the common context which we seek in order to ground our commentary. The *Ethics* is a book about blessedness; and the manner in which Aristotle formulates the question of human blessedness is utterly foundational. Aristotle approaches the question of human blessedness by way of the question of human activity (activity as contrasted both with possibility and with passivity). In order to ask whether it makes sense to speak of a specifically human blessedness, Aristotle asks whether it makes sense to speak of a specifically human activity, or work *(ergon)*.

Blessedness, as Aristotle understands it, is inseparable from being, and being is inseparable from activity To be blessed is simply to *be* full, to be fully real in accord with one's nature. To be blessed is to be blessed with and in the fullness of one's being, the fullness of one's reality. Becoming represents a condition of desire, unreality, and possibility; no one is blessed within the condition of becoming. To be blessed is to be fully actualized, to be without desire in the midst of one's full human realization. Blessedness is being and being is being-in-act *(energeia)*. Thus these three questions—What is human blessedness? What is human being? What is human activity?—are one convergent and central question for Aristotle.

In search of properly human activity, Aristotle points to a range

of activities somehow related to human being, activities in which
human beings do in fact engage. There are the activities of art or
craft; the activities of eye and hand and foot; the activities of life
itself, nutrition, growth, and sensation, and so on. In each case we
know what it would mean to be in act, to perform well the activity,
for instance, of carving wood, of making music, of smelling,
eating, growing, living; but in each case the question remains
whether human activity, human being, human blessedness resides
in any one of these activities, in the composite of them all, or in an
altogether distinct activity. In short, (one may be in fine health;
accomplished in one's art or craft or profession; fed, warmed,
sheltered, clothed, and loved and still know one's gnawing
unrealization, one's radical incompletion, one's relentless unblessedness.) Well-being in one's vital functions, in one's feelings,
in one's makings, together with the absence of pain and conflict,
does not seem to bring simple, full well-being. There seems to be
an unblessedness unique to human life, which raises the question
for us whether there might not also be a blessedness unique to
human life. And for Aristotle, as well as for Augustine, to ask
whether there is a uniquely human (blessedness is to ask whether
there is a uniquely human activity,) the proper performance of
which constitutes human being and human blessedness. Finally,
the intimate connection between "blessedness" and "word" becomes at once clear when we realize that for Augustine (as well as
for Greek thought, Hebrew-Christian thought, and modern Western thought) the uniquely human activity is speech, the uttering of
the word. The mystery of human blessedness and of human being
resides within the human word. Here we touch the center of
Augustine's thinking, and here his thinking entwines with our
own. Here commentary becomes thinkable.

Human becoming is, for Augustine, a coming to speech.
Human being and human blessedness dwell in the word, the
perfect word. Clearly, by speech Augustine has much more in
mind than the vocalization of meaningful sounds; and by the
word he has much more in mind than a written or sounded sign.
What we have here is a metaphor, a governing image for human
spiritual life. Speaking is comprehensively descriptive of all
peculiarly human activity. All thinking and all willing, every act of

the human spirit, is, at root and at center, the uttering of a word.
Thus, to inquire into human well-being is to inquire into the
proper performance of this preeminently human activity. The
question of the nature of human speech and of the word is, then,
at the same time the question of the nature of human being.
When Augustine raises this question who distinct traditions of
response, two very different understandings of human speech and
of human being present themselves to him: the Greek understanding and the (Hebrew-Christian understanding. These two
distinctly compelling experiences and visions of spiritual life
together form the context for Augustine's own questions and
reflections. It was in the face of those two images of human
possibility and reality that Augustine's mind and heart first
opened and spoke.)

There can be no prospect here of tracing the classical and
biblical influences evident or suggested in Augustine's thinking.
Rather, we must discern the two radical alternatives which
describe the boundaries of Augustine's reflections. In doing so we
must not claim, however, that Augustine would have so sharply,
even intransigently, contrasted these two alternative understandings—the classical and the biblical. For he learned neither in its
purity, bred as he was on a Hellenized Bible and a biblicized
Hellenism. It is for the sake of our own conceptual clarity and, I
think, of reflective integrity that we require to distinguish sharply
between these two possible understandings of speech: speech as
disclosure and speech as creation. Correspondingly, we may
distinguish between the disclosing word and the creative word.
The former is characteristic of Greek thinking, and the latter is
characteristic of Hebrew-Christian thinking. It is, of course, a
commonplace that Augustine, like Philo before him and Aquinas
after him, strove to reconcile Greek wisdom with Hebrew-
Christian faith. The Rome of Augustine, the spiritual Rome of the
City of God, was to be the meeting place, the common heir, of
Athens and Jerusalem. And the enduring sense and significance of
this tension as that between disclosure and creation; for this
question remains central to the development of Western thinking.

The issue of disclosure versus creation as the meaning of human
speech and of human being is as foundational for Descartes,

Hobbes, Kant, Hegel, Kierkegaard, Nietzsche, Marx, and Heidegger as it is for Augustine. Here we ought to find a compelling invitation rather than an impasse to the encounter with Augustine. The center of his philosophical concerns explores with brilliance the very center of the most serious enduring concerns in Western philosophy. The depth and range of his insight make him a most irreplaceable guide in our ownmost thinking as well us in his.

Before beginning to comment on Augustine's thinking with respect to the question of human being and blessedness, it remains to reflect more fully upon the context within which that questin emerges and makes serious sense for Augustine and for us, a context established by the polar alternatives of disclosure and creation. For Augustine, these two alternatives present themselves as Athens and Jerusalem, reason and faith, intellect and will; for us they present themselves as the ancient and the modern, the mysterious and the problematic, the sacred and the secular, wisdom and power. Regardless of the peculiar formulation, however, in which we encounter it, the enduring question of human being remains essentially invariable: Is our actual and appropriate way of being in the world one of power (such that we are called upon to create our world and our own being in it) or one of weakness (such that we dwell in a world already complete and requiring only the disclosure and recognition of human understanding for its perfection)? First, we will consider this question as it formulates itself for Augustine and then consider at least one of the formulations in which it confronts us. In the end, the kinship of our minds with Augustine's and of his with ours will be evidently close and will support our continuing his thinking and his deepening our thinking regarding the unavoidable question of our own being.

Philosophical commentary such as this seeks to participate in the work commented upon, so that here reflections upon the thought of Augustine appropriately yield to an engagement in Augustinian thinking. Thought and thinking, past and present, artifact and activity, must begin within a common context and proceed from a common source: the question of human blessedness and the meaning of the human word.

CHAPTER 1

CONTEXT

Disclosure and Creation

Blessedness and the word—we have begun with these two central Augustinian concerns, concerns which are at the same time questions; for "blessedness" is first known as desire and "word" is first known as inquiry. Further, it has been suggested that the desire for blessedness and the work of speech represent a common quest for fullness of being. Human blessedness would appear to reside in the perfection of one's being which is, at the same time, the perfection of essentially human activity, the speaking of the perfect word. Blessedness—being—activity—word: with these words the circle of our inquiry begins to open and to clarify itself.

That center, however, remains essentially questionable; for we must ask what it means to speak, how it is that we pursue the question and the possibility of our becoming under the paradigm of the word. At the outset, both for Augustine and for us, these two divergent understandings of the meaning of speech and of human being—disclosure and creation—present themselves and find their fullest embodiments within the two traditions of Athens and Jerusalem—here understood symbolically as two types or forms or ideas having their primary dwelling within the mind, the

11

"place of ideas." Thus, in describing each of these alternatives, I will be thinking a possibility to its limit rather than assessing a historical period or a corpus of literature with representative balance; for the possibilities which I have in mind are illuminated by, but not at all restricted to, the past. Since we are here together engaged in an Augustinian inquiry into blessedness and the word as well as an inquiry into Augustine's understanding of blessedness and word, these prior reflections must establish a context for thinking which is appropriate to Augustine and to us. Consequently, the substance and integrity of our thinking ought to occupy us far more than the labeling of every textual reference and the tracing of each historical remark. In the hope, then, of preserving this priority of thinking, I will use my own translations and minimal citations whenever possible.

Speech as Disclosure

The lines we draw must be reasonably sharp and careful if they are to describe a recognizable and livable house for thinking. Nevertheless, a few bold initial strokes might serve to orient our thinking in what must be a painfully distilled series of steps. Disclosure is a fundamentally nonviolent act, an activity purified of force—imposing nothing, neither shape nor purpose, upon anything. Disclosure sets its hands to nothing; rather, it is, in figure, an act of the eye in which the hands drop, idle. Disclosure is an act of participation which neither constructs nor destroys nor alters. The power of disclosure is the power not of violence *(bia)* but of being-at-work *(energeia)*. The being-at-work in each thing is the power and the being of its own unfolding, the power of its own intrinsic movement and development. The universe is a place of endless movement and change, a place of ceaseless comings-to-be and ceasings-to-be. This universe, however, in each and all of its myriad motions, is, as Plato describes it in the *Timaeus,* a living sight, a percepible divinity and an image of what only mind may perceive. The universe is the moving image *(eikōn)* of the eternal; and disclosure thus begins (as does the ascent of Plato's divided line, the ascent of wisdom) with the activity of *eikasia,* the perception of images as images. Every motion in the universe is an imitation, an imaging, of the divine and the eternal. The divine and the eternal is, then, what is endlessly coming to be in the unfoldings, in the comings to be, of all things. And human coming to be, human being-at-work, dwells in the disclosure of this universal becoming and imaging of the eternal. Human activity is at one with the activity of the universe and, in the uttering of the word of disclosure, human speech becomes the place and the time, the occasion, for the meeting of time and eternity. Human speech becomes, in the words of Martin Heidegger, the house of being. The blessedness of the universe and human blessedness, the fullness of all beings and the fulness of human being are finally a single unfolding and a single perfection in the word.

The Greek words *legein* (to speak) and *logos* (word) make no distinction between talking and thinking, between the outer word and the inner word. In the *Politics,* Aristotle distinguishes speech *(logos)* from voice *(phonē)* as sign *(sēmeion).* In the context of Aristotle's discussion, this seems to mean that speech is not to be confused with language, or the vocalization of expressive signs, which characterizes animal as well as human being. An animal, as he points out, may be quite capable of voiced expression, for instance, of hunger, anger, desire, pleasure, and pain. And animals, together, sharing this capacity for feelings and for the expression of feelings, are quite capable of communicating with one another. We speak of animal languages and are more or less accustomed to thinking of human language as a refinement of animal language, which is to say that we are more or less accustomed to thinking of human being as a refinement of animal being. From the perspectiv of observed behavior, human language belongs to the same continuum as animal language. But the activity of speech is something altogether different from the activity of vocal expression. To speak is not to express but to disclose. To illuminate, to bring to light, is the work of speech, which is something different from vocalizing or expressing.

All speech, writes Aristotle in his treatise *On the Soul,* is a matter of marking out boundaries or of showing forth. This twofold work of speech—that of defining and of illuminating—is clearly one work, however; for when the beginning and ending of a thing, its coming-to-be and its ceasing-to-be, are clearly marked, then that thing stands revealed. To know a thing in its distinct relations with all else is to know it as it is. In short, speech discloses in a particular manner: it manifests what a thing is in terms of what it is not. In speech, the being of a thing (what it is) and the nonbeing of a thing (what it is not) are inseparable.

What is it, then, that speech displays and whose limits it marks out? The appropriate object of human speech is no less than the universe, the universe as it presents itself to be perceived by the senses and the universe as it presents itself to be known by the mind. It is central to Greek thought and experience that the activity of the senses provides the paradigm and the actual foundation for the activity of the mind. "It seems," writes Aristotle, "that both theoretical understanding [*noein*] and practical understanding [*phronein*] are almost a kind of sensory understanding [*aisthanesthai*]." And he goes on to say that the relationship between the capacity for sensation and the object of sensation is the same as the relationship between the capacity for knowledge and the object of knowledge. In other words, the body's way of being in the world and the mind's way of being in the world are one; for human being is finally one being just as the world is finally one world. This vision of the unity of sensing and knowing and of the unity of the sensible and the knowable finds definitive formulation in Plato's image of the divided line in book six of the *Republic* where he describes the movement from sensation to contemplation, from the simplest perception of color and shape to the pure beholding of the divine, as movement along a single line. The line is divided but it is never broken. Sensory understanding is distinguished, but never divorced, from intellectual understanding. The ascent of this line represents, for Plato, the ascent to fullness of being, the perfection of human activity. Thus, the ascent which Plato describes is an ascent of speech, a movement of disclosure toward the uttering of the perfect word.

When Plato (and Aristotle too, for that matter) speaks of sensation *(aisthēsis),* he has sight above all in mind. Sight is the purest and most perfect of the senses, which means that the activity of sensory vision is closer than any other sensory activity to the activity of intellectual understanding, so close, indeed, that both may be called vision. Similarly, material objects, objects of sensation, insofar as they are visible, approach the immateriality of the objects of intellect. A thing is immaterial to the extent that it is not diminished as it is enjoyed and shared. The objects and the activjty of intellectual understanding are also somehow timeless, being and being known all at once, at least in rare gifted moments of wonder and contemplation; and such moments have their clear parallels and precedents in the world of sensory vision, when our eyes cease to roam in their focus and become fixed. Finally, to ascend the divided line, to approach the fullness of one's own reality and the fullness of reality itself, is to enter the world of the common and the timeless and to leave behind all that is particular and timeful, in oneself as well as in one's world. Disclosure reaches toward the eternal and the unlimitedly shareable.

Not all sight is disclosure. Rather, disclosure is rooted in what Plato calls *eikasia,* the discernment of images as images. The first insight here, the first most obvious instance of discernment, occurs when one realizes that the visual world contains both images and originals. This discovery is not simply the discovery of multiplicity but rather the discovery of multiplicity as it proceeds from unity, namely, the discovery of the cause or principle of multiplicity. For example, a willow tree sprawls over the edge of a still pond and is reflected in its waters. We have here two trees to be seen, the tree rooted in the bank of the pond and the tree spread across the waters of the pond. To commonsense discernment, the tree on shore is more real, more truly a tree than the tree in the pond; like all images, the tree to be seen afloat in the pond both is and is not what it is, in this case a tree, whereas the rooted, wooden, upright tree, it would seem, simply *is* a tree. The real or original tree is the potential source of countless images whose being (trees) is always mixed with not-being (trees). And what may we say of the many trees which will proceed from this tree, not through visual reflection, but through reproduction? Are not this one tree's many offspring in one sense its images? But are they less real than their origin on this account? After all, the original tree, in this case, is not truly original; for it is itself the offspring of another tree. Once we move from the multiplicity of visual images to the unity of the imaged original, we encounter a multiplicty of originals, a multiplicity of actual leafy trees, in this case. And the question then becomes a good deal less obvious: Could it be that the countlessly multiple material trees are in some sense only images or reflections of an original unity invisible to the eye of sense but quite visible to the inner, more truly discerning eye of spirit? Could it be that the world of sense is a world of images, a world which the activity of *eikasia* discloses to be finally derivative and dependent? Could it be that even the trees beneath which we sit for shade both are and are not trees, although they are more truly trees than are the images which those trees find upon still waters? This is precisely the question posed and answered in the affirmative by Plato in the *Republic* and throughout his writings. Disclosure is a dialectic, an unfolding vision which leads the see-er, insight by insight, from unreality to reality, from image to original, from nonbeing to being, from the many to the one. For the universe is the creation of imaging and imitation, from the first work of the demiurge, to the endless circling of the stars, to the most natural *(phusikōtaton)* of all works, the making of another like oneself in procreation.

Human becoming is, then, the uniquely human activity of disclosing the one, the common, the original being which is imaged or imitated and thus multiplied (and whose images and imitations are always still another time imaged and imitated) in the mysteriously generous overflow of time, for which, says Plato, our would-be accounts are never more than likely stories. This activity is, however, largely a passivity in which human being is led to its own disclosure as it speechfully discloses the reality of the universe, or the whole. For, if speech discloses by the marking out of limits, speech always marks out its own limits first; even the purest, most speculative thinking-and-speaking (which is one activity), *hai theoretikai noēseis,* is bounded *(horizontai)* by words. Words are, indeed, the horizon of speech, which is to say that speech discloses itself whenever it encounters, speechfully or thoughtfully, its own limits. Whatever else speech discloses, it always discloses itself (this is not to say that all disclosure is limited to self-disclosure, which is an intransigent modern claim). Speech is always wordful, fated with the temporality of sound and the materiality of images *(phantasmata).* Speech is finally itself no more than an image, the only temporal image conscious of itself as image, which Plato likens to the waters of a still lake in which the perfect light of the sun, self-disclosing being itself, is imaged, imitated, repeated in every human life striving to be fully human, full with speech.

Again it is the analogy, or rather the analogous reality, of sight which reveals to us the complicity between the disclosure of being itself and the disclosure of human being. Both Plato and Aristotle, and Greek tradition before and after them, liken the mind *(nous)*, the organ of speech and disclosure, to the eye, the organ of sight and of sensory *eikasia* or discernment. The activity of the mind, like that of the eye, is described as a receiving, a welcoming, a waiting for *(to dektikon)* the prior illumination of reality by an all-encompassing self-bestowing light for which there is no more appropriate and true image than the sun. The sun, the sheer presence of a light neither cast by the eye or the mind, nor emanating from the particular object of eye or mind, enables, empowers the bestowal of the visible, knowable universe and the self-opening hospitality of sight, sensory and spiritual. In their own most proper activity, for its right-performance, and thus for their own well-being, the eye and the mind are wholly dependent upon a power, an activity, which is sheer self-giving, in no way at their disposal. This image of human being is the most profound source of the Greek understanding of human being as weak, as, in Plato's words, a simple, gentle being whom heaven has blessed with a tranquil nature.

We clearly must have the eye before our imaginations when we think with Aristotle about the mind, that it has no other nature than its possibility *(dunaton)*. "Possibility" here means the capacity, the ability to be or, more precisely, to be like, that is, the power to image. By virtue of this possibility, the mind does not become what it knows but, rather, becomes like what it knows. The mind, says Aristotle, *is,* in the universe of beings, *nothing* before it "minds" *(noein)* and then it is one, one activity, one unfolding life *(mia energeia)* with what it "minds" or knows or, in our terms, speaks. The mind is nothing until it is mindful, until it thinks-and-speaks; and human mindfulness has as its appropriate object the universe, all things in their unity. Indeed, writes Aristotle, there is a sense in which the soul as the place of mind is somehow all things *(hē psychē ta onta pōs ta panta).*

Human being has, as its own proper being, the receiving and the imaging of all things, not in their multiplicity, but in their unity. Minding *(noein),* writes Parmenides, and being *(einai)* are the same; thus, human being and being are somehow the same. Human being in its perfection is the perfect image of being. Time finds its gathering point and eternity its fullest voice in the speechfulness of human being. Being, the divine unity, God, is spoken of by Aristotle in the *Metaphysics* as sheer activity *(energeia),* and as the minding of minding *(noēsis noēseōs),* the knowing of knowing. This activity, which is the inner life of divine being, is purely selfless, as is the inner life of human being. Only when the mind is mindful of things other than itself and thus becomes these things, which finally means only when the mind is mindful of the universe and thus becomes the universe, is the mind able to become mindful of itself. This self-knowledge, the mindfulness of mindfulness, is not introspective but contemplative. Human activity is the master image of divine activity; and the inner life of human being is in its perfection what it was to become in its beginning: the vision of image as image, now the vision of God as both God and not God.

Human being, writes Aristotle, is passive in that it becomes all things and yet active in that it makes all things. We must not, however, misread this making so as to attribute the slightest creativity to human being (or, for that matter, to divine being). Human being is above all else an openness, a wakefulness, a receiving; and the human work is above all else a being-worked-upon. Human being, writes Plato in the *Laws,* is the plaything *(ti paignion)* of God; and that, he adds, is the very noblest thing in hit. Human bringing-to-light is dependent upon the light's own endless dawning; the human disclosure of being is the ever-recurring, ever-changing image of the one, changeless self-disclosure of being. Human wakefulness is always a fleeting, mortal response to and participation in the sleepless revelation of what is eternally. For human being to conceal itself is for it to conceal being, which concealment does not lie in human power.

How, asks Heraclitus, would anyone conceal oneself in the presence of what never sets, what never conceals itself? Human being is led, indeed driven (thinking is, for Plato, a mania), to its own disclosure and thus to the disclosure of being by being's own eternal unconcealment, which is the meaning of the Greek word for truth *(alētheia)*. The true, which is the good and the beautiful, works out its own unconcealment, shines, speaks, in countless human moments, moments of human blessedness, moments of which Aristotle was said to have been so desirous that he slept with arm outstretched and with a sphere of bronze in his hand, held over a pan. A moment's giving way, and the ball would clatter upon the pan, ending his sleep. So brief and so begrudged were the interruptions which he permitted in this life of the disclosing word.

Speech as Creation

We have seen already how, in Greek understanding, human being is essentially defined by its relationship to divine being. The human activity of disclosure images, in word, the divine activity of disclosure. Thus, the human remains concealed so long as the divine lies in concealment. The pursuit of human wisdom and well-being is no less than the quest for the divine, in which the pursuer loses what is most familiar and one's own, even that most familiar and particular of spaces, one's own body; for the moment of contemplation, the pure beholding of the divine, is timeless and moodless, indifferent to the individual, devoid of particular memories, hopes, feelings, outside the body. Paradoxically, this moment of truth, the moment of ecstatic encounter, is wordless. The soul does not speak and God does not speak; there is no friendship, no fellowship, of the one with the other. The human and the divine are dark and hidden in the mystery of their final unspoken complicity.

In the biblical understanding of the order of things, the human and the divine are no less complicit. Indeed, they are personally intimate. In the beginning *(be rē'|ši)*, a radical beginning which the Greek vision of the eternal universe does not allow, God creates human being in the image of divine being *(bᵉ selem* ᵉlōhīm). Once again, we must accept that the knowledge of the human and the knowledge of the divine are entangled. Yet neither the nature of God nor the nature of human being are thematically developed. In the place of such speculation we find only an account of their activity, their work. Thus, following the mention of the image of God, there is given an explicit account of the proper or assigned work of human being, the work of dominion. The entire text reads as follows:

> Let us make man in our image, after our likeness; and let them have dominion over the fish of the sea, and over the birds of the air, and over the cattle, and over all the earth, and over every creeping thing that creeps upon the earth.
>
> (Gen. 1.26-27 RSV)

What this peculiar human work of dominion means and how it is to be exercised is nowhere in what follows this passage brought to conceptual clarity. Instead, we are left to make several assumptions. If the human work is assigned in the very moment and the very activity in which God fashions human being, then, on some level, it must be inescapable. And, if human being is fashioned in the image of divine being, then what we know of the unique divine work wherein God created (bārā'—a word used to denote only the divine creative activity) the world must interpret for us what little is said of the unique human work. Divine creation and human dominion must be somehow one original activity imaged and repeated; and this activity is clearly that of speech. The word is simply central to the biblical account of both creation and redemption, of both the beginning of time and the end of time. Creation, covenant, law, prophecy, wisdom, and gospel are all metamorphoses of the word, the word which first breaks the eternal silence, whether of being or of nonbeing, "in the beginning." And this account of the beginning has a certain simple primacy, therefore, in our reflections on the word (dabhar) of believing, which is not to be confused with the word (logos) of thinking.

All things proceed from the primal chaos (as near as the acritical reflections of the author of Genesis approach nonbeing or nothingness) by the sheer fiat of the divine word—all things, that is, except divine being and human being. God is, of course, exempt from the creative word. And human being, unique in this among all creatures, is the work of a special divine resolve and effort. The creation of human being is prefaced by the expression of a solemn resolve and accompanied by explicit labor. We read that "the LORD God formed man of dust from the ground, and breathed into his nostrils the breath of life" (Gn. 2.7 RSV); and this creation of masculine human being is completed in the creation of feminine human being, which likewise requires divine labor: "So the LORD God caused a deep sleep to fall upon the man, and while he slept took one of his ribs and closed up its place with flesh; and the rib which the LORD God had taken from the man he made into a woman" (Gn. 3.21-22 RSV). All else requires only the irresistible divine word for its creation; human being, however, requires work beyond the word. Divine being and human being are the source of words, they are described essentially by the fact that they speak. Thus, it would seem appropriate that as the creators of the word, they are not themselves the prior creatures of word. Human being is, in part, the creature of word and, correspondingly, human speech is decisively qualified and limited. Nevertheless, the work of God's hands and the breath of God's life sets apart human being, the noblest creature, for a unique fellowship with the divine life and the divine work.

The nature of divine speech and thus of divine activity is first manifest in the work of creation. The divine word is sheer absolute being *(hayah)* bringing all things to be in their own place and time. The divine word expresses the divine will, which is radically free, consulting no higher order, answerable to no cosmic forces or limits, beyond judgment and yet perfectly fair in the twofold sense of being evenhanded and lovely. The divine word is command, beyond which there is no appeal. "By the word of the LORD the heavens were made . . . the word of the LORD is upright . . . all his work is done in righteousness. . . . He loves righteousness and justice . . . let all the earth fear the LORD" (Ps. 33 RSV). The divine work is word—creative, free, powerful, just, and fearsome; and in each of these respects we may expect the divine work to be reflected in the work of human being, fashioned in the image of God. This human work, already described as dominion, is further manifest in the commission given to human being to bestow names upon all creatures.

> So out of the ground the LORD God formed every beast of the field and every bird of the air, and brought them to the man to see what he would call them; and whatever the man called every living creature, that was its name.

> (Gn. 2.19 RSV)

For the Hebrews and for much of the ancient Semitic world, to name a thing is to confer upon that thing whatever reality it possesses. To give names is to rule, to exercise dominion over what is named. To know and to utter the name of a thing is to have effective control over that thing. To be a human being is to speak over, to bestow names upon, all the other creatures brought before one. This is human being's connatural work, and we are able to give an explicit account of human being and human blessedness insofar as we are able to give an explicit account of this work of speech.

To name is to call by name; and to be named is to be at the call of that name. Every name, then, is a call, a calling, a personal command. To be given a name is to be open, vulnerable, to being called upon. Here we read that human being gives names to all other creatures, but that this giving of names is not reciprocal. For those other creatures do not, in turn, give names to human being. Thus, they are open to being called upon and are somehow at the command and service of human being without their having any corresponding right or power to name or to call upon the human. Human being, writes Philo, strikes fear into the hearts of all creatures under human dominion. For them, the beginning of wisdom, we might conclude, is the fear of human being, and wisdom would be compliance to human will and design. However, the human voice and human dominion are decisively qualified by the divine voice and divine sovereignty. God's voice shatters the eternal silence and evokes the world from the void. "The voice of the LORD is upon the waters . . . the voice of the LORD is powerful, the voice of the LORD is full of majesty" (Ps. 29.4 RSV). The human voice, however, breaks only the seeming silence of time, which is indeed alive with divine praise. The human spirit roams, not over the void, but rather over the creation which is the spoken word of God. Human dominion is subject to divine dominion, and human being is subject to divine being; for the human word is preceded and encompassed by the divine word. And the divine word names and thus calls and commands the human by name. The human word is sovereign over what lies beneath it and subject to what lies above it, just as the word of a provincial ruler is supreme within the province and yet fully answerable to the king. Such rulers were accustomeed to exercise their power seated before an *image* or standard *(sēlem)* of the king, and this word is the same as we find used for human being as the *image* of God. Human being, made in God's image, is presumably commissioned to rule also in God's image.

The position of human being in the universe is a precarious one, finely balanced between power and weakness, sovereignty and obedience. Within the ordinary course of events the commanding word is the human word, increasingly so as the human domain is established and developed; but we are reminded that God has the first word and the last word. In the absence of the divine, the human has all the appearance of the absolute. In fact, in the absence of God, human being must interpret the universe, giving name and meaning, shaping, ordering, using, destroying, creating. From day to day human being stands in the place of God, feared and obeyed by the world as God would be feared and obeyed. Human being cannot not rule. This is the human work. But to pretend to be divine, to pretend that one's words are one's own, to be unmindful of the divine power and the divine word, is to sin. It is to mistake the image for the original, to set up the image of God as an idol and to give it divine due. Only God is permitted to create a divine image; only God is entitled to name and to call upon the human. In brief, when human being speaks, creation is to listen. But when God speaks, human being is to listen.

Human being is firstly the hearer of the word, the speechful witness to divine speech, the confessor of the divine will and its mysteries. The silence which is broken by human speech is to be a human silence meditative upon the divine word, attentive to the word of creation. Human speech is appropriately *prophecy,* in which human being speaks for *(pro-phē)* divine being. Human being is appropriately *personal,* the mask of God through which the divine voice sounds *(per-sonat).* "There is One who is wise, greatly to be feared, sitting upon his throne . . . to fear the LORD is the beginning of wisdom" (Si. 1.8, 14). The prophet is one who fears the Lord and whose words are the very words of God, because, for the prophet, to attend to the divine word and to speak the human word are a single act. Thus, the prophet is the figure of human perfection, the figure of the image of God conscious of itself as image.

The world of the prophet is a world constituted by events of revelation, by the word of God speaking now and again, in and across time. The word of God bursts through the silence of human beings' lives and calls upon them to respond now. The word of God calls them into time, into the acceptable time of current revelation. Each such privileged moment is flooded with all the sacred memories and expectations, all the frustrations and dreams, of the chosen people. The world of the prophet is essentially historical, timeful, moodful, spread across the uneven, fitful texture of collective recollections and promises. The initiative in every case lies with the word of God, to build up and to tear down. The hearer must remain rooted in, and open to, the particular and the unique into which alone the word speaks. Within the context and judgment of scripture, those who presume to see, to comprehend the truth, the meaning, of the kingdom, the Messiah, the son of man, prove unequal, impervious, and unresponsive to revelation. After all, it is usually proper to sight to cointend what is not seen along with what is seen so as to comprehend the whole. It is altogether inappropriate to hearing, however, to complete what is or has been spoken for the sake of comprehension. The world of the prophet is necessarily always incomplete, always open to being revisited, even contradicted, by the word of God. The hearer's most faithful contribution is the longing silence of one who waits.

Human being as hearer of the word is altogether vulnerable to, and defenseless against, its intrusions and its claims. However, revelation is most often directed to a particular nation or congregation or family. Revelation, as event, seems to require a particular contemporaneity; revelation implies privilege. The absence of the prophets, the death of Jesus, are special crises for a community constituted by the living word of God. Whether through memory or anticipation or both, the hearer searches for contemporaneity with revelatory events, Thus, the call of Jesus to his disciples, "Come, follow me," is a unique personal invitation to enter into a time, into the lifetime of an individual man. The prophets and Jesus claim to speak directly with authority by virtue of who they are, that is, what has happened to them, by virtue of their calling. Their speech is pure command, pure declaration, without offer or promise of intelligible grounds. The prophets repeat what the lord saith; Jesus speaks only what the father has given him to say. Prophetic speech is the repetition of divine speech, the revelation of revelation. The authority of divine and prophetic speech remains unqualified. The blessed life is the life of obedient love, the life of one who hears the word of God and keeps it.

What is recognized in the anthropology of Genesis and of biblical literature more generally is the creative power of human speech or imagination as well as the altogether ambiguous character of that power. Human being fashions and controls the reality of the universe and tells a story with its own life. All things and even human being are whatever the human word and human will make of them. Yet to affirm the word of God is to claim that all things are what they are and are good prior to human imaginings and words, that human being's controlling speech and the world of its making are quite provisional. Whatever human being names and makes of things, that is what they are for human being; whereas, whatever God names and makes of things, that is what they are, simply. When human being speaks faithfully, as hearer of the word, it confesses creation as the spoken word of god. The human work, most properly, is the confession of the divine work. God, insofar as we may know and give an account of divine being, is pure speech. Human being, insofar as we may know and give an account of it, is faithful speech, speech which is fashioned by openness and obedience to divine speech.

Human being, then, if it is to be faithful, must hear the word of God before it speaks, before it lives. Human being must somehow know God's name or at least God's word, God's will, before it can know its own name, grasp its own reality, and live a life which has divine warrant, a life which escapes idolatry. However, the divine word and the divine will appear inscrutable. God gives to Moses the knowledge of the divine name *Ehyeh-asher-ehyeh* ("I will be Who I will be" or "I shall be present howsoever I shall be present," according to the renderings of Leo Strauss and Martin Buber, respectively); but it is a name which leaves the divine being radically free and undetermined and thus obscure. In Jesus a new divine name is given by which human being might call upon the divine; but an empty tomb and an all-too-fallible church leave the meaning of that name obscure to many. And as long as divine being remains obscure and radically free, human being drinks deeply of the same obsurity and freedom.

Both Greek thinking and Hebrew-Christian thinking understand the human as it is actively related to the divine. Human speech, human mind and heart, have as their most appropriate and definitive object the divine, the one, the eternal. Human being, and the blessedness which may be said to accompany it, lie in the activity of speech, the activity of uttering the perfect word, the word perfectly formed by one's seeing or one's hearing of God. The disclosing human word of Greek literature and life can be accounted for and shared only by the mind's attending to the disclosure of being; and the creating human word of Hebrew-Christian literature and life can be accounted for and shared only by the heart's attending to the revelation of will. The activity of speech, the work of human being, for both the thinking of Athens and the thinking of Jerusalem, are called forth, informed, inspired by the active presence of the divine which they reflect and image.

Finally, what we may call characteristically modern thinking, despite its theoretical provisions for the divine, is profoundly atheistic and is thus defined by the absence or the alleged absence of the divine. Martin Heidegger suggests that our thinking is not properly to be called thinking and that our loss of the capacity for proper human thinking stems from the fact that what must be thought has turned away from human being. We may recall the saying of Heraclitus ("How would anyone conceal oneself in the presence of what never conceals itself?") and ask: How would anyone disclose or create oneself in the absence of what withdraws? And it is precisely that question to which modern Western thinking has endeavored to respond. Clearly there can be no question here of surveying the myriad yet convergent paths of modern thinking. Instead, it must suffice to claim that characteristically modern thinking is defined by its atheism, which is not to slur that thinking but to perceive its core. It is indeed rooted in the absence, the withdrawal, the death, or the denial of the divine word, the presence of which gave birth to and sustained ancient thinking.

In the modern tradition, the human word, in its desires, aspirations, and assertions, remains nevertheless faithful to its ancient roots, in that the human word remains defined by the divine word, understood as disclosive light and as creative power. What is definitively modern is the claim and the experience of the identity of the human word and the divine word. The tradition of modern Western thinking has single-mindedly and single-heartedly meditated upon human being, appropriating to those reflections all the ancient divine names and powers. At the dawn of the modern era, Francis Bacon proclaimed a new science that would bring with it a new world. This science was to lay bare the secrets of the universe and, in the same moment, give to human being effective control of that universe. This new science was to represent the disclosure of human power. In this vision, the world of disclosure and the world of creation are thought to fuse and to prepare a new world or, at least, a new human being, an *Obermensch,* who is now revealed and affirmed to be not the image but the original, of which Greek being and the Hebrew-Christian God are fated and fallen images. The working of this reversal, the recentering of the universe in the human and the establishing of human sovereignty describes the modern understanding of the properly and uniquely human work, for which modern thinking has provided the theoretical foundation and elaboration. This theory is surely complete with Nietzsche, who claims that it has been human being's "most unselfish act hitherto to admire and worship and to know how to conceal from himself that it was he who created what he admired" and who raises with unmistakable clarity the question of human would-be divinity, whether human being is, after all, prepared to assume the dominion of the earth as a whole. This is, of course, a question which turns us back as well as forward. It is a question raised as sharply by what we call the past as by what we call the future. It is the question inherent in human speech, a question of our own which we bring to the study of Augustine, who knows this question well. It is here that we meet with him in the work of human thinking.

> *Informed by the traditions of Athens and Jerusalem, Augustine's speech strives to be both creative and disclosive, always in harmony with the divine will and the light of being. The life of the mind thus becomes a dialogue with God in which the word of believing and the word of thinking confront each other's claims and seek a common voice and a common truth. It is by this common truth that Augustine's life is turned back from its lesser strivings and held fast in love.*

CHAPTER 2

CONVERSION

Readings

• 1 •

Human being must first be restored to itself, so that from there, as if it had become a stepping-stone, it might rise and be lifted up to God.

(Retr., 1.8.3)

• 2 •

Recognize in yourself something which I want to call within, within you. . . . Leave behind what lies outside, leave behind your clothing and your flesh. Descend into yourself; go to your secret place, your mind. . . . If you are far from yourself, how can you draw near to God? . . . for not in the body but in the mind has human being been made after the image of God. In his own likeness let us seek God; in his own image let us recognize the creator.

(In Joann. ev., 23.10)

29

• 3 •

You are great, lord, and intensely to be praised. Great is your
strength; there is no limit to your wisdom (Ps. 147.5). And human
beings want to praise you, human beings who are but a part of your
creation and who carry with them their mortality, carry the evidence
of their sin and the evidence that you oppose the proud (Jm. 4.6).
Yet human beings, a part of your creation, want to praise you. And
you encourage us to delight in praising you, because you made us
for yourself. Our heart is restless until it finds quiet in you. Allow
me, lord, to know and to understand whether I should praise you or
pray to you first; whether I should pray to you or know you first. But
who could pray to you without knowing you? An unknowing person
might mistake one thing for another in prayer. Or is it rather
through addressing you in prayer that we know you? But how will
they believe without a preacher? (Rm. 10-14). They will praise the
lord who seek him. For in seeking him they find him, and finding
him, they will praise him (Mt. 7.7). May I seek you, lord, in prayer
and, believing in you, may I pray to you? For you have been
preached to us. My faith, which you have given me, which you have
inspired through the incarnation of your son and the ministry of
your preacher, prays to you.

(*Conf.*, 1.1)

• 4 •

It is not possible that one who loves God would not love oneself.
Indeed, on the contrary, only one who loves God knows how to love
oneself. Since we love ourselves enough if we strive earnestly to
enjoy the supreme and true good, which is, simply, God . . . who can
doubt that we love ourselves, if we love God?

(*De mor.*, 1.26.48)

• 5 •

Therefore, one who knows how to love oneself, loves God; but
one who does not love God, even if one loves oneself—a thing

implanted in one by nature—may nevertheless not unfittingly be said to hate oneself. ... For now the mind loves itself, not perversely, but rightly, when it loves God.

(*De Trin.*, 14.14.18)

· 6 ·

I have said these things so that even the slower of understanding, before whose eyes or ears this book might come, may be admonished, though briefly, how great is even the weak and erring mind's love for itself when it loves wrongly and pursues things which are beneath it. Now it could not love itself if it were altogether ignorant of itself, nor understand itself. By virtue of this image of God in it, the mind is so powerful as to be able to cleave to him whose image it is. For the mind is so ordered—in the ordering of natures, not of places—that there is none save God above the mind. When, finally, the mind will wholly cleave to God, it will be one spirit with him, to which reality the apostle bears testimony when he says: Moreover, one who cleaves to the lord, is one spirit with him (1 Co. 6.17). And this happens by virtue of the mind's drawing near to participate in God's nature, truth, and blessedness. In that nature, therefore, when the mind will have cleaved to it, the mind will live without change and will see as unchangeable everything which it will have seen. Then in accord with the promise of divine scripture to it, its desire will be satisfied with good things (Ps. 102.5), unchangeable goods, the divine trinity itself, the mind's God, whose image it is. ... But now, when it sees itself, it does not see something unchangeable.

(*De Trin.*, 14.14.20)

· 7 ·

He tells us that no other creature separates us. O man of highest mysteries! He was not content with saying "creature;" but he says "other creature," thus reminding us that whereby we love God, and that whereby we cling to God, namely, the soul and mind, is a creature. Therefore, the body is another creature. And if the soul is something intelligible, namely, something known only by intellectual understanding, the "other creature" comprises everything sensible, namely, something which, as it were, offers itself to be known through the eyes, or ears, or smell, or taste, or touch. And this latter creature is necessarily inferior to what is grasped by intellectual understanding alone.

Therefore, since God too can be known by worthy souls only through intellectual understanding—although he is more excellent than that understanding by which he is understood, for he is its creator and author—there is reason for fear, lest the human soul, by being numbered among invisible and intelligible things, should judge itself to be of the same nature as he who created it. And so it would fall away through pride from him with whom it should be united in love. For the human soul becomes like God to the extent granted by its subjecting itself to God to be honored and enlightened. And if, in that subjection by which the soul becomes like God, it approaches very near to him, it is necessarily cast far from him in the audacity by which it wishes to be more like God. It is with this same audacity that the soul refuses to observe the laws of God while it desires to be of its own power, as God is.

The further, therefore, that the soul departs from God, not in space, but in its affection and in lust for things beneath it, the more it is filled with foolishness and misery. And thus the return to God is by love, a love by which the soul strives to place itself not in contention with God but beneath him. The more urgent and zealous the soul has been in doing this, the more blessed and sublime it will be. And its freedom will be perfect with God alone as its lord. Thus the soul must know that it is a creature. For it must believe what is true, that its creator remains always in the inviolable and unchanged nature of truth and wisdom; and it must, however, confess, especially in face of the errors from which it longs to escape, that it can fall into foolishness and falsehood. Yet, on the other hand, the soul must take care lest, by the love of another creature, namely, by the love of this sensible world, it be separated from the love of God which sanctifies it for an enduring and perfect blessedness.

(*De mor.*, 1.11.20-21)

• 8 •

For a long time I had been turning over within myself many and various things. And for many days I had been earnestly seeking

myself, and my good, and what evil was to be shunned. Suddenly
someone spoke to me. Whether it was myself, or someone else from
without, or from within, I do not know. Indeed, that is the very
thing which I struggled so very greatly to know. Someone, then,
spoke to me. *Reason.*—Behold, suppose that you have discovered
something. To what will you entrust it, so that you might proceed to
other things? *Augustine.*—To memory, of course. *R.*—Is memory so
great as to preserve well all your thoughts? *A.*—That would be
difficult, nay impossible. *R.*—Then you must write them down. But
what do you do when your health does not allow for the labor of
writing? These thoughts ought not to be dictated, as they long for
unqualified solitude. *a.*—You speak truly. And thus I know not at all
what I should do. *R.*—Pray for health and for assistance in realizing
your desires. And commit this to writing so that you might be made
all the more spirited in your posterity. Then gather together
succinctly in a few brief conclusions what you find. Take no care to
invite a horde of readers. These will be sufficient for your few fellow
citizens. *A.*—I shall do as you say.

O God, you who have established the universe, grant to me first
that I might beseech you well, and then that I might bear myself
worthily of your hearing me, and finally that you might deliver me.
O God through whom all things strive to exist, things which without
you would have no existence. O God, you who let perish not even
that which destroys itself. O God, you who have created from
nothing the world which the eyes of all perceive to be most
beautiful. O God, you who do no evil and who are responsible for
the worst not happening. O God, you who show to those few taking
refuge in what truly is that evil is nothing. O God, through whom
the universe is made perfect despite its sinister side. O God, through
whom no disharmony is final, since the better and the worse are in
concert. O God, loved by everything able to love, whether knowingly or unknowingly. O God, in whom are all things; you who are
yet undefiled by the defilement of the created universe, unharmed
by its malice, unconfused by its error. O God, you who have willed
that only the pure should know the truth. O God, father of truth,
father of wisdom, father of the true and perfect life, father of
blessedness, father of the good and the beautiful, father of the
intelligible light, father of our awakening and of our illumination,
father of the pledge by which we are admonished to return to you.

I call upon you, O God, truth, in whom and by whom and
through whom all that is true is true. O God, wisdom, in whom and

by whom and through whom all who are wise are wise. O God, true and perfect life, in whom and by whom and through whom all things live which live truly and perfectly. O God, blessedness, in whom and by whom and through whom all blessed things are blessed. O God, the good and beautiful, in whom and by whom and through whom all good and beautiful things are good and beautiful. O God, intelligible light, in whom and by whom and through whom all things which shine intelligibly shine intelligibly. O God, you whose kingdom is a whole world of which our senses are ignorant. O God, whose kingdom is the source of law even in these kingdoms. O God, to turn from whom is to fall; to turn towards whom is to rise; and to abide in whom is to stand fast. O God, to depart from whom is to die; to return to whom is to come to life again; and to dwell in whom is to live. O God, whom only the deceived lose, whom only the admonished seek, and whom only the purified find. O God, the abandoning of whom is what it means to perish, the attending to whom is what it means to love, the seeing of whom is what it means to possess. O God, to whom faith summons us, to whom hope raises us, with whom love unites us, O God, through whom we overthrow our foe, I implore you. O God, whom we receive lest we perish altogether. O God, by whom we are admonished to be vigilant. O God, through whom we distinguish good from evil. O God, through whom we flee what is evil and follow after what is good. O God, through whom we do not give way to adversities. O God, through whom we serve well and rule well. O God, through whom we learn that these things that once were ours are another's and through whom we learn that these things which we once supposed to be another's belong to us. O God, through whom we do not cleave to the delights and allurements of the wicked. O God, through whom insignificant things do not render us insignificant. O God, through whom what is better in us is not made subject to what is worse. O God, through whom death is swallowed up in victory (1 Co. 15.54). O God, you who convert us, you who divest us of what is not and clothe us in what is. O God, you who make us to be heard. O God, you who protect us. O God, you who lead us to every truth. O God, you who speak to us all good things; you who neither make nor allow us to be foolish. O God, you who recall us to the way. O God, you who conduct us to the door. O God, you who cause the door to be opened to those who knock (Mt. 7.8). O God, you who give to us the bread of life. O God, through whom we drink the draught from which, when it is drunk, we shall never thirst again (Jn. 6.35). O God, you who accuse the world concerning sin, concerning justice, and concerning judgment (Jn. 16.8). O God, through whom we are not moved by those whose faith is the slightest. O God, through whom we renounce the error of those who suppose that with you souls have no merit. O God, through whom we do not serve the sick and needy elements (Ga. 6.9). O God, you who purify us, and prepare us for divine rewards, come propitiously to my assistance.

One God, come to my aid, whatever I say, one eternal and true substance, where there is no strife, no confusion, no passage, no needfulness, no death, where there is perfect concord, perfect clarity, perfect constancy, perfect fullness, perfect life. Where nothing is lacking, and nothing is superfluous. Where begetter and begotten are one. O God, served by all things which serve, and obeyed by every good soul. O God, by whose laws the poles revolve, the stars hold to their courses, the sun presides over the day, and the moon regulates the night, and the whole world keeps the great harmony of things, so far as sensible matter permits, in the orders and cycles of times—from day to day in the alternation of light and darkness, from month to month in the waxing and waning of the moon, from year to year in the succession of spring, summer, autumn, winter, from census to census in the perfection of the sun's course, and in vast circles, as the stars return to the point of their rising. O God, by whose laws standing forever, the unstable movement of changeable things is not permitted disruption and, by the reins of the revolving ages is always recalled to the likeness of stability. O God, by whose laws the soul's will is free and rewards and punishments are allotted to the good and to the evil, respectively, by an established necessity pervading all things. O God, from whom all good things proceed to us, and by whom all evil things are warded off from us. O God, above whom there is nothing, beyond whom there is nothing, without whom there is nothing. O God, beneath whom is everything, in whom is everything, with whom is everything. You who have made human being after your image and likeness, which all acknowlege who know themselves. Hear me, hear me, hear me, my God, my lord, my father, my cause, my hope, my wealth, my honor, my home, my fatherland, my health, my light, my life. Hear me, hear me, hear me in your own manner perfectly known to few.

Now you alone I love, you alone I follow, you alone I seek, you alone am I prepared to serve, because you alone are justly lord. I desire to be under your right. Order, I beseech you, and command whatever you want; but heal and open my ears that I might hear your voice. Heal and open my eyes that I might see your beckonings

Rid me of madness that I might recognize you. Tell me where to attend that I might gaze upon you; and I hope I shall fulfil all your commands. Receive, I pray, your fugitive, lord, most clement father. Already I have been punished enough; enough have I served your enemies whom you have beneath your feet. Enough have I been the sport of frauds. Accept me, you servant, fleeing from these things; for they too accepted me, a stranger, when I was fleeing from you. I sense I must return to you. Let your door swing open to me as I knock. Teach me how it is that one is to reach you. I am all will. I know only that fluid, fallen things are to be spurned and that sure, external things are to be sought after. I do this, father, because this alone is what I know. But of how to reach you I know nothing. Provide for me, guide me, give me nourishment along the way. If it is by faith that they who take refuge in you find you, then give me faith; if by virtue, then give me virtue; if knowledge, then knowledge. Increase in me faith, hope, and love. O how admirable and unique is your goodness!

I come to you. Again I ask you how one comes to you. For anyone you desert perishes. But this you do not do, because you are the supreme good, which no one has rightly sought and failed to find. Moreover, you have been rightly sought by everyone whom you have made to seek you rightly. Father, make me to seek you; set me free from error. Father, I beg, let nothing take your place for me who seek you. If, however, there is in me the desire for anything superfluous, cleanse me yourself and make me fit to see you. Moreover, regarding the health of this my mortal body, so long as it is of some use to me or to those I love, I entrust it to you, father most wise and perfect; and I pray on behalf of that which you have for a time incited. Only I beseech your most excellent clemency to convert me wholly to you, and to make nothing oppose my drawing close to you, and to command me, while I bear and carry this very body, to be pure, magnanimos, just, and prudent, a perfect percipient and lover of your wisdom, and a worthy dweller in your most blessed kingdom. Amen. Amen.

A.—Behold, I have made my prayer to God. *R.*—What, therefore, do you will to know? *A.*—All those very things for which I have prayed. *R.*—Summarize them briefly. *A.*—I desire to know God and the soul. *R.*—Nothing more? *A.*—Nothing at all. *R.*—Then begin your seeking.

(*Solil.*, 1.1.1-1.2.7)

• 9 •

Reason—It is well to be affected as you are. For reason promises what it says to you, that God will present himself to your mind as the sun is presented to the eyes. The mind has, as it were, its own eyes, senses of the soul. Moreover, the most certain truths of the learned disciplines are like things which the sun illumines so that they might be visible, such as the earth and all earthly things. And it is God himself who casts this light. I, Reason, am in minds just as the power of looking is in eyes. For to have eyes is not the same thing as to look; and to look is not the same as to see. Thus the soul has need of three things: eyes which it can already use well, looking, and seeing. The eyes are healthy when the mind is pure of every bodily disgrace, namely, when it has been set off from and purged of inordinate desire for mortal things. And this is what faith alone first exhibits. For it is not yet possible to show this to a mind sick with vices and unreasonableness. Only a healthy mind is able to see. And if the mind does not believe that in this way alone it will come to sight, then it fails to work at its own health. But even if it believes this to be the case and thus believes that, if it has been able to see, only in this way will it come to sight and yet despairs of the possibility of its being healed, does not this mind utterly degrade and despise itself and refuse to observe the physician's instructions? *A.*—Precisely so, especially since the sickness necessarily experiences those instructions as harsh. *R.*—What, then, if the mind believes all this to be so and has hope in the possibility of its own being healed, and yet does not love that very light which is promised, does not long for it, but supposes that meanwhile it ought to be content with its own darkenss, already congenial through habit, does not that mind nonetheless spurn the physician? *A.*—Yes, entirely. *R.*—Therefore, a third is necessary, love. *A.*—Nothing could be so wholly necessary. *R.*—Without these three, then, no soul is healed so as to be able to see, that is, know its God. When, therefore, the soul's eyes are healed, what remains? *A.*—That it should look. *R.*—Reason is the soul's looking. But it does not follow that everyone who looks sees. And so, right and perfect looking, which is followed by a vision, we call virtue; for virtue is right and perfect reason. But even the soul's looking cannot turn eyes, although already healed, to the light unless these things endure: faith, to believe that the soul's looking is to be directed toward what is believed so that, when it is seen, it might make that looking blessed; hope, to presume that it will see, once it has looked rightly; and love, to desire to see and to enjoy. Looking is followed by the very vision of God, which is the end of looking, not in the sense that it does not now exist but in the sense that it has nothing further to strive for. This is truly the perfect virtue, reason reaching its own end, which is the blessed life.

(Solil., 1.6.12-13)

• 10 •

Those things which we touch, or taste, or smell are less like this truth, which is more like those things which we hear and see. For every word is heard wholly by all who hear it and is heard wholly in the same time by each individual. So also every sight which presents itself to the eyes is the same for one viewer as for another, and is seen by all in the same time. But between these similar things there is a very great difference. For no utterance is sounded wholly in a single instant; rather, it is extended and prolonged through a series of times. One part of it is sounded first, and is then followed by another part. Every sight to be seen, on the other hand, is extended through a series of spatial points. It is nowhere wholly present.

And certainly all of these things are taken away despite our will; and, enslaved in difficulties, we are unable to enjoy them. Even if someone's sweet song could last forever, that one's devotees would anxiously come to hear. They would pack themselves closely together and fight over the places. The more numerous they would be the more they would fight, each one anxious to get closer to the singer. And, in the actual hearing, they would hold nothing which could remain with them; rather, they would be touched by every fleeting sound.

Moreover, if I wished to behold the sun and were able to do so persistently, it too would desert me in its very setting, or be veiled behind a cloud. And, beset with many other obstacles, I would lose, quite unwillingly, the pleasure of seeing the sun. Finally, even if the pleasure of seeing light and of hearing sound would always be with me, how would it greatly profit me, since it would be common to me and brute beasts?

But the beauty of truth and of wisdom, so long as there is present the preservering will to delight in it, does not crowd out with a

crushing multitude of hearers those who come to it. Nor does it pass
with time, nor change its place. Night never interrupts it; and
shadows never close it off. It has no converse with the senses of the
body. That beauty is perfectly at hand amd everlasting for all those
who from all the world have turned to it and love it. Nowhere is it
present, never is it absent. Outwardly it diminishes; inwardly it
teaches. It changes for the better all who behold it; by no one is it
changed for the worse. No one passes judgment on it; no one judges
well without it. From this it is manifest that that beauty is
undoubtedly better than our minds, which are made individually
wise by it. Through it they judge concerning other things; but is
itself beyond the judgment of our minds.

(De lib. arb., 2.14.38)

• 11 •

He that planted the ear, will he not hear? He who formed the eye,
will he not see? *(Ps. 93.9).* If, therefore, the word formed the eye,
since all things exist through the word; and if the word planted the
ear, since all things exist through the word, we cannot say that the
word does not hear, or that the word does not see. Otherwise, the
psalm would say to us reprovingly: Fools, someday be wise (Ps.
93.8). And, if the word hears and sees, then the son hears and sees;
but are we going to search for eyes and ears in different places?
Does he hear with one organ, and see with another? Can he not do
with his ears what his eyes do or do with his eyes what his ears do?
Or is he wholly sight and wholly hearing? Perhaps; no, not perhaps,
but truly. His seeing and his hearing are far different from ours.
Seeing and hearing are one in the word. In the word, hearing is not
one thing and seeing another. Rather, hearing is seeing, and seeing
is hearing.

And how do we come to know this, we who hear in one way and
see in another? Perhaps we return to ourselves, if we are not double
dealers to whom it is said: Return, double dealers, to your heart (Is.
46.8). Return to your heart. Why depart from yourselves and perish
from yourselves? Why go the ways of solitude? Why wander astray?
Return. Where? To the lord. It is quickly accomplished. First return
to your heart; you have wandered abroad, an exile from yourself.
You do not know yourself and yet you are seeking your maker.

Return. Return to your heart. Take yourself from your body. Your body is a dwelling for you; your heart too perceives through your body. But your body is not what your heart is. Quit your body. Return to your heart. In your body you are used to finding eyes in one place and ears in another. Do you find anything like this in your heart? Or do you have no ears in your heart? But of what was the Lord, then, speaking when he said; Whoever has ears to hear, let that one hear? (Lk. 8.8). Or do you have no eyes in your heart? How is it, then, that the apostle speaks of the eyes of your heart being enlightened? (Ep. 1.18).

Return to your heart. See there what perhaps you may perceive of God, since there is the image of God. Within the inner human being dwells Christ, therein you have been made anew after the image of God. In his own image, recognize its author.

(Tr. in Joann. ev., 18.9-10)

• 12 •

Behold, when we read this one precept: Love your neighbor as yourself (Mt. 22.39), three kinds of vision occur: one through the eyes, by which we see the letters themselves; another through the human spirit, by which we think of the neighbor, even when absent; and a third through an attending of the mind, by which we understand and see love itself. Among these three kinds of vision the first is clear to everyone. For in this vision we see heaven a d earth and all things in heaven and earth which meet our eyes. Nor is it difficult to introduce the second vision by which absent corporeal things are thought of; for we think of heaven and of earth and of those visible things in them even when we are situated in darkness. Indeed, in this situation, our eyes see nothing; yet we gaze upon corporeal images in the soul, whether those images be true, as if we saw the bodies themselves and retained them in memory, or whether those images be fictitious, as if thought could have fashioned them. Thus, we think in one way of Carthage, a place unknown to us. Now that third kind of vision, by which we understand and see love, compresses those things which do not have images resembling themselves, images which are what they themselves are. For a human being, or a tree, or the sun, or any other body whatsoever, whether heavenly or earthly, when present, is seen in its own form and, when absent, is thought of in an image impressed upon the soul. These things, then, bring about two kinds of vision: one through the senses of the body, and the other through the spirit, which contains those images. However, is love seen in one way when it is present in the form in which it exists and seen in another way when it is absent and is in some image resembling itself? Not at all. Rather, it is discerned more clearly by one and less clearly by another, depending on the capacity of one's mind to discern clearly. However, if one is thinking of some corporeal image, then it is itself discerned not at all.

We should now signify these three kinds of vision by names that are definite and consistent, so as to avoid the delays of talking around them continuously. Therefore, let us call the first kind of vision corporeal, because it is perceived through the body and is presented to the senses of the body. The second we will call spiritual; for whatever is not a body and yet is something, is rightly called spirit. The image of the absent body, although it resembles a body, is certainly not a body; nor is it itself the sight by which the body is seen. The third we will call intellectual, from the "intellect," because mental [*mentale*] from mind [*mens*], a newly coined word, is too absurd for us to speak. . . .

Therefore, these three kinds of vision, namely, corporeal, spiritual, and intellectual, are to be considered one at a time, so that reason might ascend from the lower to the higher. We have already proposed an example whereby all three kinds may be seen in one sentence. For when we read: Love your neighbor as yourself (Mt. 22.39), the letters are seen corporeally, the neighbor is thought of spiritually, and love is beheld intellectually. But the letters, when absent, can also be thought of spiritually; and the neighbor, when present, can be seen corporeally. Love, however, can be known and perceived by the mind alone, that is, by the intellect.

Clearly, corporeal vision presides over neither of the other two kinds of vision. Instead, what is sensed through corporeal vision is announced to spiritual vision, which, as it were, presides over it. For when anything is seen by the eyes, its image is immediately formed in the sprit. But this image, although produced, is not discerned, unless we find its image in the soul with eyes removed from that which we were seeing through our eyes. And if, indeed, the spirit is irrational, as is the bestial spirit, the eyes announce it only thus far; but if the soul is rational, it is also announced to the intellect, which presides over the spirit. And so, if the eyes have announced to the

spirit what they have drawn in so that its image might be formed
therein, there exists the sign of something, the meaning of which is
either immediately understood or sought out; for it can be neither
understood nor sought except by the service of the mind. . . .

There is something here to be wondered at. Although the spirit is
prior to the body and the body is prior to the image of the body, yet,
because what is later in time is formed in that which is by nature
prior, the image of the body in the spirit is preeminent over the
body itself in its own substance. And it must surely not be thought
that the body produces something in the spirit, as if the spirit were
subjected to the body making something from matter. For one who
makes something is in every way preeminent over that from which
one makes it. But the body is in no way preeminent over the spirit;
indeed, the spirit is manifestly preeminent over the body. . . .

So also, in the category of intellectual visions, there are some
which are seen in the soul itself, for example, virtues, as opposed to
vices: either enduring virtues, such as piety,or virtues useful for this
life but not for the later future life, such as faith by which we believe
what we do not yet see, and such as hope by which we patiently
await what will be, and such as patience itself by which we bear
every adversity until we come to where we wish to be. These virtues,
surely, as well as others like them, which are quite necessary now for
the sake of living through this exile, will be no longer, in that life for
the attainment of which they are necessary. And yet even they
themselves are seen intellectually; for they are not bodies, nor do
they have forms resembling bodies. Moreover, quite another thing is
that light which illumines the soul so that it might truly understand
and behold all things either in itself or in that light. For that light is
God himself, whereas this soul is a creature, which, although made
rational and intellectual after the image of God, trembles with
weakness and fails in strength when it tries to gaze upon that light.
Yet, whatever it is able to understand it understands from that
source. And when, therefore, it is withdrawn from its carnal senses
and is carried off there, it is made present to this vision in a more
express manner, not in terms of spatial proximity but in a way of its
own; and it beholds above itself that light by which it is enabled to
see whatever, in understanding, it sees, even in itself.

(De Gen. ad Litt., 12.6-7; 12.11; 12.16; 12.31)

• 13 •

I will confess, then, what I know about myself; since what I know, I know through your clarification, and what I do not know, I do not know only until my darkness becomes like midday in your countenance.

(Conf., 10.5)

• 14 •

My lord God, hear me; look down upon me and see me; pity me and heal me. I have become a subject of inquiry to myself in your eyes and that is my weakness.

(Conf., 10.33)

• 15 •

Indeed, lord, even if I wished not to confess to you, what in me could be hidden from you, to whose eyes the depths of a human's conscience are apparent? I would not be hiding myself from you but you from myself. But now, when my groaning is witness to my displeasure in myself, you shine on me and placate me; you are loved and desired so that I reject myself in shame and choose you and so that I am pleasing neither to you nor to myself, except on your account. Therefore, lord, I am manifest to you wherever I am. I have spoken of the profit in confessing to you. I do it not with words and voices of my body but with words of the soul and with the shouting of my thought, which your ear understands. When I am evil, there is nothing to confess to you, except my displeasure in myself. When I am righteous, there is nothing to confess to you but my lack of responsibility for it. Since, lord, you bless the just but first you pardon their impiety. So my confession to you, my God, is done silently in your sight—and yet not silently. In its sound it is silent; in its feeling it cries out. Anything correct I say to people you have first heard from me, and you hear no such words from me which you have not previously spoken to me.

(Conf., 10.2)

• 16 •

For to listen to you about themselves is nothing other than to know themselves.

(Conf., 10.3)

• 17 •

Where did I find you in order that I might learn of you? Certainly you were not in my memory before I learned of you. So where did I find you to learn of you unless it was in yourself and above me? There is never a place; we come and go, but there is never a place. Truth, you give audience to all who consult you and immediately respond to all the different questions. You respond clearly but all do not hear you clearly. All consult you about whatever they want, but all do not hear what they want. Your best servant is the one who pays less attention, when listening to you, to what is desired and more to what is heard.

(Conf., 10.26)

• 18 •

Let truth, light of my heart, and not the shadows within me speak to me! I slid down into that state and was in darkness, but even from there I loved you. I strayed and yet I remembered you. I heard your voice behind me, telling me to return, but I heard only faintly because of the uproar of the restless. And now I am returning, sweaty and out of breath, to your fountain. Let no one get in my way. I will drink this and I will live it. May I not be my life; I have lived badly on my own. I was my own death. I revive in you. Speak to me; discuss with me. I have believed your books and their words are full of mystery.

(Conf., 12. 10)

· 19 ·

I call on you, my God merciful to me, who made me and did not forget me when I had forgotten you. I call on you in my soul which you prepare to take hold of you from desire, inspired by you. Do not forsake me now that I am calling on you, when you have, in the past, come even before I called on you. Gathering the strength of many various voices you came before me and insisted that I hear from afar, that I be converted, and that I call upon you who were calling me.

(Conf., 13.1)

· 20 ·

We never ceased longing for philosophy and for that life which we found pleasant and harmonious. We endeavored to think of nothing else whatever; and we attended to it constantly, though less passionately. Nevertheless, we considered our efforts to be sufficient. As we were not yet in the presence of that flame which was to lay hold of us at its height, we thought that it was at its greatest such as it now warmed us. Yet behold, when certain rich books, as Celsinus says, exhaled Arabian sweetness over us, when they instilled the tiniest drops of most precious ointment into that slight flame, they at once enkindled in me an incredible conflagration, incredible, Romanianus, incredible even beyond what you may perhaps believe from my lips. What more can I say? What honor, what human pomp, what vain greed for fame, finally, what excitement or bond of this mortal life had any affect on me then? Facing forwards, I was now returning, quickly and fully, to myself. It was as if I were returning from a journey; for I confess that I looked from afar upon that religion which had been implanted in us as children and interwoven with the very marrow of our being. That religion was drawing me to itself without my knowing it. Thus, trembling, hastening, yet hesitant, I took up the epistles of Paul. For truly, I say, they couyd not have done such great things, nor would they have lived as it is manifest that they did live, if the writings and their reasons were not at odds with this such great good. I read the whole book with the greatest attention and piety.

(C. Acad., 2.2.5)

• 21 •

At that adolescent period of my life I was studying, with these companions, books on eloquence, which was a subject in which I wished to excel, an empty and blameworthy goal inspired by the glorification of human vanity. In the normal course of study I came to the work of Cicero, whose language, though not his sensibilities, almost everyone admired. However, one of his books, Hortensius, contains an exhortation to philosophy, and that book changed my thinking and transformed my prayers to you. For it gave me different longings and desires. Suddenly I despised as empty all my hopes and yearned for the immortality of wisdom with an amazing swelling in my heart. I began to ascend that I might return to you. I was eighteen and apparently spending my mother's money, two years after my father's death, for the sharpening of my tongue. However, it was not for that purpose, not for a sharper tongue, that I studied that book. For what won me over in that book was what it said, not how it spoke.

How I burned, my God, I burned to fly from earthly matters to you; yet I had no idea what you would do with me. For wisdom lived with you. But a love of wisdom the Greeks had a name for: philosophy; and with this that book inflamed me. Some men seduce with philosophy by coloring and embellishing their errors with its great, exciting, and honest name. This book reprimands and exposes almost all such men from Cicero's time and before. In addition, it illustrates that strengthening advice from your spirit, given through your good and faithful servant: Take care that no one deceive you through philosophy, as is the custom of the people and elements of this world, but not of Christ, because in him lives all the fullness of God in human form (Col. 2.8). You, light of my heart, know that at that time I was not yet aware of the scriptures; nonetheless I was delighted by this one aspect of the advice in that book, that it encouraged me not to follow this or that sect but avidly to esteem, seek, pursue, grasp, and embrace wisdom itself, whatever it may be. I was excited and inflamed by that statement and was burning with it. In my eagerness only one thing held me back. The name of Christ did not appear there. I had drunk this name, according to your mercy, lord, this name of my savior, your son, into my young heart with my mother's milk and had held it deep within me. Whatever was without that name, no matter how learned and polished and truthful, could not claim me wholly.

And so I decided to turn my attention to the holy scriptures to see what they were. What I see now is something hidden from the proud, not disclosed to children, but humble in its approach and exalted in its outcome, veiled in mysteries. But, being the person I was then, I was not able to enter the scriptures or to bow my head to their coming. At that time, when I thought about them, they seemed to me paltry compared to the dignity of Cicero. My pride shunned their mode and my acute wit did not penetrate their essence. It is surely true, that as children grow, these books grow with them. But I disdained being a child and considered myself big, though I was merely swollen with pride.

(Conf., 3.4-5)

• 22 •

Truly, lord, you exist in eternity but are not eternally angered at us since you pity dust and ashes. It was pleasing in your sight to transform my baseness. And you prodded me inside with goads so that I would be impatient until you became certain and clear to my internal vision. My bloated condition was relieved by the hidden ministrations of your medicine, and the confused and shadowed vision of my mind was daily improved by the bitter ointment of beneficial sorrows.

And because you wished first of all to demonstrate to me how you oppose the proud and give grace to the humble (Jm. 4.6), and how the path of humility has been shown to humanity through your great mercy because the word was made flesh and lived among human beings—for these reasons you made available for me through a certain man, who was huge and swollen with pride, some books by Platonists, translated into Latin verse from the Greek. There I read, not in these words but supported by many, varied arguments, this very thing: that in the beginning was the word and the word was with God and God was the word; this word was in the beginning with God. All things were made through it and without it nothing was made. There was life in what was made and life was the light of human beings. And the light shines in shadows and the shadows did not take hold of it (Jn. 1-5). And I read there that the soul of a human being is not itself the light, although it gives testimony to it; however, the word, God himself, is the true light which illumines everyone who comes into the world (Jn. 1.9). And I read that he was in this world and the world was made through him and yet the world knew him not (Jn. 1.10). But the fact that he came to his own and his own did not receive him, while to those who did receive him he gave the power to be the sons of God, as they believed in his name (Jn. 11-12), this I did not read there.

I did read in those books that God the word was not born from flesh nor from blood nor from the will of human being nor from the will of the flesh, but from God. But I did not read that the word was made flesh and lived among us. In these books I tracked down the statement, although it was phrased differently and not in various ways, that the son who was in the form of the father did not think that it was theft to be equal to God because he was by nature the same as God (Ph. 2.6). But these books did not say that he made himself empty by accepting the form of a servant, similar in his shape to human beings and in clothing to a man (Ph. 2.7). He humbled himself by making himself obedient unto death, even death on a cross (Ph. 2.8). For this God raised him from the dead and gave him a name above every name so that at the name of Jesus (Ph., 2.9), every knee in heaven, on earth, and under the earth would bend and every tongue would confess that Jesus is lord in the glory of God his father (Ph. 2.10-11).

The books said that before all time and after all time your only begotten son remains unchangeable and eternal along with you, and souls take from his fullness that they might be blessed; they are renewed by partaking in that knowledge which remains in them so that they might be wise. The books did not say that in due time he died for the wicked and that you did not spare your only son but surrendered him for us all (Rm. 8.32). You hid these things from the knowledgeable and revealed them to the insignificant so that those who labor and are burdened may come to him and be restored (Mt. 11.28); for he is gentle and humble in judgment and teaches the mild his ways. He looks upon our humility and our toil and forgives all our sins. Those who are made grandiose by the eloquence of a higher learning do not hear what he says: Learn from me, as I am gentle and humble in my heart, and you will find peace in your soul (Mt. 11.29); and, if they know God but do not glorify him or give thanks to him but rather disappear into their own thoughts and darken their foolish hearts (Rm. 1.21), then they become fools though they say they are wise. (Rm. 1.22).

I also read that the glory of your incorruptible nature was transferred to idols and various statues in the shape of corruptible humankind, of birds and beasts and serpents (Rm.1.23); to that Egyptian food, as it were, for which Esau lost his birthright, since your firstborn people honored the head of a beast instead of you and turned their hearts to Egypt, bowing down their soul, your image, before the image of a calf which chews hay (Ps. 106.20). I read these things there, and I did not chew on them. For it pleased you, lord, to remove the reproach of inferiority from Jacob so that the older might serve the younger and so you have called the gentiles into your inheritance. I had come to you from the gentiles and I turned my attention to the gold which you wished your people to bring from Egypt and which was yours wherever it was. You said to the Athenians through your apostle that we live and move and exist in you, just as certain of their poets said (Ac. 17.28). So surely these books came from Athens. I did not turn my attention to the idols of the Egyptians to which they paid homage with your gold, changing the truth of God into a lie and worshipping the creature rather than the creator (Rm. 1.25).

Thereafter, as I had been warned to return to my self, I entered into my own depths, with you as my guide. I was able to because you had made yourself my helper. I entered and with the eye of my soul, such as it is, I saw an immutable light over this same eye of my soul, over my mind. It was not the common light which is easily seen by all flesh nor was it a light like that but greater, as if it had grown more and more bright until it filled everything with its brightness. It was not of that kind at all but different, completely different from all such things. It did not shine over my mind like oil over water nor like the sky over the earth. It was above because it created me and I was below because I was created by it. If one knows truth, one knows this light; if one knows this light, one knows eternity. Love knows it. Oh, eternal truth and true love and beloved eternity! You are my God. I sigh day and night to you. When I first recognized you, you raised me up so that I might see that there was something which I should see, but that I was not yet the kind of person who might see it. You whipped back the weakness of my sight; you shone on me forcefully, and I trembled with love and horror. I found myself far from you in a place completely different, as if I heard from high above me your voice: I am food for grown people. Grow and you will chew on me. You will not change me into yourself like food for your body, but you will be changed into me.

(Conf., 7.8-10)

• 23 •

Afterwards you stroked my head without my noticing and closed my eyes so that they would not see vanity; I stepped back from myself a little and my insanity was lulled to sleep. I woke up in you and I saw you as infinite in a different way. I did not derive this vision from my flesh.

(Conf., 7.14)

• 24 •

He who made us also remade us.

(Epist., 2ᴐ1.6)

• 25 •

What will procure us salvation except your hand which remakes what you have made?

(Conf., 5.7)

• 26 •

There are, moreover, certain ones who suppose themselves, of their own strength, to be able to cleanse themselves so as to behold and to dwell in God. It is their very pride which defiles them most. For there is no vice which the divine law resists more than this one. ... These same ones promise themselves cleansing on their own, since some of them have been able to penetrate with the mind's eye beyond every creature and to touch, though ever so partially, the light of immutable truth. And they deride many Christians, who meanwhile live by faith alone, for their not being able as yet to do likewise. But how does it profit the proud to catch sight of their homeland from afar across the sea, if on this account they are ashamed to embark upon the ship of wood? And what harm is done the humble by their being unable to see their homeland across so great an expanse, so long as they are approaching it aboard that ship of wood, on which those others disdain to be carried?

(De Trin., 4.15.20)

• 27 •

Truly there is one who is everywhere present, and who, in many ways, through the creation which serves him as its lord, calls those who have turned away, teaches those who believe, encourages those who hope, exhorts those who love, assists those who strive, and listens to those who pray. You are not held to blame for ignorance which you have never willed; but you are held to blame for neglecting to seek out that of which you are ignorant. There is no blame in not binding up one's wounded members; but there is blame in despising one who is willing to heal them. Those are your own private sins. For no one has ever been given to know how to seek usefully that of which one is uselessly ignorant. And so we must confess humbly our utter weakness so that he, who neither errs nor labors in his aid, might come to the assistance of those who are seeking and who make their confession.

(De lib. arb., 3.19.53)

• 28 •

It was a wonder to me that now I was loving you, rather than some image in your place. I did not stand fixed in the enjoyment of my God. Rather, I was swept away to you by your loveliness. Soon, however, I was carried away from you by my own weight. I even rushed into those other concerns, weeping. The weight was the sheer habit of the flesh. But the memory of you remained with me. I never doubted at all that there existed one to whom I might cling but that I was not yet able to do. For the body, corrupt as it is, weights down the soul, and dwelling on earth suppresses the mind which ponders many things. I was most certain from the world's creation your invisible acts are seen, comprehended through the things which were created (Rm. 1.20); also your eternal power and your divinity. In seeking the basis on which I approved the beauty of either

celestial or terrestrial bodies, and the means by which I was able
with justice to judge mutable things and say: this ought to be so,
that not so—in seeking, then, the basis for this judgment, when I
made it, I had found the unchangeable and real eternity of truth
above my changeable mind. And so, step by step, from bodies to the
soul, which perceives through the body and from there to the inner
force of the soul to which the body's senses report eternal things—
which is the farthest step which beasts achieve—I progressed. From
there I went on to the faculty of reason by which the matter
perceived by the body is judged. Reason, also finding itself mutable
in me, raised itself up toward its own understanding and lead my
thoughts away from habit, by withdrawing from the contradictory
confusion of phantoms so that it might discover by which light it
was suffused. Then, without any hesitation, it cried out that the
unchangeable must be preferred to the changeable, from which it
had comprehended the unchangeable itself—which it would never
have preferred to the changeable if it had not comprehended it in
some way; and it arrived at that which is, in a burst of trembling
sight. Then, truly, I perceived your invisible acts which are
understood through that which is made, but I had not the strength
to make fast my gaze. I returned to my accustomed ways through a
weakness which had been momentarily beaten back and I carried
with me nothing but a loving memory and an appetite for the meat,
so to speak, which I was not yet able to eat.

I sought a way of gaining sufficient strength to enjoy you, but I
did not find it until I embraced the mediator between the divine and
the human, the man Jesus Christ (1 Tm. 2.5), who is God over all,
blessed from age to age (Rm. 9.5), and who calls and says: I am the
way of truth and the life (Jn. 14.6); who mixes sustenance which I
was incapable of taking with flesh, since the word was made flesh so
that your wisdom (Jn. 1.14), with which you created everything,
might suckle our infancy. Yet I did not have the humility to
comprehend the humility of my God, Jesus, nor did I understand
what his weakness made him master of. Your world, eternal truth,
which towers over the loftiest heights of your creation, raises up to
its own height those who are cast down. It has built for itself from
our mud a humble house among the lowly. This he did so that he
might draw away from themselves those he wishes to raise up and
might then draw them to himself, curing their swollen state and
feeding their love. His purpose was not to increase their faith in

themselves but rather to weaken it, by making them perceive face to face divinity made weak by assuming a covering of mortal skin. Then in their weakness they might throw themselves on his mortality, which, as it rises, also lifts them up.

At the time I thought quite differently. I had the same feelings about my lord Christ as I would have about a man of outstanding wisdom, to whom no one would claim to be equal. I felt especially that his birth from a virgin, which teaches us by example to despise temporal things for the sake of immortality, was a sign of divine care for us which granted him the authority of a master. But I was not able to imagine what mystery was contained in the word made flesh.

(Conf., 7.17-19)

• 29 •

But when I had finished reading these books of the Platonists and had received from them the advice to seek incorporeal truth, I perceived your invisible things, which are understood through the things which have been created. I felt, remotely but certainly, what I was not allowed to contemplate in the darkness of my soul; that you exist and are infinite but not diffused over infinite or finite space; that you truly exist, always the same, yourself, and never change in any part or with any motion; that all other things exist from you, because of this one, most certain piece of evidence, that they exist.

I was sure in these matters but too weak to enjoy you. I continued to chatter intelligibly, as if I were an expert; but, if I had not sought your way in Christ, our savior, I would have been extinct, not expert. For I had begun to want the reputation of a wise man and, though I was full of punishment, my eyes were not swollen with weeping but my body was, tremendously, with science. Where was that love which builds from a foundation of humility, which is Jesus Christ? When would these books have taught me it?

You willed, I believe, that I should come upon those books before I came to consider your scriptures, so that it would be stamped upon my memory how I had once been affected by those books. It was your will that later, when I would become responsive amidst your books, you would touch my wounds with your healing fingers. Then,

as you willed, I would learn about and mark clearly the difference
between presumption and confession, the difference between those
who see that a journey must be made and yet are blind to the way
and those who see the way leading to the beloved homeland, a land
to be dwelled in as well as perceived with the mind.

If I had first been instructed by your writings, and if you had
become sweet to me through familiarity with them, those books
might then have wrenched me from the solid foundation of piety,
when I came across them. Even if I had remained steady in that
healthy stance which I had acquired from your writings, I might
have thought that it could have been acquired just as well by
reading those books alone.

And so I seized most avidly upon the venerable writings of your
spirit, in particular the apostle Paul. Those problematic points in
which he had sometimes seemed to me to contradict himself had
disappeared. The text of his discourse no longer seemed in
opposition to the testimony of the law and the prophets. His chaste
eloquence had but one face for me, and I learned to rejoice with
trembling (Ps. 2.11). I began to discover that whatever truth I had
read in the Platonists was stated here with the recommendation of
your grace. So those who see should not therefore glorify themselves
as if they had not been given, not only what they see but also that
they see at all. For what do they have which they have not been
given? (2 Co. 4.7). So one should be advised not only to see you who
are always the same, but also to be strengthened in order to keep
hold of you. As for those who cannot see you from afar, nonetheless
they walk along the road by which they might arrive and see and
take hold. For even if someone delights in the law of God in
accordance with the inner self (Rm. 7.22), what can that person do
about the other law in the limbs which opposes the law of the mind
and which makes the mind captive to the law of sin which is in the
limbs? (Rm. 7.23). You are just, lord, but we have sinned; we have
acted unjustly; we have behaved impiously (Dn. 9.5), and your
hand is heavy upon us. We have been justly handed over to the
ancient sinner, the overseer of death, because he had molded our
will to his will, by which he did not stand fast in your truth. What
will unhappy humanity do? Who will free us from the body of this
death (Rm. 7.24), if not your grace through Jesus Christ our lord
whom you conceived to be coeternal with you and whom you
created in the beginning of your ways; in whom the leader of this

world found nothing to make him worthy of death and yet killed him? And the handwriting was erased which was in opposition to us.

(Conf., 7.20-21)

• 30 •

Oh lord, I am your servant, your servant and the son of your handmaid. You burst my chains. I will offer to you the sacrifice of my praise (Ps. 116.16-17). Let my heart and my tongue praise you. Let all my bones cry out: Lord, who is like you? Ps. 35.10). Let them cry out and you answer me and say to my soul: I am your salvation. Who am I? What kind of a person am I? What aspect of evil has not been manifested in my deeds; or, if not my deeds, my words; or, if not my words, my will. Yet, lord, you are good and full of mercy. Your right hand respected the depth of my death and dragged from the bottom of my heart the abyss of corruption. And so it came about that I resisted totally what I willed and willed totally what you willed. But where had this been for so long a time? From what deep and hidden corner was my free will summoned suddenly, with which I offered my neck to your gentle yoke and my shoulders to your light burden, Jesus Christ, my helper and my redeemer? How sweet it suddenly became for me to be without the sweetness of those vanities. Where there had been fear of their loss there was now joy in sending them away. For you dismissed them from me, you who are the true and greatest sweetness. You dismissed them and in their place you entered, who are sweeter than all pleasure, but not to flesh and blood; brighter than all light, but more private than any secret; more exalted than all honor, but not to those who are exalted in themselves. Finally my soul was free from the gnawing cares of aspiring and acquiring, of wallowing in filth and picking at the scab of lust. And I chattered to you, my glory and my wealth, my salvation, my lord God.

(Conf., 9.1)

• 31 •

Lord, I love you with a sure conscience, not a doubtful one. You have pierced my heart with your word and I have loved you. But the

sky and the earth and all things which are in them tell me from all
sides that I should love you. They never stop saying it to all people,
so that they can have no excuse. However, you will show greater
mercy to whomever you show mercy and greater compassion to
whomever you show compassion. Otherwise, the sky and the earth
speak your praises to deaf ears.

(Conf., 10.6)

Who Will Seize the Heart and Hold It Still?

Augustine, in his *Soliloquies,* claims to desire nothing except to
know God and the soul *(Solil.,* 1.2.7). This is the sum and scope of
his prayer to God. This same desire for knowledge of God and of
self finds a peculiarly illuminating formulation in the tenth book
of the *Confessions.*[1] There Augustine relates:

> I directed myself to myself and to myself I said, "You, who are
> you?" And I responded, "A human being." *(Conf.,* 10.6)

> *What* am I, then, my God? What nature am I? My life is many and
> various and violently without measure. *(Conf.,* 10.17) (Italics
> added.)

Self-knowledge appears to be twofold: knowledge of *who* one is
and knowledge of *what* one is: we may note that Augustine
addresses the question "Who am I?" to himself and the question
"What am I?" to God. I would suggest that this distinction
between the who *(quis)* and the what *(quid)* of human being
corresponds rather closely to the distinction which we have
already drawn between the biblical and the Greek conceptions of
human being, that is, between human being as hearer and human
being as see-er, respectively. The elaboration and substantiation
of this claim, however, requires the entire scope of our reflections
upon Augustine. In these reflections, for facility of expression, I
will use the word *person* as synonymous with the *who* of human

---

1. I am indebted here to Hannah Arendt's brief but germinal commentary
upon these texts in *The Human Condition* (Chicago: The University of Chicago
Press, 1958), pp. 12-13 and 302, n. 2.

being and the word *nature* as synonymous with the *what* of human being.

Who a human being is describes the unfolding of a person in time. Augustine likens the creation of personality to the begetting of an inner word (cf. *De Trin.*, 9.7). Who Augustine is, is somehow the creation of Augustine himself; and thus the question "Who am I?" is addressed properly, though perhaps only provisionally so, to himself. A person is altogether timeful, spread across seemingly infinite moments.

> I have flown apart into moments whose order I know not; and my thoughts, the deepest workings of my soul, are shredded by the havoc of change. *(Conf.,* 11.29)

Time is the continuity of unfolding of the soul, the expanding and dividing of the life of the soul into countless distinct moments. A person is all of those moments which comprise a lifetime, past and future; and a person's "moments" are its loves.

> Human being is a great bottomless depth. And yet, lord, you keep count of every human hair, not one of which is slighted. And yet it is easier to count the hairs of the head than to count the movements and stirrings of the heart. *(Conf.,* 4.14)

For Augustine, a human being is, though never wholly and never finally, what it loves.

However, to know who one is, to recall and perceive the loves of one's moments, is not to know oneself. To know that one exists and lives and remembers and understands and loves is to know that one is a human being. And to know this is to have a question. Thus, Augustine's final response to the question addressed most properly to himself, the question "Who are you?," is simply "a human being." One cannot know who one is until one knows what human being is, what God has made human being to be. Augustine cannot know what it means to be Augustine until he knows what it means to be a human being. Augustine's "creation," his person, becomes radically questionable, accountable, before God, before God's creation, human being; in God's eyes

Augustine has become a question to himself (cf. *Conf.*, 10.33). To give an account of one's life is not simply to chronicle one's loves but to speak as well of the faithfulness or the perversity, the appropriateness or the inappropriateness, of those loves. "Such was my life, but was that a life, my God?" (*Conf.*, 3.2). To speak of one's own regarding one's life is to lie (cf. *De Gen. c. Man.*, 2.6); to confess one's life, one's loves, before God is to speak wisely and faithfully.

To give an account of one's life and thus of one's person presumably requires self-knowledge, which for Augustine, within the classical tradition, would mean "self-sight." However, such knowledge could hardly be thought possible; for such would be a contradiction. Insight or theoretical knowledge is understood by Greek thought to be of the timeless and changeless; whereas, recalling a passage cited above, Augustine realizes that he is torn apart, scattered into diverse moments in the confusion of constant change. Self-knowledge would, then, be timeless understanding of what is altogether timeful, changeless understanding of what is altogether changeable. Self-knowledge would require a moment in which the whole of one's life would be simultaneously present and available to sight. Augustine attributes such knowledge and such a moment, an eternal moment, to God. It is interesting to note that Augustine sees eternity not as the absence but rather as the fullness of time, the simultaneous presence of all time (cf. *Conf.*, 11.11).

> You are supreme and beyond change. In you the present day is never spent; and yet it is spent in you. For in you even these moments all exist. Indeed, if you did not contain them, they would have no way of transpiring. Your years are a today, because they never pass. And however numerous our days and our fathers' days have been, they have passed through your today and received from it their limits and the character of their existence. So too will others pass the same way, receiving their limits and the character of their existence. You, however, remain yourself the same, while in your today you have once fashioned and will once again fashion all our yesterdays and all our tomorrows. *(Conf.*, 1.6)

Corresponding to the eternal present, to God's undying day, Augustine describes the presence of one's past and future, all of one's yesterdays and tomorrows, to mind, once the mind has expanded itself by the activities of memory and expectation to receive this full personal presence.

> The presence of past things is memory; the presence of present things is attention; and the presence of future things is expectation. (*Conf.*, 11.20)

Augustine, in the eleventh book of the *Confessions,* proposes an analysis of time as an inner phenomenon, a phenomenon of the mind. He says that he finds these three things—what we call the past, the present, and the future—to be only in the mind. These reflections on time, or on times, are clearly raised and guided by the central question of person, the question "*Who* am I?" After all, time is the medium, the very fabric, of the person. The person is a creature of time and time a creature of mind. If time does not exist because it is no longer; if the future does not exist because it is not yet, and if the present does not exist because it is without extension; namely, if time does not exist, then the human person cannot be said to exist. This series of hypotheses would then force the conclusion that the question "Who am I?" is simply not a legitimate philosophical question. However, if the present moment is not altogether immediate, dimensionless, emptied of all concerns regarding one's past and future, then the present may be said to exist. And if past and future moments are brought to mind, gathered into a present moment dilated by the activities of memory and anticipation so as to embrace a lifetime, then past and future too may be said to exist. In such a moment, flooded with the memories and hopes of a lifetime, the person may be said to exist in some sense within the mind. Such, it seems, is the proper scope and locus of the question "Who am I?" Augustine confesses the entirety of his lifetime, his person, to God; for in God is found the present and presence in which nothing dies. And, as we have seen, Augustine suggests how it may also be said that for human being too nothing dies. Thus he explains how:

> Continuing on to this point from infancy, did I not enter boyhood? Or, rather, was it boyhood which itself came to me and took the place of infancy? No, infancy never left; for to what place did it

depart? Yet, it was now no more. For I was no longer an infant, speechless; but I was a boy, speaking. *(Conf.,* 1.8)

The *I,* the person, embraces and contains a lifetime somehow as the eternal God embraces and contains all time. Indeed, if the past and the present were not so contained, they would have no way, no place, of transpiring.

Augustine does not equate, however, the eternal presence of *the* past and *the* future with the temporal presence of one's personal past through memory and of one's personal future through expectation. For memory and expectation are necessarily wilful and interpretive. Any present moment flooded with memories and expectations is itself a particular moment in which one construes the concerns and loves of one's past and projects the concerns and loves of one's future in the peculiar image and light fixed by the concerns and loves of that one present moment. Memory and expectation are a dilation of attention rather than a purification of it. Past and future moments are finally delivered over to, and prismed through, the present moment. And it would seem that there is no privileged present, no true present; for what one calls the present was future a moment ago and will be past a moment hence. Thus, a person's self-knowledge is always subject to the tyranny of present wilfulness and love. The response one receives to the question "Who am I, simply?" is always no more than a response to the question "Who am I, now?"

> They endeavor to taste the eternal, but still their heart flits about groundlessly in the past and future flow of things. Who will seize the heart and hold it fast so that for a while it might stand still and for a moment grasp at the splendor of eternity which stands still always? In comparison with time which is never still, the heart would see that eternity is incomparable . . . that in eternity nothing passes and all is present while no time is ever wholly present at once. The heart would see that every past is cast out from the future and that every future follows upon the past. It would see that every moment, past and future, is created by and proceeds from that which is always present. Who will hold the human heart so that it might stand still and see how eternity, which is neither future nor past, commands the future and the past? Does my hand have this kind of power, or

can the manipulations of speech perform so great a feat? (*Conf.,* 11.11)

What is decisive is that memory and expectation are wilful undertakings of human being. The present moment of extended consciousness which they make possible represents finally a particular creation of the person rather than a privileged perspective upon the person. To resolve upon a particular moment in which one will pose the question "Who am I?" and in which one will survey one's past and future for a unified response is to place a particular prejudice upon that response. Augustine realizes and makes clear that the human mind must be seized and held still by the miracle of eternal being.

Truth must appear or speak to the person. Augustine's account of his conversion may be interpreted as an account of his being seized and held still both by the vision and by the voice of truth. Augustine recounts numerous moments of seeing and hearing which build toward the culminating experiences of his conversion, the vision at Ostia and the voice in the garden (cf. *Conf.,* 8.12; 9.10). The moment of conversion is a moment in which a person is given to glimpse the splendor of eternity which is forever still. As later reflections will point out and clarify, to glimpse eternity is to gaze momentarily, not only upon God, but also upon human being as the creation of God, upon the *what* or nature of human being. And to know the *what* or the nature of human being is to possess a privileged perspective upon the *who* or the person of a human being, upon oneself. It is from this privileged perspective, grounded in the experience of conversion, that Augustine confesses his lifetime, his person. His decision to bring to mind all his yesterdays and all his tomorrows is founded upon his experience of being held still. The presence of lifetime to mind is founded upon the experienced presence of mind to God. Augustine's gathering together of all of his moments is inseparable from his seeing the face and his hearing the voice of God "in whom all of my scattered fragments are gathered together into one" *(Conf.,* 10.40). Augustine is able to speak of, to judge, his life, his loves, only because he is able to say: "My lord God, judge of my conscience ... my heart and my remembrance lie open before you" *(Conf.,* 5.6). And it was the experience of God's creative and providential love rather than any or all of Augustine's own loves that allowed him to claim that now "caring and cared for, each drop of time becomes precious to me" *(Conf.,* 11.2). The love through which Augustine's person is prismed is not the definitive love of a particular, arbitrary present but the creative and redemptive love of God's eternal present. Thus Augustine explains his response: "I make these confessions for love of your love" *(Conf.,* 11.1).

Augustine's conversion, as the experience of being seized and held still, embraces both his human nature and his human person and thus involves both seeing and hearing. Augustine's conversion suggests a convergence of eternity and time, of the miracle of being and of the miracle of the word. The word of God invaded Augustine's life in the peculiar vulnerability of childhood and thus became a dimension of the person of Augustine, veritably part of *who* Augustine was, Indeed, "religion ... had been implanted in us as children and interwoven with the very marrow of our being" *(C. Acad.,* 2.2.5). Indeed, Augustine says of the name of Christ that "already with my mother's milk my infant heart had drunk it in" *(Conf.,* 3.4). The authority of the Word remains unquestioned and is received by, is woven into, the timeful fabric of the human person. With the dynamic eventfulness of sound, the word follows Augustine as his life unfolds: "Whose but yours were those words which you sang repeatedly into my ears through the voice of my mother, your faithful servant?" *(Conf.,* 2.3). There is a sense in which the personal authority of the word is never questioned at any point in Augustine's life; for he explains, concerning the name of Jesus Christ, that "whatever was without that name, no matter how learned and polished and truthful, could not claim me wholly" *(Conf.,* 3.4). For the name of Jesus Christ, as we have seen, is part of *who* Augustine is. The truth of that name is a *personal* truth, the truth belonging to what has a claim upon the person of Augustine. The name of Jesus Christ and the name of God lie deep within the memory of Augustine.

> Never, from the time when I first learned of you, was I forgetful of you. For wherever I found truth, there I found my God, truth itself,

of which, from the time when I first learned of it, I was never
forgetful. *(Conf.,* 10.24)

Augustine's accounts of his conversion to the religion of his
infancy are rich in images of the heart and of hearing, recalling
the Bible and our earlier reflections on biblical anthropology.

You cried to me from afar: In deepest truth, I am who I am. And I
listened as one listens in the heart. *(Conf.,* 7.10)

You have pierced my heart with your word, and I have loved you.
(Conf., 10.6)

Gathering the strength of many various voices, you came before me
and insisted that I hear from afar, that I be converted, and that I call
upon you who were calling me. *(Conf.,* 13.1)

Finally, the culminating experience of Augustine's conversion
to the religion of Christ is the experience in the garden. Again, the
imagery is that of event, sound, interruption, hearing, and heart.

And behold I hear a voice (whether a boy's voice or a girl's I do
not know) from a nearby house, saying melodically and repeating
over and over: "Take and read; take and read." *(Conf.,* 8.12)

Augustine's response to this event may be interpreted as his
endeavoring not to qualify the altogether unsolicited and "eventful" character of this experience with personal wilfulness. He
narrates:

Holding back a flood of tears, I arose, interpreting this event as
nothing other than a divine command to open my book of scriptures
and to read the first passage upon which my eyes would have fallen.
(Conf., 8.12)

Augustine evidently wishes the book to speak, to be a word
striking his eye as a voice breaks upon one's ears, indeed as the
voice in the garden is described as having suddenly interrupted
him. We may note as well that he reads the passage (Rm. 13.13) in
silence, which was Ambrose's customary manner of reading the
scripture (cf. *Conf.,* 6.3), but which was unusual for Augustine and

contrary to then common practice. Again this seems to be an expression of Augustine's clear desire to *hear* the word of God, to experience revelation.

Although Augustine's references to conversion through hearing and the heart are distinct and explicit, they are never divorced from references to conversion through seeing and the mind. Understanding and faith, seeing and hearing, mingle freely and converge in the account of his conversion. Augustine's first glimpse of the life of free insight in his reading of Cicero's *Hortensius* and the ardor which it enkindled was qualified by the absence of the name of Christ (cf. *Conf.*, 3.4). It is this same lack that he later notices in the Platonic writings (cf. *Conf.*, 7.21). Still, when Augustine describes the "incredible conflagration" enkindled in him by these writings, he adds, in a commingling of metaphors that:

> Facing forwards, I was now returning, quickly and fully, to myself. It was as if I were returning from a journey; for I confess that I looked from afar upon that religion which had been implanted in us as children and interwoven with the very marrow of our being. *(C. Acad.,* 2.2.5)

Augustine wishes to live a life of free insight, a life of understanding, without, however, departing from the name of Christ and the religion of his youth, which is to say from that religion which is *personally* his. He wishes to steer his own course by the light of his own insights and yet to recognize the authority of scripture and remain a child, open and vulnerable to its Word.

> I was altogether unwilling to entrust the care of my languishing soul to the philosophers, because they were without the saving name of Christ. I resolved, therefore, to be a catechumen in the Catholic Church, the church urged upon me by my parents, until it became clear beyond doubt how I was to direct the course of my life. *(Conf.,* 5.14)

The authority which the scriptures seem to have for Augustine at this point is what we have called a *personal* authority. They represent the religion of Augustine's parents and of his own infancy and youth; they are, by his own, account, part of *who* he is. However, he will not embrace them any more than he will abandon them (cf. *Conf.,* 6.4). The heart, if it is to be free of wilfulness, must love only what is truly seen and heard. The heart like the mind, the *who* like the *what,* must be held still.

Augustine longs for a certainty which may be interpreted as the deliverance from wilfulness over to love, a decisive revelation of being and word, a holding still and uniting of his nature and his person. He had many times before made things to be true for himself, conferred personal truth upon things, by loving them. But such wilfulness had proved futile and foolish.

> Fearful of another fall, I held back my heart from accepting anything. But this suspending of my will was even more deadly. For I wanted to become as certain of what I could not see as I was certain that seven and three are ten. *(Conf.,* 6.4)

Augustine is granted the vision which he requires; and the *Confessions* are richly laden with accounts of the experience of contemplation, which seem to culminate in his account of his and his mother Monica's vision in the garden at Ostia (cf. *Conf.,* 7.10,17; 8.1; 9.10; 10.27). Often these accounts of vision mingle with accounts of hearing. In the end, the conversion to wisdom (to the truth of the nature of human being) and the conversion to the word (to the truth of the person of Augustine) are one. They are one, finally, because the word of God spoken in eternity is one with the word of God spoken in time.

> You cried to me from afar: In deepest truth, I am who am. And I listened as one listens in the heart, no longer finding the slightest grounds for doubt. It would have been easier to doubt that I am alive than to be in doubt whether truth might not exist. For the truth is made visible to the intellect in all created things. *(Conf.,* 7.10)

> With your calling and your crying you broke through my deafness. Your shining and your splendor drove out my blindness. *(Conf.,* 10.27)

And yet what marks this experience of contemplation is its

altogether fleeting character (cf. *Conf.*, 7.17,20; 8.1; 9.10). Such a moment is a moment outside of time; and only the memory of it belongs to the lifetime and to the person.

> It was a wonder to me that now I was loving you, rather than some image in your place. I did not stand fixed in the enjoyment of my God. Rath r, I was swept away to you by your loveliness. Soon, however, I was carried away from you by my own w ight. I even rushed into those other concerns, weeping. This weight was the sheer habit of the flesh. But the memory of you remained with me. *(Conf., 7.17)*

The passing of such a moment returns the individual to time, to the loves that define and dominate the person. What Augustine finds lacking in the experience of contemplation is reflected in what he finds lacking in the philosophical texts corresponding to the life of insight and contemplation. The philosophers point to the goal, eternity, and contemplation glimpses it; but they fail to indicate the way to that goal and fail to furnish the personal strength required to journey that way. Christ is himself that way and it is his care,[2] his purifying love, that empowers the person to follow him.

> You willed, I believe, that I should come upon those [Platonic] books before I came to consider your scriptures, so that it would be stamped upon my memory how I had once been affected by those

---

2. Cf. Augustine, *Confessions*, 7.14. Robert J. O'Connell in his work *St. Augustine's Confessions—the Odyssey of Soul* (Cambridge, Mass. Harvard University Press, 1969) points out the biblical character of the relationship of *care* on the part of God and of *trust* on the part of the soul (p. 100). This mutuality of care and trust finds a clear parallel in the twofold meaning of *care* in a passage (11.2) already cited from the *Confessions.* The full Latin text reads: *caro mihi valent stillae temporum.* The critical word here is *caro,* which is able to mean both *caring* and *cared* for; and both meanings are intimately related for Augustine. Both in the living and in the confessing of his life, Augustine has come to know God's care for him in each single moment; and this care enables Augustine, both in the confessing and in the living of his life, to care for and to find precious each moment of his lifetime. The *Confessions,* the speaking of a life, is for Augustine an act of human and personal care, which is an image, a creation, of divine care.

books. It was your will that later, when I would become responsive amidst your books, you would touch my wounds with your healing fingers. Then, as you willed, I would learn about and mark clearly the difference between presumption and confession, the difference between those who see that a journey must be made and yet are blind to the way and those who see the way leading to the beloved homeland, a land to be dwelled in as well as perceived with the mind. *(Conf., 7.20)*

Thus Augustine "seized most avidly upon the venerably writings of your spirit, and above all especially upon the apostle Paul" *(Conf., 7.21)*. For there Augustine found account not only of the Truth of the philosophers but also of the person divided and scattered by its loves and of the praise of the delivering grace of Jesus Christ. Like Paul, Augustine longed for the power and strength of personal conversion, the conversion of one's loves. Augustine possessed the certainty of vision (cf. *Conf., 7.17)*; but that certainty belonged to eternity. Only the memory of it belonged to time, to the person. What remained to be sought was the certainty of the heart, steadfast personal love.

I was now certain of your eternal life, although I saw that life only obscurely, as if through a mirror. Nevertheless, every doubt concerning incorruptible substance, that from it every substance proceeds, was lifted from me. I desired then, not to be more certain of you, but to be more secure in you. Everything about my properly temporal life was uncertain and my heart required to be purged by the old leaven. The way, our very savior, pleased; still I was disinclined to pass through its straits. *(Conf., 8.1)*

What Augustine found lacking in contemplation and in the Platonists' accounts of the life of philosophy was the entire dimension of the person, the will, the heart, the concerns and conflicts of past and future loves, the need for humble submission to authority and grace, the moral necessity of revelation and deliverance.

Of all this, those writings say nothing. Nowhere in their pages is the face of this pity, the tears of confession, your sacrifice, the afflicted spirit, the contrite and humbled heart, the salvation of a people, the espoused city, the earnest of the Holy Spirit, the chalice of our ransom. Therein no one sings: *Will not my soul be submitted to God? For from him is my salvation. Indeed my very God and my savior, my defender: no more shall I be moved.* In those books, no one hears someone calling: *Come to me you who labor.* They disdain to learn from him, *for he is meek and humble of heart. For these things you have hidden from the wise and prudent and have revealed them to the little ones. (Conf.,* 7.21) (Italics added.)

Augustine, from his early youth, was sensitive to the reality and claims of the personal dimension of human being. He recalls his fascination over the wanderings of Aeneas, his tears over the death of Aeneas's Dido (cf. *Conf.,* 1.13), and his fascination with the spectacle of the theater (cf. *Conf.,* 3.2). Central to Augustine's own conversion are the stories of others' conversions—the conversions of Victorinus (cf. *Conf.,* 8.1), Anthony (cf. *Conf.,* 7.21), and Paul (cf. *Conf.,* 7.21)—stories which challenge, inflame, and torment Augustine. Each account turns him back upon himself; each such story traces the temporal paths, the way, that must be gone by the person. It is this way, the return from contemplation to speech, from eternity to time—the conversion of the person— that the philosophers fail to recognize and ponder. Finally this way is Christ, whose name is so notably absent in their writings.

It is hoped that this brief initial consideration of Augustine's conceptions of nature and person, particularly as they figure in Augustine's account of his own conversion in the *Confessions,* may serve as a bridge spanning our earlier contextual analyses and the detailed discussions which follow. Augustine's conversion, or at least his various accounts of it, represent a mingling of Greek and biblical understandings of human being, of nature and person, of contemplation and revelation, of being and word, which characterize the whole of Augustine's Christian philosophy. What remains is to ground more surely and to develop more fully our understanding of this mingling and mutuality, particularly through a study of the latter books (8-15) of Augustine's work *On the Trinity.* It is there that his pursuit of the knowledge of God and of self, which initiated our remarks on Augustine, finds its most profound and sustained elaboration.

Seized and held still by the light of divine truth and by the voice of divine will, Augustine sees himself as both creator and creature, both subject and substance. His word is both his own work and the work of God. In the order of time, the question of his own word and his own work arises first.

CHAPTER 3

PERSON

Readings

• 1 •

We must remain firm in that good and cling to it with love so that we might enjoy the presence from which we take our being and in the absence of which we could not exist. For, when we walk now by faith, not by sight (2 Co. 5.7), we surely do not yet see God . . . face to face. . . . Unless we love him now, we shall never see him.

But who loves the unknown? Something can be known without being loved. What I seek to know is whether something can be loved without being known. Because, if this is not possible, no one loves God prior to knowing God. And what is it to know God except to see him in the mind and to look upon him steadfastly? For he is not a body to be sought out with bodily eyes.

But even before we are able to look upon and to see God as he can be looked upon and seen, a thing granted to the pure of heart; blessed, therefore, are the pure of heart, becau e they shall see God (Mt. 5.8). Unless God is loved through faith, the heart cannot be cleansed so as to be fit and well-suited to the vision of God. Where do those three exist—faith, hope, and charity, for the building up of which in the soul the workings of all the divine books join together— except in the soul believing what it does not yet see and hoping in

70

and loving what it believes? Therefore he who is unknown, yet believed, is loved. . . .

How, then, by believing do we love that trinity which we know not? According to some generic or general knowledge . . . ? What generic or general knowledge of that excellent trinity do we have, as though there were many such trinities in some of which we have come to be experienced, so that through a pattern of similarity impressed upon us or through either generic or general knowledge we might believe that trinity also to be such, and in that way might love a thing, which we believe and do not yet know, from its resemblance to a thing which we do know? . . . The question here is: From what likeness to or comparison with things known may we believe so that we might love God even when he is not yet known?

We are certainly seeking a trinity, not any trinity at all, but that trinity which is God, the true, supreme, and only God. Whoever you are, therefore, who hear these words, wait with longing. For we are still seeking and no one justly reproaches anyone for seeking such things provided that one is most firmly secured in one's faith while seeking what is most difficult either to know or express.

We are not yet speaking of heavenly things, not yet of God the father, the son, and the holy spirit. Rather, we speak of this unequal image, an image nevertheless, which is human being. For the mind's weakness perhaps looks upon this image with more familiarity and facility. . . . Let us attend as much as we can and call upon the heavenly light to illumine our darkness so that we might see, as much as we are permitted, the image of God in us.

(De Trin., 8.4.6; 8.5.8; 9.1.1; 9.2.2)

• 2 •

Who will understand the almighty trinity? Yet who does not speak of it, if it is, in fact, of it we speak? Rare is the soul which speaks of it and knows of what it speaks. People argue and fight but no one sees the vision of it without peace. I wish that humankind would think of itself as having these three things inside. The three things are far different from that trinity but I am speaking of a way in which they may exercise and test themselves to discover how far away they are. I am speaking of these three things: being, knowing, and willing. For I am; I know; and I will. I am a knowing and willing being. I know that I am and that I will. And I will that I be and know. So let anyone, who can, perceive that between these three things there is an inseparable life—one life, one mind, one essence—and that in the end there is an inseparable distinction, but a distinction nonetheless. It is open to anyone. Let people but turn their attention inside themselves and see and then tell me. But when they have found something in these things and have spoken of it, let them not think they have found the unchangeable above these things which exists unchangeably, knows unchangeably, and wills unchangeably. Whether there is a trinity in God because of these three things, or whether these three things exist in individuals so that individuals are made up of threes, or whether in a miraculous way it is both simple and manifold, infinite but with its own boundary within itself, by which it exists and knows itself and is itself sufficient unto itself without change and with the generous magnitude of its unity—whether any of these are so, who can easily understand? Who might speak of it in any terms? Who might dare in any terms to give one's opinion boldly?

(Conf., 13.11)

• 3 •

In these thr e—mind, love, knowledge—a trinity remains, when the mind knows itself and loves itself. And no commingling brings about confusion, although each one is in itself, and all are mutually in all, whether each one in the other two or two in the other one. Thus, all are in all. For the mind is surely in itself since it is said to be a mind with respect to itself, although relative to its own knowledge, it may be said to be knowing, known, or knowable. And with reference to that love with which it loves itself, the mind may be said to be loving, loved, or lovable. And knowledge, though referred to a mind that is knowing or known, is still with respect to itself spoken of as known or knowing; for the knowledge by which the mind knows itself is not unknown to itself. And love, though referred to a mind that loves, whose love of itself it is, is nevertheless love with respect to itself too so that it is also in itself. For love also is loved, nor can it be loved except by love which it is itself. And so these three are singly in themselves. Yet they are in each other in

such a way that the mind in loving is in love, and love is in the
knowledge of one who loves, and knowledge in the knowing mind.
And so each one is in the other two, because the mind that knows
and loves itself, is in its own love and knowledge. And the love of
the mind loving and knowing itself is in the mind and is knowledge;
and the knowledge of the mind knowing and loving itself is in the
mind and in its love, because it loves itself as knowing and knows
itself as loving. And on this account each two are in the other one.
For the mind which knows and loves itself is in the love with its
knowledge and in the knowledge with its love. And the love itself
and the knowledge are at the same time in the mind, which loves
and knows itself. We have already shown above how all are in all,
when the mind loves itself as a whole and knows itself as a whole
and knows its whole love and loves its own whole knowledge, when
these three are perfect with respect to themselves. Thus these three
are in a marvelous manner inseparable from one another; and yet
each one of them is a substance, and all at the same time are one
substance or essence, while the three are spoken of relatively with
respect to one another.

But when the human mind knows itself and loves itself, it does
not know and love something unchangeable. The individual human
being, attending to what goes on within itself, speaks in one way
when disclosing its own mind and speaks, moreover, in a different
way when defining the human mind in terms of a generic or general
knowledge. Therefore, when, someone speaks to me of their own
mind concerning whether it understands or does not understand this
or that and whether it wills or does not will this or that, I believe
what is said. But, indeed, when someone says something true about
the human mind generically or generally, I recognize and affirm
what is said.

(De Trin., 9.5.8; 9.6.9)

• 4 •

With the mind's sight, then, we see in that eternal truth, from
which all temporal things have come to be, the form according to
which we are and according to which either in us or in bodies we
effect something with true and right reason. And the true knowledge
of things thence conceived we have within us as a word which we

beget inwardly by speaking and which does not leave us in being born. When, however, we speak to others, we apply to the word remaining within us the ministry of our voice or of some other corporal sign so that through a kind of sensible remembrance, some such thing may come to be even in the soul of the listener as that which d es not leave the soul of the speaker. Thus we do nothing through the members of our body, whether in deeds or in words, to approve or to disapprove of human conduct, which we do not anticipate with a word uttered within us. No one, then, willingly does anything which one has not first spoken in one's heart.

That word is conceived with love, whether it be the creature's or the creator's, that is, whether it be of a changeable nature or of an unchangeable truth. Thus it is conceived either with inordinate desire or with charity. Not that the creature is not to be loved. But if that love is referred to the creator it will no longer be inordinate desire but charity. It is a matter of inordinate desire, when a creature is loved for its own sake. Then, instead of aiding one who uses it, the creature corrupts one who would enjoy it. For when a creature's place is equal to our own, it is to be enjoyed, but enjoyed in God; and when a creature's place is beneath us, that creature is to be used for the sake of God. For just as you ought to enjoy yourself not in yourself but in him who made you, so you also ought to enjoy one whom you love even as yourself. And therefore let us enjoy ourselves and our brethren in the lord and let us not dare to send ourselves back from there to ourselves nor dare to slacken downwards. The word, moreover, is born when what is thought pleases us either for our sinning or for acting rightly. Thus love, as a means, joins our word and the mind from which it is born and, as a third being, bonds itself together with them in an incorporeal embrace without any confusion.

(De Trin., 9.7.12; 9.8.13)

• 5 •

When the mind itself knows itself and affirms itself this same knowledge is its word in such wise that it is altogether like and equal to it, even identical to it, because it is not the knowledge of a lower essence, such as a body, nor the knowledge of a higher essence, such as God. And since knowledge has a likeness to that thing which it knows, namely, that thing of which it is the knowledge, then this knowledge has a perfect and equal likeness; for the mind itself which knows is known. This knowledge is, therefore, both the mind's image and its word, because it is the expression of the mind and, in knowing, is rendered equal to the mind and because what is begotten is equal to its begetter.

(De Trin., 9.11.16)

• 6 •

What, then, is love? Will it not be an image? Will it not be a word? Will it not be begotten? For why would the mind beget its knowledge when it knows itself and not beget its love when it loves itself? For if the cause of its knowledge is that it is knowable, then the cause of its love is that it is lovable. Why it has not therefore begotten both is difficult to say. This is indeed a question even with respect to the supreme trinity itself, God the most omnipotent creator, after whose image human being is made—a question which customarily troubles human beings whom the truth of God, through human speech, invites to faith. Why they ask is not the Holy Spirit also either believed or understood to be begotten by God the father so as also to be called the son? This is what we are now endeavoring to investigate in the human mind in such a way that, beginning with an inferior image in which our nature, as though interrogated, responds in a manner more familiar to us, we may direct the then more exercised keenness of our own mind from the illuminated creature to the unchangeable light. This is assuming that the truth itself has persuaded us that, just as the son is the word of God, which no Christian doubts, so the holy spirit is charity. Therefore, let us return to that image, which the creature is, namely, the rational mind which is to be interrogated and considered regarding the matter. There, the temporarily existing knowledge of some things which were not previously loved, open to us quite distinctly what we might say. Indeed, it is easier for speech, which itself must be directed in time, to explain a thing which is comprehended in the order of time.

Firstly, this should be manifest—that it is possible for something to be knowable, namely a thing which can be known, and yet for it not to be known. It is not possible, however, for something which is not knowable to be known. Thus it should clearly be maintained that everything whatsoever which we know generates in us its own knowledge. For knowledge is born from both the one knowing and the one known. The mind, therefore, when it knows itself, is alone the parent of its own knowledge; and the mind itself, then, is both the known and the knower. It was, however, itself knowable to itself, even before it knew itself; but that knowledge of itself was not in it when it did not know itself. When, therefore, it knows itself, it begets a knowledge of itself which is equal to itself. For it does not know itself as less than it is, nor is its knowledge of another essence, not only because it is itself the knower but also because it is itself the known, as we said earlier.

What, then, should be said of love, why it too is not seen to have begotten the very love of itself, even when it loves itself? For it was to itself lovable, even before it loved itself, because it has been able to know itself. For if it were not knowable to itself, it could never have been able to know itself; so, if it were not lovable to itself, it could never have been able to love itself. Why, then, is it not said also to have begotten its own love by loving itself, just as by knowing itself it has begotten its own knowledge? Perhaps in this it is manifestly shown that this is the principle of love from which it proceeds. It does, indeed, proceed from the mind which is lovable to itself before it loves itself. And thus the mind is the principle of its own love with which it loves itself. Perhaps, then, it is not rightly said to be begotten by it as is that knowledge of itself with which it knows itself, because that which is said to be born or discovered has already been found by knowledge and often follows an inquiry which is put to rest by what is found which is its goal.

For inquiry is the desire to find, which is equivalent to saying the desire to discover. Moreover, things which are discovered are, as it were, brought forth. Hence they are similar to an offspring. But where are they brought forth unless in knowledge itself? For therein they are formed as things expressed. And even if things were already existing when we searched and found them, still the knowledge itself did not previously exist which we are calling an offspring being born. Further, that desire, which is in seeking, proceeds from the seeker and, in a certain sense, remains in suspense, never resting in that object toward which it strives, until that which is sought has been found and is united with the one who seeks. That desire, namely, that inquiry, does not seem to be love, by which that which is known is loved; for up to this point the effort is to know it. Nevertheless it is something of the same sort as love. For it can already be called will, since everyone who seeks wills to find. If that is sought which pertains to knowledge, then everyone who seeks wills to know. And if one wills ardently and earnestly, one is said to study, which is how we customarily speak of those who pursue and attain to any sort of learning. Therefore, a kind of desire precedes the mind's giving birth and by means of this desire that which we will to know in our seeking and finding is born as an offspring, namely knowledge itself. And for this reason that desire, by which knowledge is conceived and born, is not rightly called a birth and an offspring. And this same desire with which one longs to know a thing becomes love for the thing once it is known, while it holds and embraces the beloved offspring, knowledge, and conjoins it to its begetter.

There is, then, a certain image of the trinity: the mind itself, its knowledge, which is its offspring and its word from itself, and, thirdly, love. And these three are one and one substance. The offspring is not less so long as the mind knows itself as a thing as great as it is; nor is the love less so long as the mind loves itself as a thing as great as it knows and as great as it is.

(De Trin., 9.12.16-9.12.18)

· 7 ·

We must, therefore, come to that word of human being, to the word of a rational animate being, to the word of an image of God, not born of God, but made by God. This word is neither expressible in a sound nor thinkable in the likeness of a sound, which must belong to one language or another. This word perceives all the signs by which it is signified and is begotten by the knowledge which remains in the soul, when that same knowledge is spoken inwardly, just as it is. For the vision of thought is very much like the vision of knowledge. For when it is spoken through a sound or through some corporeal sign, it is not said just as it is but as it can be seen or heard through the body. When, therefore, that is in a word which is in knowledge, then there is a true word and the truth, such as is expected from human being, so that what is in the knowledge is also in the word and what is not in the knowledge is not in the word. Here we recognize what is meant by: Yes, yes; no, no (Mt. 5.37).

Thus, as much as it can, this likeness of the image that was made approaches that likeness of the image that was born, whereby God the son is proclaimed to be substantially like unto the father in all things.

The likeness of the word of God is also to be noticed in this enigma, namely, that just as it has been said of that word: All things were made through him—where it is proclaimed that God made the universe through his only begotten word—so there are no works of human being which are not first spoken in the heart. Whence it is written: The beginning of every work is the word (Si. 37.20). But even here, when the word is true, then it is begotten from the knowledge of doing a good work, so that even here the saying may be observed: Yes, yes; no, no. For if it is "yes" in that knowledge by which one is to live, then it is "yes" too in the word through which the work is to be accomplished; if it is "no" in the former, then it is "no" too in the latter. Otherwise, such a word will be a lie, not the truth; and from it sin, and not a right work.

In the likeness of our word there is also this likeness of the word of God, namely, that our word can be without a work following it. However, a work cannot be, unless a word proceeds it, just as the word of God could be without the existence of any creature, but no creature could exist except through that very word through which all things were made. Therefore, not God the father, not the holy spirit, not the tri ity itself, but the son alone, who is the word of God, was made flesh, although this was the doing of the trinity, so that, when our word follows and imitates its example, we might live rightly, which is to say, we might have no lie either in the contemplation or in the operation of our word. Truly, this perfection of this image is for sometime in the future.

(De Trin., 15.11.20)

• 8 •

When I hear . . . that a soul is said to be good, just as there are two words, so from these two words I understand two things: one by which the soul is a soul and the other by which the soul is good. Clearly the soul did nothing to bring about its own existence; for at that time it did not yet exist so that it might do something toward its own existence. However, if the soul is to be good, I see that the will must act. This is not to say that that by which the soul exists is not something good. For otherwise how is the soul already said to be better, and most truthfully said to be better, than the body? Rather the soul is indeed not yet said to be good because there still is lacking to it an act of the will whereby it may become more excellent. And should it neglect this act, it, then, is justifiably blamed and is rightly said not to be a good soul.

For one who does not do this differs from one who does—the latter is deserving of praise, while the former is truly deserving of blame. When the soul truly acts with this intent and does become good, it cannot accomplish this unless it turns itself toward something which it is not. And to what may the soul turn itself so as to become good except to the good, which it does when it loves, desires, and attains to the good? Should it then turn away from the good, and by its very turning away become not good, and should it later wish to amend, there would be nothing to which it might turn unless the good from which it turns away remains in it.

There would, therefore, be no changeable goods unless there were an unchangeable good. Thus, when you hear of this good and of that good which in other respects can be said to be not good, if apart from those things which are good by virtue of their participation in the good, you were able to look upon the good itself in which by participation other things are good—for when you hear of this or that good you also in the same moment understand the good itself— if therefore you could put aside those other goods and look upon the good in itself, you would look upon God. And if in love you could cling to God, you would at once be blessed.

(De Trin., 8.3.4-5)

• 9 •

Arise, seek, sigh, pant with longing, knock at what is shut. If, moreover, we do not yet long, not yet desire, not yet sigh, we shall only be casting pearls to whomever, or we shall ourselves find pearls of some sort. Therefore, dearest beloved, I would stir up longing in your heart. Right living leads to understanding. It is a matter of a way of life leading to a way of life. One kind of life is earthly, another is heavenly. There is a life of beasts, another of human beings, and another of angels. The life of beasts rages with earthly pleasures, seeks only earthly things, and is cast headlong into them. The life of angels is reserved to what is heavenly. The life of human beings is midway between the angels and the beasts.

If human beings live according to the flesh, they are comparable to beasts; if they live according to the spirit, they are companions to angels. When you live according to the spirit, inquire too whether you are small or great in that angelic life. If you are still small, the angels say to you: Grow. We eat bread while you are nourished on milk, the milk of faith, so that you might attain to the bread of sight. If, moreover, there is still a desiring of sordid pleasures, if deceits are still being thought, if lies are not avoided, if lies are added to perjuries, will a heart so foul dare to say: Explain to me how one sees the word and if I too might be able, if I too might now see?

Still, even if I am perhaps not of this sort, I am far from that vision. But how ravaged with earthly longings are they who are not yet seized with this desire from above. There is a great difference between one who loathes and one who longs, as also between one who longs and one who enjoys. One who loathes this vision, lives as a beast, while the angels enjoy it. If, however, you do not live as a beast, you have no loathing for it; rather it is something for which you long without grasping it. In that very longing you have begun to live the life of the angels. May it grow and be brought to perfection in you. And may you grasp this, not from me, but from him who made us both.

(In Joann. ev., 18.7)

• 10 •

No one comes to me except whom the Father has drawn (Jn. 6.44). Do not think that you are drawn against your will. The soul is drawn also by love . . . I say that it is not enough to be drawn by the will. You are drawn also by pleasure. And what does it mean to be drawn by pleasure? Delight in the lord and we will grant you your heart's desires (Ps. 36.4). . . . Moreover, if Vergil was permitted to say, "Each one is drawn by one's own pleasure" (Vergil, *Eclogues,* 2)—not necessity, but pleasure; not obligation, but delight—how much more forcefully ought we to say that one is drawn to Christ when one delights in the truth, in blessedness, in justice, and in everlasting life, all of which Christ is?

Is it the case, instead, that our bodily senses have their own pleasures, while the soul is left without pleasures of its own? If the soul has no pleasures of its own, how is it said that: The sons of human beings shall trust under the cover of your wings; they will be filled with the fulness of your house, and you will give them drink from the torrent of your pleasure? In your light we shall see light? (Ps. 35.8-10). Give me one who loves, and that one perceives what I am saying. Give me one who desires, one who hungers, give me one who wanders in this exile and thirsts, one who sighs for the fountain of the eternal homeland; give me such a one and that one knows what I say. But if I speak to one whose heart is cold, that one is ignorant of what I am saying.

(In Joann. ev., 26.4)

• 11 •

I say that there was in that first-formed human being the will's freedom of choice. He was so made that nothing whatever would resist his will, if he wished to observe the precepts of God. However, after he sinned of his own free will, we, who have descended from his stock, were cast down headlong into necessity. Each one of us, moreover, with a little reflection, can discover the truth of what I say. For today in our actions, before we are tangled in any habit, we have a will free to do something or not to do it. But when we have exercised that freedom and done something, and the pernicious sweetness and pleasure of that deed have seized the mind, the mind is so entangled by its own habit that it cannot afterwards overcome what it fashioned for itself by its own sinning. We see many who do not wish to swear an oath; but, because the tongue has already held fast to habit, they cannot restrain those things from leaving the mouth, things which we must say belong to the root of evil. . . .

This is what wars against the soul, habit made with the flesh. This is undoubtedly the discretion [*prudentia*] of the flesh, which, so long as it is such that it cannot be brought under the law of God, is for so long a time the discretion of the flesh. But when the soul is illumined, it ceases to be that discretion of the flesh. For thus it is said that the discretion of the flesh cannot be made subject to the law of God, which is as if to say that snow cannot be warm. For, so long as snow is snow, it can in no way be warm. But just as the snow is melted by heat and ceases to be snow, so that it might become warm, so also that discretion of the flesh, namely, habit made with flesh—when our mind has been illuminated and when God has subjected for himself the whole human being to the will of the divine law—forms a good habit in place of that evil habit of the soul.

Wherefore, it is most truly said by the lord that those two trees, the good tree and the evil tree, . . . have their own fruit, namely, that the good tree cannot bear evil fruit nor the evil tree good fruit. Rather, so long as the evil tree is evil, it can bear only evil fruit. Let us take two human beings, the one good and the other evil. So long as one is good, one cannot bear evil fruit. And so long as one is evil, one cannot bear good fruit.

But so that you might understand that those two trees are presented by the lord in such a way that therein free will might be signified; and so that you might understand that those two trees are not natures, but our wills, the lord himself says in the gospel: Either make the tree good, or make it evil. Who is there that could make a nature? If, then, we are commanded to make the tree either good or evil, what is ours to do is to choose in accord with our will.

(C. Fort., 22)

• 12 •

Regarding the authority of the New Testament—by which we are commanded to love nothing of this world (1 Jn. 2.15), especially in that passage wherein it is stated: Be not conformed to this world (Rm. 12.2); for at the same time it must be shown that one is conformed to whatever one loves—if I look in the Old Testament for something comparable to this authority, I find, indeed, many things. But one book of Solomon, called Ecclesiastes, at very great length brings all earthly things into the highest contempt. It begins thus: vanity of the vain, vanity of the vain; and all is vanity. What profit is there for one in all one's labor, in all that one labors under the sun? (Qo. 1.2, 3). If we attend to all of these words, weigh and examine them carefully, we find many things altogether necessary for those who long to flee this world and to find refuge in God. But that takes a long time; and our discussion hastens elsewhere.

Yet, beginning as he did, he explains "all things" by asserting that the vain are those who are deceived by things of this sort. Moreover, that which deceives them he calls vanity, not that God did not create those things, but because human beings, through their sins, wish to subject themselves to those things which by divine law are subjected to them through right conduct. For, when you consider things which are less than ôneself as things to be marvelled at and sought after, is this not to be toyed with and deceived by false gods? The man, therefore, who is temperate in mortal and transient things of this sort has a rule of life supported by both testaments: that he should love none of them, that he should not regard any of them as something to be sought after for its own sake, but, rather, that he should make sufficient use of them so far as is necessary for the duties of this life, provided that he does so with the moderation of a user and not with the affection of a lover. These remarks on temperance are brief in view of the magnitude of the matter; and, yet, in view of the work I have undertaken, they have been perhaps too extensive.

Concerning fortitude, we must, indeed, be brief. The love, then, of which we speak, which must be wholly ablaze with piety toward God, is said to be temperate in not seeking those twisted things and in putting them aside. But among all the things which are possessed in this life, by God's most just laws and on account of the ancient sin, the body is human being's heaviest bond. Nothing must be proclaimed more openly and understood more secretly. Lest this bond be shaken and shattered, it disturbs the soul with the fear of toil and grief; and lest it be removed and destroyed, it disturbs the soul with the fear of death. For, through force of habit, the soul loves the body, without understanding that, if it uses the body well and knowledgeably, its resurrection and renewal will, by divine law and work, be made subject to its authority without any antipathy. But when the soul turns wholly to God with this love, these things are understood; and it not only will despise death but even truly long for it.

But there remains a great struggle with pain. Yet there is nothing so difficult and iron-fast that it cannot be overwhelmed by love's fire. And when in this love the soul hastens toward God it will fly free and wondrous above all torture on the loveliest and healthiest of wings, with which chaste love soars into God's embrace. Otherwise, God would allow lovers of gold, lovers of praise, and lovers of women to exercise more fortitude than his own lovers, although those loves would more appropriately be called not love but lust or wantonness. And yet even in this it is clear how great is the drivenness of the soul toward those things which it loves as it strives unweariedly on its path through immense obstacles. And the point is made to us how we must prefer anything to deserting God, if those others endure so much in order to desert him.

(De mor., 1.21.39-1.22.41)

• 13 •

They began to be evil in secret with the result that they slipped into open disobedience. For there is no evil deed which is not preceded by an evil will. And what would be at the beginning of an evil will if not pride—pride, which is the beginning of all sin. Yet what is pride but a seeking for distorted exaltation? Distorted exaltation comes when one deserts him to whom the soul ought to cling as a beginning and end; then somehow one becomes and exists as a beginning and end for oneself. This happens when one is too pleased with oneself; and one pleases oneself in this way when one has receded from that unchangeable good which ought to be more pleasing than oneself. This receding is spontaneous. For if the will had remained stable in its love of that higher, unchangeable good, by which it is illumined so that it may see and by which it is warmed so that it may love, it would not have turned from the good to pleasing itself and so would not have grown dark and cold. Then Eve would not have believed that the serpent spoke the truth nor would Adam have placed the will of his wife before the command of God and thought that it was a venial transgression if he did not abandon the companion of his life even in a partnership of sin. Therefore the evil deed was performed—I mean the transgression of eating forbidden fruit—by people who were already evil. And likewise that fruit would not have been evil if it had not come from an evil tree. For that tree to be evil it had to be created against nature, because without a failure of the will, which is against nature, it could not have become evil. But nature cannot be perverted by vice unless it is created from nothing. Thus the fact that it has a nature comes from its creation by God; but the fact that it has fallen away from what it is comes from its creation from nothing. So humankind did not fall away into nothingness; but the more it turned to itself the more it became less than it was when it clung to him who is highest. And so to abandon God and to be alone in oneself—that is, to be pleasing to oneself—is not quite to be nothing but to come close to it. For this reason the proud are called by another name according to the holy scripture: those who are pleasing to themselves. It is good to have a heart lifted up, but not to oneself, for this creates pride; it is good to lift one's heart up to God, for this creates obedience which belongs only to the humble. Some part of humility, therefore, in a marvelous way makes high the heart, while some part of pride lowers it. It seems to be backwards that pride should lower and humility raise up. But pious humility makes one submit to one's superior; and there is nothing superior to God. Therefore humility, which makes one submissive to God, raises one up. But pride, which is a vice, rejects submission to God and falls away from him who is superior to all. For this reason it will be inferior and what is written will come about: You have thrown down those who are being raised up (Ps. 72.18). It does not say "when they had been raised up," meaning that they are first raised up and then thrown down. Rather they are thrown down as they are raised up. So, in fact, the very raising up is already a throwing down. For this reason humility is commended now in the city of God and to the city of God as it journeys in this age, and in its king who is Christ it is greatly celebrated, while the opposite of this virtue, the vice of pride, is said by the sacred scriptures to dominate Christ's adversary, who is the devil. Certainly this is the big difference by which each of the cities about which we are speaking is distinguished: one is a city for the pious, the other for the impious; each has its angels which belong to it, in whom, in the city of God, love of God excels, while in the other city love of themselves excels.

Therefore evil would not have captured humankind by a manifest and open sin, in which an act was committed which God had forbidden, if humankind had not begun already to be pleasing to itself. For this reason it delighted them to hear: You will be as gods (Gn. 3.5). But this they could have become far more easily by clinging to the highest and true beginning and end through obedience, rather than by putting themselves forth as their own beginning and end through pride. For gods are created not by their own truth but through participation in the one true God. By seeking more, human beings become less when they fall away from him who truly satisfies them and choose to satisfy themselves. And so that evil by which human beings, when they please themselves as if they were the light, are turned away from the light, although that light would indeed make them the light, if it were pleasing to them—that evil, I say, existed first in secret, with the result that an evil followed which was openly performed.

(*De civ. Dei*, 14.13)

• 14 •

Therefore, because God's command was despised—God, who had created human beings in his own image; who had placed them above the other animals; who had established them in paradise and had provided them with an abundance of health and of all things; who had not burdened them with precepts which were plentiful, great, or difficult but had given support to healthy obedience by giving them one, very short, very light precept in which he reminded his creation, to whom free service would be profitable, that he was God—a just damnation followed, one in which human beings, who would have been spiritual even in the flesh, had they kept their commandment, became carnal even in their mind and were given to themselves through the justice of God, since through their own pride they had become pleasing to themselves. This damnation did not bring about the independence of human beings in their own power but rather in dissatisfaction with themselves they were to lead a hard and miserable servitude under him to whom they had yielded by sinning, instead of the life of liberty which they desired. They died in spirit through their own will and would die in body unwillingly, deserters of the eternal life, damned to eternal death if the grace of God had not freed them. Everyone of this world who thinks that damnation excessive or unjust does not know how to measure correctly the degree of wickedness in sinning when it was so easy not to sin. Just as the obedience of Abraham is justly called great because the commandment to kill his son was a very difficult thing to obey, so the complete ease of the commandment in paradise makes the disobedience there that much greater. And just as the obedience of the second man was more praiseworthy in that it was obedience even unto death, so the disobedience of the first man was more abominable in that it was disobedience even unto death. When the punishment established for disobedience is great and the order given by the creator easy, who can sufficiently explain how great is the evil in disobedience to such an easy command made by so great a power and enforced with the threat of so great a punishment?

Finally, to be brief, what punishment was given in return for the sin of disobedience but disobedience? For what other misery exists for human beings besides their own disobedience to themselves, so that they wish for something of which they are incapable, since they refused the thing of which they were capable? Although in paradise before the sin humankind was not capable of everything, yet it did not desire what it was not capable of; and similarly all that it desired it was capable of. Now, as we perceive in the offspring of Adam and as is written in the holy scriptures, humankind was made similar to vanity (Ps. 144.4). Who can count the number of things they want of which they are incapable, as long as they do not obey themselves; that is to say, as long as their soul and their flesh which is even weaker is disobedient to their will?

Although we do not want it, our soul is often disturbed, our flesh knows pain, grows old and dies, and we suffer in many other ways. We would not suffer against our will if our nature were to obey our will in every way and in all its parts. But the flesh experiences something because of which it is not allowed to serve. What does it matter how it happens, as long as, through the justice of the lord God, whom we did not willingly and submissively serve, our flesh, which had been submissive to us, has become harmful to us by not serving us? All this happened even though we could only hurt ourselves and not God by not serving him. For he does not need our service, as we need the service of our bodies; and so our punishment is what we received, while what we did is no punishment to him.

(De civ. Dei, 14.15)

· 15 ·

To whom and how will I talk of the lust which drags us down into a precipitous abyss and of the love which raises us up through your spirit which was carried over the waters? To whom? How? For there are no places into which we are dragged, no places out of which we rise. It is similar and yet dissimilar to this. There are emotions, there are loves and there is the uncleanness of our spirit rushing downwards, full of love for daily cares; there is your holiness raising

us up with love of freedom from cares, so that we may hold up our
hearts to you, where your spirit was carried over the waters, and so
that we may arrive at far-reaching peace when our soul has crossed
the waters which are without substance.

The angel fell, the soul of humanity fell; and they both pointed
out the chasm in the dark depths where the entire spiritual creation
would have ended up, if you had not said: Let there be light, and
there was light (Gn. 1.3). And each obedient intelligence in your
heavenly city clung to you and lay quiet in your spirit which is
carried unchangeable over all that is changeable. Otherwise the
heaven of heavens itself would have been a dark chasm in itself; but
now there is light in the lord. Even in that wretched disquiet of
falling spirits who point out their own darkness divested of your
light, you show sufficiently how great a rational creation you have
made, since nothing which is less than you suffices to bring your
creation blessed peace; and so it cannot bring peace to itself. You,
our God, will illuminate our darkness; our vestments rise up from
you and our darkness will be as noonday light. Give yourself to me,
my God; return to me. For I love; but if it is too little, let me love
more strongly. I cannot measure my love to know how much it
needs before it is enough for my life to run into your arms and never
turn away until it is hidden in the secret place of your countenance.
This much I know, that without you I suffer ill, not only externally
but also internally. And all my wealth which is not my God is
poverty.

Was neither the father nor the son carried over the waters? If this
movement is like the movement of a body in space, not even the
holy spirit was moved across the waters. If the movement is the
suspension of unchangeable divinity over all that changes, then the
father, the son and holy spirit were carried over the waters. Then
why is it only talked of in connection with your spirit? Why is it only
in connection with your spirit that a sort of place is mentioned
where he exists, though it is not a place? Why is it said of him alone
that he is your gift? We rest in your gift. We enjoy you there. Our
rest is our place. Love carries us there, and your good spirit raises up
our humility from the gates of death. We have peace in your
goodwill. A body finds it own place by entrusting itself to its own
weight, which carries it not to the place that is lowest but to the
place that is its own. A flame rises and a stone falls. They are moved
by their weights and seek their own proper places. When things are
less than perfectly ordered they are restless; and, when they are in

order, they are at rest. My weight is my love. By love I am drawn to
wherever I am drawn. By your gift we rise up and are carried above.
We burn and we go on. We scale the heights in our hearts and we
sing a song of steps. We burn with your fire, your good fire, and we
go on since we go to the peace of Jerusalem. For I rejoiced in those
who said to me: We will go to the house of the lord. Good will shall
put us there so that we want only to remain there forever.

(Conf., 13.7-9)

• 16 •

I sighed for this thing, though bound not by external chains but
by my own iron will. An enemy held my will and had made a chain
of it and had bound me. In fact, lust was created by my perverse
will, and I got into the habit of serving my lust. From submission to
this habit I acquired an addiction. Through such a progression, like
links joined together—hence my use of the term chain—a harsh
bondage held me captive. And a new will which I had begun to
possess, a will to enjoy and to worship you without reward, God,
sole assured joy, was not yet fit to overcome my earlier will, which
had the strength of familiarity. And so my two wills, one old and the
other new, the former carnal and the latter spiritual, struggled with
each other and by their discord sapped my soul.

So I came to understand what I had read through my own
experience; I understood how the flesh had desires which were
opposed to the spirit and the spirit had desires opposed to the flesh.
I found myself conflicted in both ways but more often on the side of
the self of which I approved than on the other side. The carnal side
was no longer really me, because, for the most part, I experienced it
unwillingly rather than created it wilfully. Nonetheless habit
became such a strong opponent against me through my own doing,
because I had willingly come to the point which I now wanted to
reject. Who could justly complain when just punishment follows a
sin? I no longer had the excuse by which I was accustomed to
consider myself not yet ready to serve you and reject the world: that
my perception of the truth was as yet unclear. For now the truth was
certain. But I was still linked to the earth and so refused to enlist in
your army. I feared to be freed from hindrances when I should have
feared being hindered.

Like a person in a dream I was pleasantly weighted down with the burden of the present age. Thoughts in which I dwelt upon you were similar to the struggles of a person who wants to wake up but who is submerged again into the depths of sleep. And, to continue the analogy, there is no one who wants to sleep continually—everyone with sane judgment prefers to be awake—yet one often postpones shaking off sleep, when one's limbs are heavy, and though dissatisfied with one's self, one sinks back into sleep, although it is time to get up. So I was certain that it would be better to give myself over to your love than to yield to my desires. But though the former course of action seemed right and convincing to me, the latter seduced and bound me. I could not respond when you said to me: Get up, you who sleep, and rise from the dead. Christ will give you light (Ep. 5.14). When you surrounded me with proofs that you spoke the truth, there was nothing at all I could answer, since I was convinced, except these few somnolent and slow words: In a minute. I'll be there in a minute. Just a moment. But the moments had no limit and the minutes stretched on for ages. In vain I rejoiced in your law in accordance with the inner person, while the other law in my limbs resisted the law of my mind and led me captive into the law of sin, which was in my limbs. The law of sin has the violence of habit, by which even an unwilling soul is dragged and held and deserves it, because it has slipped willingly into that habit. Who might deliver me, wretched as I was, from the body of this death, if not your grace from Jesus Christ our lord?

(Conf., 8.5)

• 17 •

Then, in the midst of that great struggle inside me, which I had started between myself and my soul in our shared bedroom, my heart, I turned with my appearance and my mind in turmoil, to Alypius, and I cried out: What is happening to us? What did you just hear? The ignorant rise up and seize the heavens but look at us, with all our learning, wallowing in flesh and blood. Because others have preceded we are ashamed to follow and yet not ashamed not to do that, at least? I jabbered on like that and my rampage tore me from him, while he stood silent and astonished, watching me. I was not talking in my usual manner. But my forehead, cheeks, eyes, complexion, tone of voice expressed my soul more eloquently than the words which I uttered. Our lodging had a garden which we used as freely as the house. Our host, the master of the house, did not live there. The uproar inside me had brought me to the garden where no one would get in the way of the burning conflict which I had launched against myself, until it was settled—but how, only you, not I, knew. My intense insanity, however, was healthy; my dying, life-bringing. I was aware of what a miserable thing I was, but I was ignorant of how good I would shortly become. So I withdrew into the garden and Alypius followed my every step. His presence did not destroy my isolation; and how could he leave me in such a state? We sat as far from the buildings as we could. In my spirit I was raging with violent indignation because I would not enter into your will and covenant, my God, although every bone in my body cried out to be there and praised it to the skies. One does not need ships, chariots, or feet to go there, and it is not as far as the distance from the house to where I was sitting. One needs nothing either to set out for that place or to arrive there but the will to go: a strong and honest will, not a half-wounded will which roams here and there, falling down and then struggling on, with one part falling as the other rises.

Finally, in the heat of my struggle, I performed with my body many things which people sometimes want to do but cannot because they haven't the right bodies or their limbs are bound in chains or weakened by lethargy or otherwise impeded. But if I tore my hair or beat my forehead or locked my fingers around my knee, I did so because I wanted to. However, I might have willed it but not done it, if the flexibility of my limbs had not obeyed my will. So I performed many acts when to want to act and to be able to were not the same. Yet I did not do that which was far more pleasing to me and which I would have been able to do as soon as I willed it, because the moment I willed it, I did so completely. In this case the ability to will it and the ability to do it are one and the same. And yet I did not do it; my body obeyed the slightest wish of my soul to move a limb more easily than the soul obeyed itself in carrying out its own great will, which might be done by will alone.

Where does this extraordinary event come from? Why has it come? Let your mercy enlighten me. Let me ask in case the shadows of human suffering and the darkest griefs of the sons of Adam might answer me. Where does this extraordinary event come from? Why does it come? The soul commands the body and is immediately obeyed; the soul commands itself and is opposed. The soul commands the hand to move and it happens with such quickness that it is hard to distinguish the command from the execution. Soul is soul and hand is body. The soul commands the soul to will. It is not other, and yet it does not obey. Where does this extraordinary event come from? Why does it come? The soul commands the soul to will, as I say, and it does not do what it commands. But it does not command completely. For it commands as far as it wills, since the will commands that there be will—not another will, but itself. But the will is not complete when it commands, and for this reason what it commands does not happen. If it were complete it would not command it to be, because it would already exist. Therefore, it is not an extraordinary event to will partially and to refuse partially; rather it is a sickness of the soul that it does not completely rise when it is elevated by truth, because it is weighted down with habit. And so there are two wills, and one is not complete. So one has what the other lacks.

May they pass away from your presence, God, as those empty babblers and seducers of the mind pass away, who assert that there are two natures in us from two minds, one good and the other evil, since they have noticed that there are two wills involved in the process of deliberation. They themselves are, in fact, evil when they have such evil beliefs. These same people will be good if they perceive the truth and consent to it so that your apostle may say to them: You were once shadows but now are light in the lord (Ep. 5.8). As long as these people want to be the light not in the lord but in themselves by assuming the nature of their soul to be the same as God, they become deeper shadows. For they have receded farther from you in their terrible arrogance, from you who are the true light which illuminates everyone who comes into this world (Jn. 1.9). Listen to what you say and blush; approach him and be enlightened and your faces will not blush with shame (Ps. 34.5). When I thought about serving the lord my God, as I had long determined to do, it was I who willed it, I who resisted it. I was myself. I neither fully willed it nor fully resisted it. So I struggled within myself and was destroyed by myself. Yet this same destruction happened against my will. But it revealed not the nature of someone else's mind but the punishment of my own mind. Not I myself but the sin which lives in me caused the punishment, which derives from the punishment of the more voluntary sin of Adam, whose son I was.

If there are as many conflicting natures as there are wills which oppose each other, there would be several natures, not just two. If a person debates whether to go to the Manichees' conventicle or to the theater, these men cry out: Look! Two natures: the good one leads this person here, the other, evil one, leads to the theater. Where else does this doubt of wills in opposition to each other come from? I say that both the will which leads to the conventicle and the will which leads to the theater are bad. But they do not believe that the will which leads to them could be anything but good. But suppose a Christian is considering whether to go to the theater or to the church and is in doubt because of two wills fighting each other. Would they not be in doubt as how to respond? Either they will admit against their will that the will which leads to our church is good, as is the wi l which leads people to theirs and causes them to participate in and be bound to their sacraments. Or they must say that there are two evil natures and two evil minds in conflict inside one person. But then their claim that there are two natures, one good and one evil, will not be true. Or they will convert to the truth and will no longer deny that when a person debates something there are two wills in conflict within one soul.

Therefore let them not say that there are two opposed minds in one person when they perceive two wills in conflict with each other. Let them not say that these two minds are made of two opposing substances and that they are struggling for two opposing substances and that they are struggling for two opposing principles, one good and one bad. Truthful God, you disprove them, confute them, convict them. For example, when both wills are bad someone may be debating whether to kill someone with poison or a sword; whether to rob this or that piece of property, since to do both is impossible. Or the problem may be whether to buy extravagant pleasure or to keep the money out of greed; or whether to go to the theater or the races if both are happening at once; or, as a third example, whether to rob someone else's house, given the opportunity; and, a fourth one, whether to commit adultery, if that possibility exists also. And suppose all these things become possible at the same moment, and all are equally desirable, but it is impossible to do all at once. Then such an abundance of desirable things causes the soul to be torn apart, because there are four or more wills in conflict with each other. But they do not admit that there is such a proliferation of different substances.

The case is the same for good wills. I ask of them this: Is it good to be delighted by reading an apostle *and* by reading a solemn

psalm *and* by discussing the gospel? They will answer in each case
that it is good. But suppose all these things give us pleasure equally
and at the same time. Are not different wills struggling in our heart
while we decide which attracts us most strongly? All these wills are
good and struggle with each other until one emerges the victor and
unites into one will what was before several. In the same way when
eternity offers higher pleasure and the enjoyment of temporal goods
keeps us below, the same soul wants both pleasures but not with
complete will. Therefore the soul is torn apart by terrible vexation,
as long as truth puts forward one side, while habit will not abandon
the other.

So I was ill and tortured. I accused myself more harshly than
usual. I tried to twist and turn in my chains until the thin strand by
which I was still held would break. But I was held nonetheless. And
you pursued me in my hidden corners, lord, increasing in your
severe mercy, the lashes of fear and shame in case I might give in
again and allow that thin, slender strand which remained not to
break but to grow strong again and bind me tighter. I kept saying to
myself: Come on, let it happen now, right now. And with the words
came resolution. I almost did it but then did not; yet I did not step
back into my former state but stood nearby and caught my breath. I
tried again. I was almost there. I was just touching it, just holding
it—but I was not there; I neither touched it nor held it, because I
hesitated to die to death and live to life. The worse part in me was
stronger from habit than the better part which was a novelty. That
moment in time in which I was to become something else struck
more and more fear into me the closer it got. But I was not struck
down or turned back. I was held in suspension.

The most insignificant of trifles held me back; the most vain of
vanities, those old favorites of mine, were plucking at the garment
of my skin and murmuring: Are you sending us away? From now
on will we never be with you, not ever? From now on will this or
that be forbidden to you forever? What were they hinting at with
their "this or that"; what did they mean, my God? Keep these
things from the soul of your servant. Have mercy. What filthy,
shameful things they hinted at! But now I heard them from twice as
far away and farther; they did not contradict me so openly nor
approached me face to face. Rather they muttered behind my back
and pinched me so that I would look back as I left furtively. Still
they slowed me down in my attempt to tear myself away and to

shake them off and jump to where I was being called. Violent habit
kept jeering: So, you think you can live without them?

But then it was speaking very faintly. For, in the direction I had
turned my face and was hesitating to go, the chaste dignity of
continence appeared, happy but not wildly gay; it honestly encouraged me to come without hesitation, and it held out to me pious
hands overflowing with good examples, to receive and embrace me.
There there were lots of boys and girls; youths and people of all
ages; serious widows and old spinsters; in each one continence itself
appeared, not sterile but a fertile mother of children, her joys from
you her husband, oh lord. And she smiled on me with an
encouraging expression, as if to say: Can you not do what these men
and women have done? Are these people really capable in and of
themselves rather than in their lord God? The lord their God gave
me to them. Why do you stand by yourself and yet not by yourself?
Throw yourself on him. Do not fear. He will not pull away and let
you fall. Throw yourself without fear and he will receive you and
heal you. I was blushing because I kept on hearing the whispering of
those vanities, and I was suspended in hesitation. And again she
seemed to say: Deafen yourself to the murmuring of your members
so that they may be mortified. They speak to you of delights but
none like the ones the law of the lord your God tells you of. This
was the argument raging in my heart, created by myself against
myself. Alypius stuck to me, waiting in silence for the result of my
peculiar agitation.

(Conf., 8.8-11)

• 18 •

There is in scripture a certain passage which is very closely related
to this matter of present concern to us and which gives marvelously
confirming witness to this same discussion. It is in the book which
some call Jesus Sirach and which others call Ecclesiasticus. There it
is written: All human beings are of the ground and Adam was
created from earth. In the fullness of his knowledge, the lord
separated them and changed their ways. Some of them he has
blessed and exalted. Some he has hallowed and drawn near to
himself. Some he has cursed and humbled; and he set them to

quarreling. As clay is in the potter's hand to mold and fashion it, always according to the potter's own pleasure, so is human being in the hand of its maker. And he shall render to human being in accord with his judgment. Good is at odds with evil; and life is set against death. So too the sinner is set against the just one. Thus look upon all the works of the most high, two by two, contraries one to the other (Si. 33.10 ff.).

First, the knowledge of God is commended, when he says: In the fullness of his knowledge the lord separated them—from what else than the blessedness of paradise?—and changed their ways—so that they might now live as mortals. Then, from them all, one mass was formed, coming from a legacy of sin and from the punishment of mortality, even though God formed and created what is good. For there is in all things a form and corporeal coherence in the concord of bodily members such that the apostle draws from it a metaphor for the attainment of love (1 Co. 12.12). For in all things there is a vital spirit which enlivens the earthly members. And the whole of human nature is in a marvelously regulated condition when the soul rules and the body serves. But now, as a result of the penalty of sin, carnal desire reigns, and has hurled the entire human race into confusion, like one total lump, in every element of which there endures the original and lasting state of the condemned. And yet there follows: Some of them he has blessed and exalted. Some he has hallowed and drawn near to himself. Some he has cursed and humbled; and set them to quarreling. This is very like the apostle's saying: Does not the potter have power over the clay, from the same lump to make one vessel for honor and another for disgrace? (Rm. 9.21). Thus, when he continues, he keeps the same metaphor, saying: As clay is in the potter's hand to mold and fashion it, always according to the potter's own good pleasure, so is human being in the hand of its maker. But in that the apostle says: Surely there is no iniquity on God's part (Rm. 9.14); see too what Sirach adds here: And he shall render to human being in accord with his judgment. But when the damned are allotted their just deserts, even this is nevertheless put to use, so that they might profit from it who are shown mercy. Listen to the rest: God is at odds with evil; and life is set against death. So too the sinner is set over against the just one. Thus look upon all the works of the most high, two by two, contraries one to the other. This too is so that in contrast with those worse ones, the better might stand out and profit. And yet they who are better are so by grace; for he speaks of a remnant being saved.

Then he goes on and speaks as one of that remnant: And I was the last to keep vigil, like one who gleans after the vineyard workers (Si. 33.16). But how does he prove that this was due not to his own nature but to God's mercy? To which he says: In the blessing of God I too have hoped; and like one who gathers grapes I have filled the winepress (Si. 33.17). For although they were the last to keep vigil—yet also because, as has been said, the last shall be first—a people gleaned from the remnant of Israel hoped in the blessing of the lord and filled the winepress from the abundance of the harvest, which extends to every corner of the earth.

The Apostle, therefore, and all of the justified who have shown to us the understanding of grace have no other intention than that whoever glories might glory in the lord (2 Co. 10.17). For who will tear down the works of the lord, who from the same lump damns one and justifies another? Free exercise of the will is what matters most. Indeed, it truly exists; but of what avail is it among those sold under sin? (Rm. 7.13). The Apostle says: The flesh lusts against the spirit and the spirit against the flesh, so that you may not do what you will to do (Ga. 5.17). We are commanded to live rightly; and the reward is set before us, that we might deserve to live blessedly forever. For who, unless justified by faith, can live rightly and do good works? We are commanded to believe, so that we might accept the gift of the holy spirit and be able to work through love. But who can believe unless touched by some calling or some real testimony? What person has power to touch its own mind with such a sight as would move the will toward faith? Who is able to embrace with the soul what brings no delight? And who has power to ensure either that what is delightful will happen or that what happens will be delightful? When, therefore, those things delight us which bring us closer to God, this is inspired and brought about by the grace of God, and is not provided for by our asserting nod, nor by our industry, nor by the merits of our works. For the fact that our will nods its assent and that we study industriously, and that our charity is fervently at work is his doing, the result of his largesse.

We are commanded to ask that we might receive, and to seek that we might find, and to knock that it might be opened to us (Mt. 7.7). Is not our prayer at times so tepid or rather so cold and close to being nothing—indeed at times it is nothing at all—that within us we do not even notice this with sorrow? For if we grieve over this, we are already praying. What else, therefore, are we being shown except that he who commands that we ask and seek and knock grants to us the doing of these things? Therefore, it is not of the one willing, nor of the one running, but of the God showing mercy, since we could neither will nor run without his moving and stirring us.

If there is election of some sort here—such that we understand the apostle's saying that: a remnant has been saved through the grace of election (Rm. 11.5) to mean not that there occurs an election of the justified for eternal life but that they are chosen who are to be justified—surely this election is hidden so as not to be in the least apparent to us, portions of the same lump. Or if it is apparent to some, I confess my powerlessness in this regard. For if I am permitted to examine in thought the election of human beings in accord with the grace of salvation, I have nothing whereby to see into this election unless it be either greater genius, or fewer sins, or both. And, if you please, we might add honest and useful doctrines. Therefore, it appears that whoever is entangled and stained with the slightest possible sins—for who can be without sin?—and is keen of wit and refined in the liberal arts should be elected to grace.

But when I will have set forth this opinion, he who has elected the weak things of the world to confound the strong and has elected the foolish things of the world to confound the wise (1 Co. 1.27) will laugh at me, so that, looking at him and set straight in my shame, I might laugh at many who are both more pure by comparison with certain sinners and are orators by comparison with certain fishermen. Do we not notice that many of our faithful who walk the way of God are in no respect comparable in genius even to certain comic actors, to say nothing of certain heretics? Likewise, do we not see certain ones, men and women, living chaste marriages free of contention and who are yet either heretics or heathens or who are in the true faith and in the true church so tepid that we wonder at how they are surpassed not only by the patience and temperance but also by the faith, the hope, and the charity of suddenly converted harlots and actors?

The only conclusion to be drawn is that wills are elected. The will itself, moreover, unless something comes before it which delights and draws the mind, can in no way be moved. To make this happen does not lie within the power of human being. What did Saul used to want except to attack, seize, subdue, and slay Christians? How raving, how furious, how blind was his will! And yet with one word from on high he was hurled prostrate. And such a vision came to him whereby his savagery was opposed and that mind and will were turned round and set straight. Suddenly, from a notorious persecutor of the gospel, he was made into a still more notorious proclaimer of the gospel (Ac. 8.3; 9.1). And yet what are we to say? Surely there is no iniquity on God's part (Rm. 9.14), who exacts from whom it pleases him, and who gives to whom it pleases him? He never exacts what is not due and never gives what is not his. Surely there is no iniquity on God's part? Far be it (Rm. 9.14). Yet why to this one in this way, and not to that one? O human, who are you? If you do not render what is owed, you have cause to be grateful; if you do not render what is owed, you have no cause to complain.

Let us only believe, even if we cannot grasp, that he who made and established the created universe, both spiritual and corporeal, disposes of all things by number, weight, and measure. But his judgments are inscrutable and his ways beyond investigation (Rm. 11.33). Let us say: Alleluia; and let us sing together his praise. And let us not say; why is this, or what is this? For all things have been created each in its own time (Si. 39.19, 26).

(Ad Simpl., 1.2.20-22)

Who Am I?

For Augustine, as truly as for Aristotle, "the nature of a thing is its end. For what each thing is when its becoming is complete, we call its nature, whether it be a human being, a horse, or a household." [1] The way of life proper to human being, life in accord with human nature, is, however, only one of several general possibilities available to individual human beings. This existential ambiguity accounts for the possible disparity between one's character and nature (Aristotle) or between one's person and nature (Augustine). Aristotle suggests the range of these possible ways of life when he says that "one who is unable to live a common life, or is self-sufficient and has no need to do so . . . must be either a beast or a god." [2] Augustine too has in mind types of life actually available to individual human beings when he

---

1. Aristotle, *Politics*, 1.1; 1252^b 32-35.
2. Ibid., 1.1; 1253^a 27-29. cf. also 1.2; 1253^a 2-3.

explains: "One kind of life is earthly, another is heavenly; there is a life of beasts, another of human beings, and another of angels" *(In Joann. ev.,* 18.7). Both Aristotle and Augustine assign human nature to a middle position between the animal and the divine,[3] although they testify as well to the immoderate and somehow inappropriate possibility of a human being's sharing in the life of the divine. What is clear, however, from the passages cited above and what is more to our immediate purposes, is that there is no necessity to human development and thus no assurance that an individual human being's life is or will be truly or fully human life. From this we may conclude that what defines and determines one's character or person is distinguishable and separable from what defines and determines one's nature. According to Aristotle, character (what it means to be *who* one is) is determined by conduct and conduct by character. This circularity of conduct and character determines, in time, one's posture toward the passions, fixed by the will's choice of objects. According to both Aristotle and Augustine, one is responsible *to* one's nature, which is not at all of one's making, while one is responsible *for* one's character, which is qualifiedly of one's own making. What remains for the present is to focus upon Augustine's understanding of the person—its formation, and its fulfillment—particularly as it unfolds in the last eight books of his *De Trinitate.*

Parallel to Aristotle's understanding of the circularity of character and conduct, Augustine proposes a corresponding circularity of person and love or will. One's love determines one's person, and one's person determines one's love. What I love is both constitutive and expressive of who I am, of what kind of person I am.

A body finds its own place by entrusting itself to its own weight, which carries it not to the place that is lowest but to the place that is

---

3. Augustine would have been familiar with this conception of human being as occupying a middle position among essences in its Plotinian formation: "Human being lies mid-way [*en mesō*] between gods and beasts and inclines towards both. Some human beings become like gods and others become like beasts. Most, however, remain in the middle." *(Enneads,* 3.2 9-11; cf. 4.6.3; 4.8.3; 5.3.3. cf. also Augustine's *De mus.,* 2.23; *De Trin.,* 12.11.16.)

its own. A flame rises and a stone falls. They are moved by their
weights and seek their own proper places. . . . My weight is my love.
By love I am drawn to wherever I am drawn. (*Conf.*, 13.9)

In this passage the movement is from the general to the particular,
the appropriate to the actual, nature to person.

Augustine, in likening the good and evil human being to the
two trees in the Garden of Eden, has occasion to distinguish
explicitly between nature and will or person. He paraphrases
scripture to the effect that as good trees bear good fruit and bad
trees bad fruit, so also do good human beings bear good fruit and
bad human beings bad fruit. This is clearly to say that one's
actions are determined by the type of human being one is. And
the type of human being one is, is not a matter of nature, a matter
of *what* one is, but rather is it a matter of person, a matter of *who*
one is; for Augustine goes on to explain:

Those two trees are not natures, but our wills . . . the lord himself
says in the gospel: Either make the tree good, or make it evil. Who
is there that could make a nature? If, then, we are commanded to
make the tree either good or evil, what is ours to do is to choose in
accord with our will.

(*C. Fort.*, 22)

It is necessary to distinguish here two senses of the manifoldly
ambiguous term *love:* One kind of love desires what is not
possessed, and the other delights in what is possessed. It is love as
desire (or delight in prospect) which is the weight, the influence,
driving one to do what one does and to seek what one seeks. Each
human being is understood to live and to act with a view toward
what seems to be most pleasant. Augustine indirectly concurs with
Vergil's saying, "Each one is drawn by one's own pleasure," [4] and
adds, "not necessity but pleasure; not obligation, but delight" *(In
Joann. ev.,* 26.4). Desire is clearly for the sake of pleasure or
delight; and thus Augustine assigns primacy to delight or enjoyment over desire. Delight, as its end, is the very core of the person.

---

4. cf. Vergil, *Eclogues,* 2.

Every love has its own force; and it cannot lie idle in the soul of the lover. Love must draw the soul on. Do you, then, wish to know the character of a love? See where it leads.

(En. in Ps., 121.1)

Delight is, as it were, the weight of the soul. For delight orders the soul ... where the soul's delight is, there is its treasure. Where the heart is, there is either blessedness or misery.

(De mus., 6.11.29)

Augustine in his *De Trinitate* presents his understanding of the inner life of human being with a view toward coming to some understanding of the inner life of God. The crucial foundation for this extended analogy is the scriptural and traditional reference to human beings as created *ad imaginem Dei*.[5] Thus each successive conception of human being has a tripartite or trinitarian structure. Most fundamentally, what is asserted throughout is that human being is a relational creature—its very life consists in its relatedness to itself and to others, which is also Augustine's fundamental assertion regarding the life of God. In the course of his reflections it is clear that, while his stated purpose is to pursue an understanding of human being in the hope of gaining insights into scriptural and traditional testimonies to God, those very testimonies lead and formulate his inquiries into the life of human being. Augustine surely considers it appropriate that faith should inform understanding as well as that understanding should inform faith. For those who cannot accept this circularity in principle, it is still possible in practice to consider and appreciate Augustine's consequent understanding of human being.

The first conception of spiritual life which Augustine considers at length is his conception of human life as mind [*mens*]—knowledge (of mind) [*notitia*]—love (of mind) [*amor*]. According to

---

5. Augustine regards the word to be the primary if not the sole proper referent of the title *Imago Dei,* while human being is created after, or approximate to, the image of God.

this conception, both the fullness and the unity of human life would be perfect when knowledge and love would be exactly coextensive with the mind of human being.

> Therefore the mind itself, and the love of it, and the knowledge of it, are three things, and these three are one; and when they are perfect, they are equal.
>
> *(De Trin., 9.4.4)*

However, Augustine recognizes the inadequacy of this conception on the grounds that the mind is, in fact, related to things other than itself. The mind is potentially and actually "mindful" of a world. Again the analogy between human being and God, between human experience and scriptural testimony, is sustained.

> The mind, moreover, with that love with which it loves itself, is able to love too something beyond itself. So too, the mind knows not only itself but also many other things. For this reason, love and knowledge do not inhere in the mind as in a subject. Rather, they have their own substantial existence, as does the mind itself.
>
> *(De Trin., 9.4.5)*

Augustine eventually collapses the threefold structure of mind-knowledge-love into the structure of mind [*mens*]—word [*verbum*]—love [*amor*] (cf. *De Trin.*, 9.8). Speech, understood in a peculiarly comprehensive sense, then becomes the guiding metaphor for human life. Human being begets its life as a word which it speaks. Its life proceeds from and unfolds before it as a spoken word. The life which one leads, one's loves, are as one's offspring, as words spoken from the heart. Again Augustine's account of human being parallels scripture's account of God; both human being's and God's inward and outward relations preeminently involve speech. God utters the word from eternity; and it is through that same word, spoken in time, that God creates the world, redeems the elect, and judges the damned. Speech is altogether primary too for human being, in that:

> We do nothing through the members of our body, whether in our deeds or words, to approve or to disapprove of human conduct,

which we do not anticipate with a word uttered within us. No one, then, willingly does anything which one has not first spoken in one's heart.

(De. Trin., 9.7.12)

To speak is to think of with love, to be mindful of with love, to attend to with love, in fact, to bestow oneself upon. This is critically different from to know and to love; for speech is itself clearly ambiguous regarding either its truthfulness or its appropriateness. Human being often speaks foolishly and perversely, which is to say that its life is often the story of ignorance and concupiscence. If human life were simply the knowledge and love of mind and of what is immediately accessible to mind, then there would be no creative, temporal dimension to human life, no dimension of the person. Insofar as human being is a person, its life is a word unfolding across time.

Augustine's understanding of human life as the mind and its word embraces both nature and person, respectively. *Who* one is represents a particular, temporal creation which may or may not be faithful to the humanity of its creator, just as the mind's word, its love, may or may not express wisdom and virtue. Augustine's understanding of human life as the mind and its word preserves both the creative, originative power of the person as well as the claims placed upon each person by its nature. Indeed the life of human being is a relation between time and eternity, between creation and createdness, between the fashioning of one's life in time and the fact of one's givenness from eternity. Only for God is it one thing to be and to be wise (cf. *De Trin.,* 15.13). For human being these are both distinct and separable. The person, *who* one is, is somehow one's own creation, one's own word, spoken in lifetime, while nature or mind, *what* one is, is God's own creation, God's own word, spoken for all time.

Love determines person, *who* one is. In time, the mind's word, its own self-created image, comes to represent the mind. Mind becomes as its own word; mind becomes, unfolds in time, in relation to what it loves. This word, the person, *is* the mind's concrete mindfulness or wakefulness. A person becomes what it thinks about with love.

So great is the force of love that, once the mind has long thought of
things with love and has cleaved to them, held fast by its care, the
mind drags those things with it even when it somehow returns to
think of itself.

(De Trin., 10.5.7)

The mind, moreover, loses its way, when to those images it conjoins
itself with such love that it considers even itself to be something of
the same sort. And so it is somehow conformed to them, not by
being this but by supposing it.

(De Trin., 10.6.8)

This imagined, but nonetheless real, conformity of mind with its
word is closely related to Augustine's confessed inability, prior to
his conversion, to conceive of spiritual substance, of a God who is
pure spirit, and of a human blessedness that is other than sensual.

Person, like Aristotelian character, is a creature of habit. One's
own loves, whether appropriate or not to *what* one is, fashion and
fit *who* one is. One's own life or word, whether finally a lie or not,
acquires a certain personal truth. Although nature places no
necessity upon person, person generates a necessity of its own.
Although the fact that I am a human being does not force me to
be this or that kind of person, the fact that I have become a
particular kind of person somehow necessitates that I live a
corresponding kind of life. This personal necessity, the momen-
tum of one's loves, is what Augustine calls habit or custom
(consuetudo). Habit, though originating in the will, a creature of
the will, becomes virtually natural (cf. *De civ. dei*, 12.3). In fact,
"there are as many contrary natures [in human being] as there are
wills which resist one another" *(Conf., 8.10)*.

For today in our actions, before we are tangled in any habit, we
have a will free to do something or not to do it. But when we have
exercised that freedom and done something, and the pernicious
sweetness and pleasure of that deed have seized the mind, the mind
is so entangled by its own habit that it cannot afterwards overcome
what it fashioned for itself by its own sinning.

(C. Fort., 22)

But I am dragged back again into these things by my own toilsome
gravity and am swallowed up in things customary. I am held fast.
My tears are many but so are my bonds. So greatly does the burden
of habit oppress me. For this condition I have the capacity but not
the will; and for another condition I have the will but not the
capacity. In both cases I am miserable.

(Conf., 10.40)

To see human life as a word is to recognize the deep ambiguity
and inevitable risk involved in personal existence. Human being
cannot but speak in time. Mind must attend to its world, become
mindful of that world, implicate itself by its loves, and live in the
web of its own necessities. The pursuit of self-knowledge and self-
acceptance, the concerns of the autobiographer which is everyone,
initially focus on the person. Self-knowledge and self-acceptance
mean knowledge and acceptance of *who* one has become. This
dimension is evident in the *Confessions.* It is in some immediate
sense appropriate to retell the story of one's life in that one's life is
simply a story which one tells. What is told once bears a second
telling, for the sake of clarity and consortium. One can know and
find pleasing what one has made; and so one can know and accept
and give an account of *who* one has become. However, although
this is one possible interpretation of human life, of mind-
knowledge-love, this is not Augustine's understanding of it. The
person, personal life, is ambiguous, arbitrary, and thus radically
unknowable and unacceptable apart from nature. Consequently
Augustine asks "Such was my life; but was that a life, my God?"
(Conf., 3.2). Augustine knew the type of person he had become
and the type of life he had lived; but he did not count this to be
true knowledge. Augustine must know how to regard critically or
to judge such a life. To say "Such was my life" is closer to truism
than to truth; it is sheer repetition; a second telling of one's life no
wiser than the first.

Speech had once meant for Augustine merely the articulation of
personal truths. All that one could hope to do was to speak
eloquently and persuasively. He said of his own parents' ambitions for him that their only concern was that he should learn to
make as fine and persuasive speeches as possible. Augustine's

conversion may be seen, in part, as a gradual discovery of the possibility of truthful speech. Regarding his study of Cicero's *Hortensius*, he relates: "I was eighteen and apparently spending my mother's money, two years after my father's death, for the sharpening of my tongue. However, it was not for that purpose, not for a sharper tongue, that I studied that book. For what won me over in that book was what it said, not how it spoke" *(Conf.,* 3.4). Similarly, he tells of his listening to Ambrose preaching: "And while I was opening my heart to hear how eloquently he spoke, what entered my heart at the same time, though only gradually, was how truly he spoke" *(Conf.,* 5.14).

Apart from factual and eloquent speech there is, then, wise, truthful speech. If human being alone speaks, then the silence which it breaks with its words is the absolute silence of nothingness. This is to say that if human being is simply a person, without a nature, then the story which it tells with its life is its own pure creation, personal fiction; and to give an account of that story is simply to retell it. If, however, God also speaks, then the silence which human being breaks with its words renders those words profoundly ambiguous. This is to say that if human being has also a nature, if it means something to say that a person is human, then the life story of any person must be judged in the light of what a truly human life is. This is clearly what Augustine has in mind when he says that he becomes a question to himself before God (cf. *Conf.,* 10.33). God's word, what it means to be human, renders Augustine's word, what is has come to mean to be Augustine, profoundly questionable. The person of Augustine, *who* Augustine is in time, becomes a question, a questioning of self and time. To speak properly is to speak truthfully, which calls for the pursuit of wisdom, the personal pursuit of one's own nature.

Speech, then, for Augustine also means judgment. Judgment is directed toward the temporal, toward the person and its world; and yet it is itself informed by the eternal, by nature and its creator. Augustine interprets human being's promised dominion in Genesis to rest upon the human capacity and inclination to judge all things which are to be judged. Without understanding and judgment, human being "is compared to the insensate beasts, and is become like to them" *(Conf.,* 13.23).

Those who live spiritual lives, whether in positions of authority or in positions of submission, make spiritual judgments. They do not judge on spiritual knowledge which shines in the firmament (for it is not proper to judge on so sublime an authority); nor do they judge on your book, even if something therein is obscure. For we submit our understanding to that book in the certainty that even what is closed to our sight is said rightly and truthfully. Such is human being . . . required to be a doer of the law but not its judge. Human being . . . judges, approving what it finds right and condemning what it finds wrong.

(Conf., 13.23)*

To give an account of one's life, then, is not simply to say "such was my life" but to confess the faithful or faithless character of that life. To live a human life is to speak, to narrate one's life from moment to moment, but also to judge one's life in moments of confession. Whatever further meanings of speech for Augustine will appear, we can now see the inadequacy, in Augustine's own terms, of any conception of the human word and of human life as unqualifiedly creative, that is, the inadequacy of an account of person apart from an account of nature.

The person is capable of denying the claims of nature but incapable of negating those claims. If the mind's word is faithless, that word, despite its undeniable personal truth, is a lie.

When a human being lives unto itself . . . it surely lives out a lie. This does not mean that human being is itself a lie; for its author and creator is God, who is certainly not the author and creator of a lie. Rather, human being has been made upright so that it might live not unto itself but in accordance with its maker, doing his will rather than its own. Not to live in this way, as one was made to live, this is a lie. . . . every sin is a lie.

(De civ. Dei, 14.4)*

The limits placed upon person by nature, upon human creation by divine creation, are finally ineluctable. The human place in the order of things is fixed. Human being is already named; and its name is its calling and its truth. To deny one's calling is to lose one's place and purpose.

By refusing to serve, they do not avoid serving altogether but avoid only the service of the lord. For if anyone will not serve love, that person will of necessity serve evil.

(En. in Ps., 18.2.15)

Beginning from a perverse desire for likeness to God, [human being] arrives in the end at likeness to the beasts.

(De Trin., 12.11.17)

The human being who will not respond freely to the claims of its creator will lose its freedom gradually to the self-made necessities of its own creation. "For the soul is higher than the body, and higher than the soul is God. ... Let it serve its lord, lest it be trampled on by its own servant" *(In Joann. ev.,* 23.5). The creative power of human being reaches no further than the person, the mind's word, which is finally accountable to the creative power of God, God's word, which returns in final judgment. The first word and the last word are the divine prerogative.

Accordingly, if all natures would observe their own proper measure, form, and order, there would be no evil. If, on the other hand, anyone would wish to make evil use of these good things, the will of God is not thereby overturned. For God knows how to order justly even the unjust, so that if they through perversity of will were to misuse God's good things, then God through the power of his own justice would use well their evils, rightly assigning to punishments those who perversely assigned themselves to sins.

(De nat. boni, 37)

In no way, therefore, do evil persons either change or overturn the will of the omnipotent God. ... For just as they make evil use of their own good nature which is his good work, so the good God makes good use of their evil words, lest the will of the omnipotent one be in any respect overcome.

(Serm., 214.3)

The scope and sense of our reflections upon the person may be caught and summed up by appealing to a distinction which Augustine draws between the mature mind and the immature mind. He does so within the context of a later conceptual structure of mind: memory [*memoria*]—understanding [*intelligentia*]—will [*voluntas*].

> In childhood, the more tenacious and facile one's memory, the keener one's understanding, and the more ardent one's study, all the more is one praised as talented. But when it is a question of learning, one is not asked how surely and easily one remembers or how keenly one understands. Rather, one is asked what one remembers and what one understands. And since the soul is praised not only for how learned it is but also for how good it is, attention is given not only to what one remembers and understands, but also to what one wills. What matters is not how enthusiastically one wills but first what one wills and only then how much one wills it. For a soul is to be praised for the vehemence of its love only when what it loves deserves to be loved vehemently.
>
> *(De Trin.,* 10.11.17)

In youth one's concerns are focused upon one's unique person, upon the measure and challenge of one's capacities. It seems most urgent and sufficient to create one's own response to the question *"Who* am I?" However, whether or not this is in some way acceptable for a youth, more than this is to be asked of a grown person. One's capacities and their achievements become questionable for a human being who realizes that one is answerable for them and for oneself. What one has said with one's life, what one has come to love, is altogether crucial. The question arises whether there is such a thing as a truthful life, or simply, whether one can respond at all to the question *"What* am I?" The question of nature arises from the final ambiguity of person.

It is perhaps interesting to suggest briefly that the terms of Augustine's discussion of person may, indeed, be applied to his discussion of societies or people, as in *The City of God* (cf. *De civ. Dei,* 19.24). A society is defined and constituted by its common love or concern. Regardless of the character of that love or concern, a society acquires from it a certain unity and identity. Such a society may be seen as a person blown large. Thus the question emerges whether or not there is a true society, a true communal person, whose common concern and commitment is to act in accord with the demands of justice, charity, and piety proper to human community. Just as it must be asked of a person what does one know and love, what does one remember, and understand, and will, so a society must be interrogated regarding its concerns and loves. The ambiguity and confusion of the person is multiplied and deepened when the story being told is that of a human society rather than that of an individual human being. Augustine concludes that the only true society is the society of the elect in heaven, just as the only true human being is one renewed and fulfilled by the heavenly vision of God.

The first act of human being in time is to speak, to image itself in its own word, to bestow itself in love upon otherness and so to inform that otherness with an order of love. The first question of human being is to inquire into its own word and its own love—a question and an inquiry which must reach beyond the person, beyond personal will and work, to nature, the will and work of God. The human creator must come to know and to love itself as a divine creation.

CHAPTER 4

NATURE

Readings

• 1 •

The mind, when it thinks and sees itself as understood, certainly does not beget this, its own understanding, as though it had previously been unknown to itself. Indeed the mind was known to itself as things are known which are contained in the memory, even if they are not being thought of. ... Moreover, these two, the begetter and the begotten, are united by love as a third, which is nothing other than the will desiring or retaining the enjoyment of something. Therefore, we have thought that the trinity of the mind is to be penetrated with these three names: memory, understanding, and will.

(De Trin., 14.6.8)

• 2 •

For if we refer ourselves to the inner memory of the mind by which the mind remembers itself, and to the inner understanding with which the mind understands itself, and to the inner will with

which the mind loves itself, where these three are always together at
the same time, and have always been together at the same time from
the first instant when they began to be, whether they were being
thought or whether they were not being thought, indeed, the image
of that trinity too will be seen to pertain to the memory alone; but
because the word cannot be there without thought—for we think
everything which we say, even if it be with that inner word which
belongs to no nation's tongue—this image is rather to be recognized
in these three: memory, of course, understanding, and will.

(De Trin., 14.7.10)

• 3 •

Those shadows are also to be mourned in which the ability inside
me lies hidden from me. As a result, when my soul asks itself about
its own strengths, it does not easily credit its own worthiness. For
what lies within it is mostly hidden, unless experience has revealed
it. And no one ought to be sure in life, which is called a continuous
trial, that if one can become better from a worse state, one cannot
also be made worse from a better one. Our one hope, our one
security, our one firm promise is your mercy.

(Conf., 10. 32)

• 4 •

Let me know you, you who are so cognizant of me; let me know
you as I am known. (1 Co. 13.12). Strength of my soul, enter it and
fit it to yourself, so that you may hold and possess it without stain or
wrinkle. This is my hope; so I speak and rejoice in that hope now
when my rejoicing is sane. Indeed the more we lament the other
things in life the less should they be lamented; and the less we
lament them, the more should they be lamented. For, look, you
have loved the truth, since whoever performs it comes to the light. I
want to perform it in my heart before you, in confession, and with
my pen, before many witnesses.

Indeed, lord, even if I wished not to confess to you, what in me
could be hidden from you, to whose eyes the depths of a human

being's conscience are apparent? I would not be hiding myself from
you but you from myself.

(*Conf.*, 10. 1-2)

. • 5 •

The human race is curious to know about other peoples' lives but
lazy in correcting its own. Why do they ask me who I am, when they
don't want to hear from you who they are? How do they know
whether I speak the truth when they hear about me from my own
mouth, since no person knows what takes place inside a human
being, except the spirit inside that very human being (1 Co. 2.11).
But if they should listen to you about themselves, they could not
say: The lord lies. For to listen to you about themselves is nothing
other than to know themselves.

(*Conf.*, 10.3)

• 6 •

Lord, you judge me because, although humans, except for the
spirit inside them, know nothing about themselves, there is some
part of a human being which even this spirit does not know; but you
who created human beings know every part of them. And though I
despise myself in your sight and value myself as dust and ashes, yet
I know something about you which I do not know about myself.
Now, indeed, we see through a glass darkly, not yet face to face (1
Co. 13.12). And so, as long as I wander away from you, I am closer
to myself than to you. Yet I know that you cannot be violated. I do
not know which temptations I have the strength to resist and which
not. Yet I have hope because you are faithful and do not allow us to
be tempted beyond our capabilities. Always you create the release
as well as the temptation, so that we can bear it. I will confess, then,
what I know about myself, and I will confess what I do not know
about myself; since what I know, I know through your clarification,
and what I do not know, I do not know only until my darkness
becomes like midday in your countenance.

(*Conf.*, 10.5)

• 7 •

I directed myself to myself and to myself I said: You, who are you? I responded: A human being. Look, I have a body without and a soul within. With which of these should I have sought my God, whom I had already sought with my body from the earth to the sky, as far as I could send as messengers the sight of my eyes? But what is inside is better. To it all my body acted as a messenger, while it presided over and judged the answers of the sky and the earth and of all the things which are in them when they said: We are not God, and, God made us. My inner self knew these things through the ministry of my outer self. I, my inner self, my soul, knew these things through the senses of my body. I asked the world about my God and it answered to me: I am not he, but he made me . . . nor every corporeal thing. The very nature of these things declares this. It is evident that the burden of the part is less than the whole. Now you are better, I tell you, soul, because you give life to the burden of the body, which no body can do for itself. But for you, too, your God is the life of life.

(Conf., 10.6)

• 8 •

In my opinion I am not to be called upon now to provide a definition of human being. Rather, the question here seems to me to be this: . . . What is human being? Is human being both body and soul, or body only, or soul only? For although body and soul are two and neither should be called human being without the other—for the body would not be human being without the soul, nor would the soul be human being without its ensouling the body, nevertheless it is possible for one of these to be regarded as and called human being.

What, then, do we call human being? Soul and body, like a pair of horses harnessed together, or like a centaur? Or the body alone, for the use of the soul which rules it, as when we assign the name "lamp" to an earthen vessel, not to the flame and vessel together, but to the vessel alone, even though we do so on account of the flame? Or do we mean by human being nothing other than the soul, but this on account of the body which it rules, just as by "equestrian" we mean not horse and human being together, but only human being, yet as given over to the mastery of a horse? This controversial matter is not easily resolved. Or, if a resolution comes easily to reason, it comes slowly to speech. But this is a labor and a detour which we need not accept and take upon ourselves. For whether the name of human being belongs to both soul and body, or to the soul alone, the highest good of human being is not the body's highest good. Rather, whatever is the highest good either for body and soul together or for the soul alone is the highest good of human being.

If, moreover, we ask what is the highest good of the body, sure reason compels the response that it is that which brings the body to its perfect state. But of all those things which enliven the body, none is better or more excellent than the soul. Thus the supreme good of the body is not bodily pleasure, nor the absence of bodily pain, nor power, nor beauty, nor swiftness, nor whatever else is usually counted amongst bodily goods, but simply and wholly the soul. For it is the soul's presence that brings to the body those things listed above and, what surpasses them all, life. Wherefore it does not seem to me that the soul is the supreme good of human being, whether by human being we mean soul and body together or the soul alone. For just as reason discovers the supreme good of the body to be something better than the body, furnishing the body with vigor and life, so, whether body and soul or the soul in itself is human being, we must discover whether there is anything which goes before the soul itself, in following which the soul reaches its own proper perfection. And if we can find this, all obscurities will vanish and it will surely have to be called, with all due right and merit, the supreme good of human being.

(De mor., 6.4.6-6.5.7)*

· 9 ·

It is a wonder that, although there is for all human beings a single will to lay hold of and possess blessedness, there exists so great a variety and diversity of wills concerning that blessedness itself. It is not that anyone does not will blessedness; rather, it is that not everyone has come to know it. For if all knew it, it would not be supposed by some to be excellence of soul, by others bodily pleasure, by others both: by some here, by others there. Thus, whatever has delighted them most, therein they have constituted the blessed life.

How is it, then, that all human beings love with the greatest fervor what not all know? Who can' love the unknown? ... Why, therefore, is blessedness loved by all, yet not known by all? Or is it perhaps that all know what blessedness itself is but do not know where it is; and from there arises the dispute? It is as if it were a matter of some place in this world where one who wills to live blessedly ought to will to live, so if in seeking what blessedness is there would be no question regarding where blessedness is. For surely if blessedness is in bodily pleasure, one is blessed if one enjoys bodily pleasure; and if blessedness is in excellence of soul, one is blessed if one enjoys excellence of soul; if blessedness is in both, one is blessed if one enjoys both.

Thus, when someone says that to live blessedly is to enjoy bodily pleasure and when, moreover, someone says that to live blessedly is to enjoy excellence of soul, is it not the case either that both are ignorant of what blessedness is or at least that not both of them know what blessedness is? Or is what we have set down as most true and most certain—that all human beings will to live blessedly— perhaps false? For if to will blessedly is, for example, to live in accord with excellence of soul, how does one will to live blessedly when one does not will this? Would we not more truly say: This human being does not will to live blessedly on account of not willing to live in accord with excellence, which alone is what it means to live blessedly? Not all, therefore, will to live blessedly, indeed few will this, if there is no way to live blessedly except by living in accord with excellence of soul, which many do not will.

Will that, then, be false which not even Cicero the Academician doubted, although the Academicians doubt everything? For, when he wished to begin his argument in the dialogue *Hortensius* from some certain point concerning which no one would have doubts, he said: Certainly we all will to be blessed. Far be it from us to say that this is false. What then? Should it be said that, even if to live blessedly is nothing else than to live in accord with excellence of soul, even one who does not will this nevertheless wills to live blessedly? This indeed appears to be too absurd. For this is as if we were to say: Even one who does not will to live blessedly wills to live blessedly. Who would listen to this contradiction; who would propose it? Regardless, this is where necessity thrusts us, if it is true both that all will to live blessedly and that not all will to live in the only way in which life may be blessedly lived.

(De Trin., 13.4.7)

• 10 •

These premises have been firmly established: that the rational soul is made blessed only by God, that the body is enlivened only through the soul, and that the soul is somehow intermediate between God and the body . . . There is nothing more powerful than this creature, which is called the rational mind; nothing more sublime. Whatever is above it is certainly the creator.

(In Joann. ev., 23.6)

• 11 •

The Old Testament, with its earthly promises, seems to advise that God should not be loved for nothing but, rather, that God should be loved because he gives us something on earth. What do you love so as not to love God? Tell me. Love, if you can, something w ich he has not made. Look round the whole creation. See whether you are anywhere held by the birdlime of lust or hindered from loving the creator, except by a thing which he himself whom you neglect has created. Why, moreover, do you love those things except because they are beautiful? And can they be as beautiful as he who made them? You marvel at these things, because you do not see him. Through those objects of your marveling, love him whom you see not. Interrogate the creation. If it is of itself, remain in it. But if it is from him, it is pernicious to one who loves it only because it is preferred to its creator.

(En. in Ps., 79.14)

• 12 •

All wills bound together are, moreover, right if that one will is good to which each of the others is referred. If, however, that final

will is depraved, then all the other wills referred to it are depraved.
And thus, in the unity of right wills, those who ascent to blessedness
have a kind of path, made, as it were, of quite sure steps. The
entanglement of depraved and distorted wills is, moreover, a chain
by which one who acts in this way is bound so as to be cast into the
outer darkness.

Blessed, therefore, are they who in their deeds and ways sing the
canticle of the steps; and woe to those who draw sins as a long rope.
Thus there is a repose of the will which we call a goal, even if it is
still referred to something else ... yet if something is pleasing such
that the will rests in it with a certain delight, it is nevertheless not yet
that toward which the will is inclined to strive. Rather, this
something is referred beyond itself so that it might be regarded, not
as a homeland for the citizen, but as a place of renewal, or even as a
place of lodging for the traveler.

(De Trin., 11.6.10)

· 13 ·

The force of this memory is great, God, so very great—a huge and
infinite sanctuary. Who ever reaches the bottom of it? And its force
is the force of my soul and belongs to my nature, but I do not take
hold completely of what I am. Therefore the soul is too limited to
hold itself. But then, where is the part it does not hold? Surely it is
not outside rather than inside itself? How then does it not take hold
of it? Great wonder rises up in me at this; astonishment grabs me.

(Conf., 10.8)

· 14 ·

If, even for a short time, I stop calling to mind the things which
we are said to know, they sink back again as if they were
disappearing into a faraway sanctuary, so that I have to think them
through all over again, as if they were new thoughts; I must force
them back from that same place—there is nowhere else for them to
go—so that they can be known. It is as if they must be collected after
being scattered. This we call thinking.

(Conf., 10.11)

• 15 •

I name memory, and I recognize what I name. But where do I recognize it, if not in this same memory? For surely it cannot be in its own presence, through an image of itself, and yet not through itself.

And what of forgetfulness? If I name it and in the same way recognize what I name, how do I recognize it, if not in my memory? I do not mean the sound of the word but the thing itself, what it means. If I had forgotten the meaning, the sound would have no use, as I should not recognize it. When I remember memory, it is itself present through itself. When I remember forgetfulness, then both memory and forgetfulness are present: memory, for which I have remembered, and forgetfulness, which I am remembering. But what is forgetfulness but loss of memory? How, then, is it present so that I remember it, when in its presence I have no memory? But if memory retains what we remember and if, unless we have remembered forgetfulness, we could never be able, on hearing the word, to recognize the meaning of it, then memory retains forgetfulness. Therefore, what we forget, when it is present, is itself present, so that we do not forget. From this argument we understand that forgetfulness is not present in memory through itself, when we remember it, but through itself it would bring about not memory but forgetfulness. Who can discover the solution to this, or understand how it could be?

To be sure I struggle with this, lord; I struggle inside myself. I have become to myself a piece of field to sweat over. For we are not now examining the heavens, or plotting out the constellations, or inquiring into the suspension of the earth. It is I, my soul, who remember. So it is not remarkable if what I am not is far away from me. But what could be closer to me than myself? But, look, I do not understand the force of my memory, although without it I could not say that I am myself.

(Conf., 15-16)

• 16 •

Is it the same kind of thing as when I, who have seen Carthage, remember it? No. Eyes do not see a blessed life, because it is not corporeal. Then is it like remembering numbers? No. The person who already has a knowledge of numbers does not search to acquire it further; but if we have a blessed life and therefore love it, we want nevertheless to acquire it further, so that we may be blessed. Well then, is it like remembering eloquence? No. For, although people who are not yet eloquent remember the thing itself when they hear the name, and although there are many people who want to be eloquent and so apparently have some knowledge of it, yet these people have noticed, with their bodily senses, the eloquence of others and so have enjoyed it and want it for themselves. Now it is true that unless they had some inner knowledge of eloquence they would not delight in it, nor would they want it, if it did not delight them; but a blessed life we do not experience either with our senses or through other poeple. Then it is like remembering joy? Perhaps that's it. For I have remembered my joy when I am sad, as I have remembered my blessed life when I am miserable. And never through the senses of my body have I seen or heard or smelled or tasted or touched my joy; but I have experienced it in my soul, when I am blessed, and the knowledge of it has stuck in my memory, so that I am able to remember it, sometimes with contempt and sometimes with yearning, in keeping with the different sorts of things I remember having enjoyed. At times I have been overcome with joy at disgraceful things, and when I now remember these times, I detest them and curse them. At times my joy has come from good and honest things, and when I remember these, I yearn for them although they may no longer be present. Then I remember past joy with sadness.

So where and when have I experienced my blessed life, so that I can remember and love and yearn for it? It is not my wish alone, or mine and a few other people's, to be blessed; absolutely everyone wants it. We would not want it with such a sure will, if we did not have sure knowledge of it. But why is this? Why? If two people were asked whether they wanted to join the military, it would be possible for one to say yes and the other no. If, however, these two were asked if they wished to be blessed, each would immediately and without doubt say yes; yet their motivation for wanting or refusing to join the military is nothing other than blessedness. So perhaps people rejoice in different things? So all agree that they want to be blessed, just as they would agree, if asked, that they want to rejoice; and this joy is what they call the blessed life. And joy may be acquired through different means but there is one goal which everyone strives to achieve: a state of joy. Joy is a thing which everyone claims to have experienced, and therefore it lives in the memory and is recognized when the words "blessed life" are heard.

Let it be far, lord, far from the heart of your servant, who confesses to you; let it be far from me to think that I am blessed whenever I experience joy. There is a joy which is not given to the wicked but to those who love you for your own sake, whose joy you yourself are. To rejoice in you and to you and because of you, this is the blessed life. There is no other. Those who think that there is another pursue another joy, which is not pure joy. But their will is turned toward some form of joy.

So it is not a sure thing that everyone wants to be blessed, since those who do not want to rejoice in you—which is the only way to lead a blessed life—do not truly want a blessed life. But perhaps everyone wants this but because the flesh has desires which are not in accordance with the spirit and vice versa one cannot do what one wants (Ga. 5.17), and so one falls into whatever one can do and is content with it; because what one is not able to do one does not want enough to make one able to do it. I ask all of humankind whether they would prefer to rejoice in the truth or in falsehood. Without hesitation they say they prefer to rejoice in truth, just as they say without hesitation that they would like to be blessed. Indeed a blessed life is joy in the truth. For this is joy in you who are the truth, God, my light, health of my countenance, my God. All people want this blessed life, this one which is alone blessed; everyone, yes, all people, want joy in the truth. I have met many who want to deceive but no one wants to be deceived. So where have they known this blessed life, if not in the same place that they have known truth? They love truth because none of them wishes to be deceived. And when they love a blessed life, which is nothing other than joy in the truth, they also love truth; nor could they love it if some knowledge of it did not exist in their memory. Why do they not rejoice in it? Why aren't they blessed? Because they are more involved in other things which make them miserable than in that which makes them blessed but which they remember only vaguely. For there is only a small light inside each human being, who must walk, walk so that the darkness does not overcome the light.

But why does truth give birth to hatred? Why is your servant made out to be an enemy when he preaches the truth, although a blessed life, which is nothing other than joy in the truth, is beloved? Perhaps because truth inspires the kind of love in which whoever loves something wants that thing, whatever it is, to be the truth. And because they have no desire to be deceived they are unwilling to admit that they have been. So they hate the truth for the sake of that thing which they love instead of it. They love the truth when it gives light; they hate it when it contradicts. Because they wish to deceive and not to be deceived, they love truth when it informs on itself and hate it when it informs on them. And so, in return, truth will reveal those who do not want to be revealed by it, but it will itself remain hidden to those people. This, yes, this is the way of the human soul. In the same way it is also blind and lazy, base and indecent; it wishes to hide itself, but that it should have anything hidden from it, that it does not want. The result is quite the contrary: The soul does not lie hidden from the truth, but truth lies hidden from it. And even so, despite its misery, it prefers to rejoice in true things than in false things. It will, therefore, be blessed if without malicious interference, on its own, it comes to rejoice in the one truth through which all things are true.

Look how far I have traveled in my memory in search of you, lord; I have not found you outside of it. Never, from the time I learned of you, have I discovered anything about you except in my memory. Never from the time when I first learned of you was I forgetful of you. For wherever I found truth, there I found my God, truth itself, of which from the time when I first learned it, I was never forgetful. And so you remain in my memory from that moment on, and I find you there whenever I recall you and delight in you. These are the holy delights which you, because you are thoughtful of my poverty, have given me in your mercy.

Where in my memory do you reside, lord; in what part? What kind of resting place have you created for yourself there? What sort of sanctuary have you built? You have given my memory honor by residing in it, but I wonder in what part of it you reside. I have passed beyond the parts of memory which beasts also have when I remember you, because I never found you among the images of corporeal beings. I came to the part where I had deposited the feelings of my soul, and I did not find you there. I entered the very seat of my soul—which is in my memory, since my soul also remembers itself—and you were not there. For just as you are not an image of a corporeal being neither are you a feeling of any human being's, like the feeling we have when we are blessed or sad, or when we lust or fear, remember or forget, or anything of that sort. And so you are not the soul itself because you are God the lord of the soul. All these things change, but you remain unchangeable over everything. Yet you deigned to live in my memory from the moment I learned of you. Why do I seek the place where you live as if there were truly places there? It is certain that you live there, since I have remembered you from the time I learned of you, and I find you in my memory when I recall you.

Where did I find you in order that I might learn of you? Certainly you were not in my memory before I learned of you. So where did I find you to learn of you unless it was in yourself and above me? There is never a place; we come and go, but there is never a place. Truth, you give audience to all who consult you and immediately respond to all the different questions. You respond clearly but all do not hear you clearly. All consult you about whatever they want, but all do not hear what they want. Your best servant is the one who pays less attention, when listening to you, to what is desired and more to what is heard.

Too late I loved you, beauty so old and so new, too late I loved you! Look! You were within, and I was far away looking for you. And I, in my ugliness, rushed headlong into your beautiful creations. You were with me, and I was not with you. Those very things kept me far from you which would not even have existed if they had not been in you. With your calling and your crying you broke through my deafness, your shining and your splendor drove out my blindness. You breathed perfume and I took in a breath; and now I gasp for you. I tasted you and now I hunger and thirst. You touched me and I burned for your peace.

(Conf., 10.21-27)

• 17 •

Human nature, therefore, has been so formed that never does it not remember itself, never does it not understand itself, and never does it not love itself.

(De Trin., 14.14.18)

• 18 •

Indeed, in the mind's memory, understanding, and willing of itself, we discovered the mind itself to be such that, just as it was preserved always to know itself and always to love itself, so at the same time it was preserved always to remember itself, always to understand and to love itself, although it does not always think of itself as distinct from those things which are not what the mind itself is. And, through this difficulty, the distinction is made in the mind between the memory of self and the understanding of self. It would appear as though there were not two things but one thing, being called by two names, in the mind wherein they are so closely conjoined, and wherein neither precedes the other in time. Love itself, when need does not make it evident, is not sensed in this way, for what is loved is always present.

(De Trin., 10.12.19)

• 19 •

What is so present to thought as what is present to the mind? Or what is so present to the mind as the mind itself? If we trace back the origin of the word "discovery" [*inventio*], what other response, what other meaning does it offer than this: To discover is to come upon that which is sought? Therefore, things which enter the mind, as it were, spontaneously are not usually said to have been discovered, although they can be said to have been known. This is because in our seeking we were not striving toward those things so that we might come upon them, namely, discover them. On this account, just as the mind itself seeks those things which are sought out by the eyes or by any other corporeal sense—for the mind itself also directs bodily sense, and, moreover, discovers in that same moment when that same sense comes upon the things sought after— so the mind discovers other things which it ought to know, not through corporeal sense as a messenger but through itself. And it discovers when it comes upon them, either in a higher substance, that is, in God, or in other parts of the soul, as when it forms a judgment concerning the images of bodies, which it discovers within, in the soul, where they have been impressed through the body.

Therefore the marvelous question is this: How may the mind seek and find itself, where might it strive so as to seek or where might it come so as to find? For what is so on the mind as the mind itself? But, because it is in those things which it thinks about with love, the mind, grown accustomed with love to sensible things, namely, to corporeal things, cannot prevail to be in itself without the images of those things. From this arises the shame of its error so long as it cannot separate from itself the images of sensory things so that it might see only itself. For in a manner to be marveled at the glue of love has stuck them fast to the mind. And its uncleanness is such that, while it strains to think of itself alone, it regards itself as that without which it is unable to think of itself.

Therefore, when the mind is instructed to think of itself, it should not seek itself as if it were removed from itself. Rather, it should remove what it has added to itself. For it is itself more deeply within itself not only than those sensible things which are manifestly outside the mind but even than the images of those things, images that in some part belong to the soul which even animals have, although they lack intelligence, a thing proper to the mind. Since, then, the mind is more inward, it somehow departs from itself when it sets forth the affection of its love upon those things like the footprints of many acts of intention. And these footprints, so to speak, are impressed upon the memory when the corporeal things which are outside the mind are sensed so that, even though they are absent, their images are nevertheless present to those who think of them.

Therefore, let the mind come to know itself. Let it seek out itself, but not as a thing absent. Rather, let the mind fix itself upon the will's intending, by which the mind wandered elsewhere, and let the mind reflect upon itself. In this way, the mind will see that it has never not loved itself, never not known itself. But, by loving something else with itself, the mind confused itself with something else and in the same way grew together with it. And thus while it embraces diverse things as if they were one, it has regarded as one things which are diverse.

Let not the mind, therefore, seek to discern itself as though it were bsent, but let it take care to discern itself as present. Neither let it know itself as if it doesn't know itself. Rather, let it distinguish itself from what else it knows. For when it hears: "Know thyself," how will it take care to do that, if it does not know what "know" means or what "thyself" means? If, moreover, it knows what both mean, it also knows itself. For "know thyself" is not said to the mind as it is said to the mind to "Know the Cherubin and Seraphim." They are not, after all, present and concerning them we believe in accord with the teaching that there are certain heavenly powers. Neither is it the same as when the mind is told: "Know that man's will," which will is not in any way present to us to be observed or understood unless made known with corporeal signs. And even then it is more a matter of believing than of understanding. Nor is it the same as when a human being is told: "See your face," which cannot be accomplished unless in a mirror. For our face itself is also absent from our glance, because it is not where our glance can be directed. But when it is said to the mind: "Know thyself," in that very moment when the mind understands what has been said, " Thyself," it understands itself, for no other reason than that it is present to itself.

(De Trin., 10.7.10-10.9.12)

· 20 ·

In the source of all these temporal things which we have mentioned, certain knowable things precede knowledge by a space of time, just as there are those sensible things which were already among things before they were known, or as there are all those things wh ch are known through history. Certain things, however, begin to be at the same moment as they are known. For example, if something visible, which previously had no existence at all, arises before our eyes, it certainly does not precede our knowledge; or, if something makes a sound in the presence of a hearer, then certainly both the sound and its being heard begin at the same moment and cease at the same moment. Nevertheless, whether they exist prior in time to their being known or whether they begin to be at the same time as they are known, knowable things beget knowledge, and not the reverse.

But when knowledge is accomplished and those things which we have come to know are placed within memory and seen again in remembrance, who would not see that the retention in memory is temporally prior to the sight in remembrance as well as to the joining together of both by the will as a third? Again, however, such is not the case for the mind. For the mind itself is not adventitious to itself, as though to the mind itself which already was existing, there should come from elsewhere the very same mind which was not

already existing; or as though it should not come from elsewhere
but in the mind itself, which was already, there should be born the
same mind which was not, just as in the already existing mind, faith,
which was not, arises; or as though the mind sees itself constituted,
as it were, in memory, after knowing itself in remembrance, as if it
were not there before it knew itself. For certainly from the first
instant when it began to be, the mind has never ceased remembering itself, never ceased understanding itself, and never ceased loving
itself. . . .

And, therefore, when the mind is converted to itself in thought,
there arises a trinity in which a word, too, can now certainly be
understood; for it is formed from thought itself, while the will joins
both together. And it is therein that the trinity which we seek is even
more to be recognized.

(De Trin., 14.10.13)

• 21 •

There is nothing more present to the mind than the mind itself . . .
it thinks itself to live, to remember, to understand and to will itself
. . . if it adds nothing to itself so as to regard itself as something of
the kind, whatever of itself remains for itself this alone is the mind
itself.

(De Trin., 10.10.16)

• 22 •

Yet so great is the power of thought, that not even the mind has
any way of placing itself in its own sight except by thinking of itself.
Wherefore, nothing is in the mind's sight, unless it is being thought
of, such that the mind itself, by which whatever is thought is
thought, cannot be in its own sight in any other way than by
thinking of itself. Moreover, how it would not itself be in its own
sight when it is not thinking of itself—for it can never be without
itself—as if the mind itself is one thing and its sight another, I cannot
discover. For it is not absurdly said of the bodily eye that since the
eye is fixed in its own place in the body, its gaze is directed toward
those things that are beyond it and is extended even to the stars. The
eye is not in its own sight, inasmuch as it does not see itself, unless in

a mirror held out before it ... which certainly does not happen when the mind constitutes itself in its own sight by thinking of itself.

Or is it, therefore, that the mind, when it sees itself by thinking of itself sees one part of itself with another part of itself, just as with some of our members, our eyes, we see others of our members, which can be in our sight? What can be more absurd to say or to think? For whence is the mind carried away if not from itself? And where is it placed in its own sight, except before itself? It will not, therefore, be where it was, when it was not in its own sight; for, having been placed here, it was brought there. But if it changed locations to be seen, where will it remain to see? Or is it, as it were, doubled so as to be both there and here, namely, both where it can see and where it can be seen, in itself seeing and before itself to be seen? When the truth is consulted, it responds to us with none of these things. For when we think in this manner, we are thinking only in terms of the fictive images of bodies; and that the mind is not such is certain to a few minds which can consult the truth on this matter.

It remains, therefore, that the mind's beholding of itself is something pertaining to its nature and that the mind is recalled to it, when it thinks of itself, not as it were across a spatial interval but by an incorporeal conversion. But when the mind is not thinking of itself, it is indeed not in its own sight, nor is its gaze formed from it; but still it knows itself, as if it were itself a memory for itself of itself. It is like the situation of one skilled in many disciplines. One knows the things contained in one's memory. And yet, of these things, only that is in one's sight which one is thinking about; the rest are put away in a kind of secret knowledge, which is called memory.

We were, therefore, proposing a trinity such that we placed in the memory that from which the gaze of the one thinking was formed. Then there was the corresponding formation itself, like an image impressed therefrom; and finally that by which both are joined together, namely love or will. When the mind, therefore, sees itself in thought, understands and recognizes itself, it thus begets this understanding and its own thought. For an incorporeal thing is seen in being understood and in this act of understanding is recognized. Yet the mind, when it thinks and sees itself as understood, certainly doe not beget this, its own understanding, as though it had previously been unknown to itself. Indeed, the mind was known to itself as things are known which are contained in the memory, even if they are not being thought of. For we say that a human being knows letters, even when one is thinking not about letters, but about other things. Moreover, these two, the begetter and the begotten, are united by love as a third, which is nothing other than the will desiring or retaining the enjoyment of something. Therefore, we have thought that the trinity of the mind is to be penetrated with these three names: memory, understanding, and will.

(De Trin., 14.6.8)

· 23 ·

What should I do now, you who are my true life, my God? I will go beyond this power of mine which is called memory; I will go beyond it so that I may reach for you, sweet light. What are you saying to me? As I rise through my soul to you who reside above me I will go beyond that strength of mine called memory. For I wish to reach you where you can be reached, and I wish to cling to you where it is possible to cling. Memory even cattle and birds have; otherwise they would not be able to find their stalls or their nests, nor could they do the other things which they are used to doing. It is only through memory that they may become used to anything. So I will go beyond memory to reach him who has distinguished me from the beasts and has made me wiser than the birds of the air. I will go beyond memory so that I may find you. But where, when will I find you, truly good and sure sweetness? If I find you beyond my memory, I have no memory of you. And how will I find you then, when I have no memory of you?

(Conf., 10.17)

· 24 ·

This trinity, then, of the mind [i.e., memory-understanding-love] is the image of God, not because the mind remembers itself, understands itself, and loves itself, but rather because it can remember, understand, and love its maker. And when it does this, the mind is made wise. If it does not do this, even if it remembers, understands, and loves itself, the mind is foolish. Let the mind, then, remember, understand, and love its God after whose image it has been made. To say the same thing more briefly, let the mind worship God, who is not made, and who has made the mind capable of God and made possible the mind's participation in God. For this reason it is written: Behold, wisdom is the worship of God. (Jb. 28.28).

(De Trin., 14.12.15)

What Am I?

The life of the human person is, according to Augustine, a fictitious fabric of will, a web of self-made, self-imposed loves. Life's personal unfolding is the mind's own work, the mind's word, loving mindfulness. Mind is always mindfulness, if it is anything at all. May we speak, however, of life's natural unfolding, of the mind as itself a work, a word? The mind's own inherent questionableness inevitably focuses itself upon the possibility, or the impossibility, of full self-knowledge and of full self-love, loving knowledge of both person and nature. Can there be a mindfulness of mind? If the eye of the soul cannot look into itself, is its vision not truly its own shadow, its own wilful projection, and nothing more?

Augustine sees the knowledge and love of mind as its own word to be finally groundless and arbitrary without the mind's knowledge and love of itself as God's word. The image of mind as creator must be qualified by the image of mind as creature, namely, by mind as merely the image of the creator. One's knowing and loving what one has made of oneself must come to nothing if they do not come to one's knowing and loving oneself as sheer gift, as a moment of divine wilfulness. Without such knowledge and love, the only human truth would be altogether personal, even private; all faithfulness would be faithfulness to oneself, what we call sincerity, which is finally no more than conscious consistency, habit made explicit and accepted as a way of life. But if knowledge and love of human nature, a personal human love and knowledge, are somehow possible, then why, we might ask, ought the mind to pursue it? In other words:

Why, then, is the soul admonished to know itself? This, I believe, is the reason: so that it might reflect upon itself and live in accord with its own nature. To live thus, would mean for the soul to desire for itself that it be ordered in accord with its nature, beneath him to whom it is rightfully subject and over those things placed in its charge, again, beneath its proper ruler and over its proper subjects.

(De Trin., 10.5.7)

If mind is, however, already conformed to its own word, already become what it has thought of with love, then mindfulness of mind must mean the mind's renewal, the conversion and re-generation of mind.

In a variety of contexts and formulations, Augustine asserts that the mind can never wholly violate or forfeit its own nature. On the contrary, he affirms the enduring presence and accessibility of nature to knowledge and to will. He claims, for instance, that it is one thing for the mind not to think of itself and quite another thing for it not to know itself (cf. De Trin., 10.5.7), and that it is one thing for the mind to think of itself as material and quite another for the mind actually to be material (cf. De Trin., 10.7.8). Augustine claims, as well, that the mind's knowledge of itself (cf. De Trin., 10.8.11) and its power of judgment (cf. De Trin., 10.5.7) are never lost; for "what is so much in the mind as the mind itself?" (De Trin., 10.8.11). The fall of the mind into its entangle-ment with material things and material images is never total and thus never includes the full loss or dissolution of mind.

To its fashioning of things the soul gives away something of its own substance. Still the soul retains what it needs to judge freely the species of such images. What the soul retains for the sake of its judging is rational intelligence. And this is more truly mind than is what the soul gives away.

(De Trin., 10.5.7)

Therefore, let the mind come to know itself. Let it seek itself, but not as a thing absent. Rather, let the mind fix upon itself the will's intending, by which the mind wandered elsewhere, and let the mind reflect upon itself. In this way, the mind will see that it has never not loved itself, never not known itself. But by loving something else with itself, the mind confused itself with something else and in some way grew together with it.

(De Trin., 10.8.11)

The mind in pursuit of itself first begins to escape the tyranny, the lie, of the absolute person, when that person becomes to itself ambiguous and questionable. What follows is a knowledge of the person which reaches heuristically beyond the person.

As soon as the mind seeks to know itself, it knows itself at once as seeking itself. Now it does, indeed, know itself. On this account too the mind cannot be altogether unknowing of itself: It is knowing itself when it knows its own unknowing. Moreover, if it should not know its own unknowing, then the mind does not seek to know itself. Wherefore, the very fact that the mind seeks itself argues convincingly that the mind is more known than unknown to itself. For the mind, as it seeks to know itself, knows its own seeking and its own unknowing.

(De Trin., 10.3.5)

Augustine thus further modifies the initial trinitarian structure of mind-knowledge-love by proposing that knowledge be thought of as inquiry or study and that love be thought of as whatever sort of love one has for that which is the object of innermost inquiry or study. To paraphrase Augustine, this trinity then becomes: mind—the knowledge of one who seeks [*quaerit*]—the love of one who seeks. The ambiguity of this phrasing is intentional. Knowledge has come to mean here both the mind's knowledge of the person as seeking and that knowledge of the mind which belongs to the person and enables the person who seeks to know the mind. And love has come to mean both the mind's love of the person as seeking and that love of the mind which drives the person in its search.

It is important to note here a distinction Augustine draws regarding the mind's knowledge of itself as seeking and as not knowing itself. He insists that this knowledge is partial knowledge of the whole rather than knowledge of a part.

What, therefore, shall we say? That the mind knows itself in part, and in part does not know itself? But it is absurd to say that the mind, when it knows itself, does not know itself as a whole. This is not to say that the mind is wholly knowing but that in its knowing the mind is whole. Thus, when the mind knows anything concerning itself, which it cannot know unless it is itself whole, it knows itself as a whole. Moreover, the mind knows itself as knowing something; and it cannot know anything unless it is itself a whole. Thus it knows itself as a whole.

(De Trin., 10.4.6)

The significance of this distinction is to make clear that person and nature are not parts of a whole. Rather, both person and nature somehow embrace the whole of one's life. True knowledge of the person, then, knowledge of the person as provisionally creative but finally ambiguous and answerable, is imperfect knowledge of the whole (rather than perfect knowledge of a part). The interrelationships between person and nature are complex and contextual. There is no ready law by which to subordinate the one to the other, no simple formula to register once for all their respective properties. Augustine recognizes the peculiar and inalienable legitimacy of both person and nature, of both questions: Who am I and what am I? The preceding reflections and those that follow focus upon the centrality and the interplay of these questions in certain of Augustine's works and considerations. This analysis is intended to display rather than dissolve the inseparable unity of the questions of person and nature for Augustine. "As the mind, therefore, is a whole mind, so it lives as a whole" *(De Trin.*, 10.4.6).

The claim has already been made and lightly passed over that the person possesses a certain knowledge of the mind, which knowledge directs and motivates its search. We must now listen to a fuller articulation of this claim before considering its implications and grounds.

But see, the mind does not know itself to be mind. Rather it seeks itself and it knows itself only in that it seeks itself. For if it does not know this, the mind may well seek one thing in search of another. However, lest it seek one thing mistaking it for another, the mind

without a doubt knows what it is seeking. But if it knows what it
seeks, and if it seeks itself, then it surely knows itself. What, then, is
it still seeking? If it knows itself in part, but in part is still seeking
itself, then it does not seek its very self but a part belonging to it. But
when the mind is spoken of, it is spoken of as a whole. And because
it knows itself as not wholly discovered by itself, it knows the
dimensions of the whole. And so it seeks what is still missing, much
as we are accustomed to inquire in such a way as to bring to mind
what has fallen out of mind but is not entirely gone. For, when this
once again comes to mind, the mind can recognize it to be what it
seeks.

(De Trin., 10.4.6)

What the mind seeks in seeking itself is a wholeness or fullness
which is proper to it and which is therefore still sufficiently present
to it to enable it to know what it lacks and seeks. Augustine does
not claim that this knowledge is specific or articulate but only that
it is adequate for the mind to know that what is truly being sought
has not yet been found and to recognize what is being sought once
it has been found. Augustine suggests here and elsewhere the
phenomenon of forgetfulness as an appropriate metaphor for
understanding the mind's imperfect grasp upon itself.

At this point it is illuminating to consider still another of
Augustine's trinitarian proposals for understanding the life proper
to human being: memory [memoria]—understanding [intelligent-
ia]—will [voluntas]. The crucial qualification of earlier proposals
which is made here seems to be the introduction of memory in the
place formerly occupied by mind. What is perhaps partially
intended here is still another assertion of the extent to which the
mind becomes conformed to its concerns. Augustine has spoken
elsewhere of the mind's loves as confusing and convincing
accretions to its substance. Thus, the collapse or falling away of
mind into forgetfulness tells even more of the provisional power
of the person in human life; for it says that human being is
somehow what it has done, made, and attended to. Over against
this, however, by affirming memory here, Augustine claims that
the whole mind remains accessible to thought (or understanding)
and to love (or will) in the experience of memory. Here it is
important to distinguish between the memory of things past and

the memory of things present. In ordinary discourse, memory has reference only to past experiences, to a past which remains somehow ours and available to our reflection through our retention of it in what we call memory. Memories are not simply absent from thought, nor are they simply present. Rather, they remain somehow both always past or absent and always present, or else they could never be recalled. Augustine sees a likeness here with the mind's or human nature's simultaneous absence and presence in the life of human being. Augustine has already spoken of the mind's forgetfulness of itself (cf., e.g., *De Trin.*, 10.5.7), which implies the mind's availability to itself in memory.

> Regarding things past, what we call memory is that which brings it about that those past things are able to be recalled and remembered. So too, regarding a thing present as the mind is to itself, it makes sense that we should call memory that by which the mind is present to itself, so that it might be understood by its own thought and so that both might be joined together by the mind's love of itself.
>
> *(De Trin.*, 14.11.14) [1]

Quite appropriately, then, Augustine considers this question at length in his *Confessions* and elsewhere: whether blessedness lies within the memory of human being. And, for Augustine, as we have already reflected upon, to speak of blessedness is to speak of human being, the desired end of human becoming; for the nature of anything dwells in its proper end which, in the case of human being, we call blessedness. On this point, Augustine's own reflections require no further commentary here.

> Great is the force of memory, my God, a thing to be wondered at, a profound and infinite multiplicity. This thing is the soul. This thing am I myself. What am I, then, my God? What nature am I? My life is many and various and violently without measure. See, in the innumerable fields and caves and hollows of my memory, innu-

---

1. Augustine, after rejecting the Plotinean teaching regarding the soul's preexistence and its reminiscence of its condition before the fall, could not speak of the mind's memory of itself without explicitly distinguishing memory of what is present from memory of what is past.

merably full of innumerable things . . . through all of these things I
flit and flutter, this way and that. I reach as far as I am able but
never do I reach a boundary. So great is the force of memory. So
great is the force of life in the mortal life of human being!

(Conf., 10.17)

I remember how I have often searched for and found what was lost.
And I know that, when I was searching for something and someone
was asking me "Is it this? or Is it that?," I would continue to answer
"No" until I was offered what it was I sought. Now, unless I were
mindful of that thing and remembered what it was, I would not find
it even if it were offered to me; for I would not recognize it. And this
is the way it always happens when we search for and find something
that is lost. If by chance something passes away from the eyes but
not from memory (as any visible body might do) the image of it is
held inwardly, and it is sought until it is restored to our sight. And
when it has been found, it is recognized from the image of it which
dwells within us. For we do not claim to have found what had been
lost if we fail to recognize it. And we cannot recognize it, if we do
not remember it. Indeed, what had been lost to our eyes was
retained by our memory.

(Conf., 10.18)

How, then, do I seek you, lord? For when I seek you, my God, I am
seeking the blessed life. I shall seek you so that my soul might live.
For my body draws its life from my soul and my soul draws its life
from you. How, then, do I seek the blessed life? For it is not mine
until, when it is for me to speak, I shall say, "Enough. It is there."
How do I seek it? Through remembrance, as though I have
forgotten it and regard myself to be forgetful still? Or through the
appetite for finding it out as something unknown, something which
either I have never known or I forgot so fully that I do not
remember my having forgotten it? Is it not the blessed life that is
willed by everyone and for which no one is unwilling? But where
did they come to know it so that they might will it? Where did they
see it so that they might love it? Somehow (I do not know how) they
have come to know it and thus possess it in some kind of knowledge
. . . what I seek to know is this: Whether the blessed life dwells
within memory. For we would never love it unless we knew it. . . .
The blessed life is known, then, to all; for, if in a single tongue, all

human beings could be asked whether they will to be blessed, they would doubtlessly respond yes. And this could not happen unless the very thing named in that tongue [namely, the blessed life] were held fast within their memory.

(Conf., 10.20)

The key to Augustine's claim that there is a residual or innate knowledge and love of mind accessible to every person, and so dwelling in the life of every human being, seems to lie in his assertion of the universality of the will for blessedness. According to Augustine, the desire for blessedness is a dimension, indeed is the center, of every human desire. The will for blessedness belongs most properly to nature. Yet, since human being always lives in some sense as a whole, the unique and private character of personal will is unable to exclude from itself altogether the natural and common desire of human being for blessedness.

... even among those persons who will the same thing, although one's own will lies open to one's own sight, the will of another lies hidden, despite the fact that that other person wills the same thing as oneself.

(De Trin., 13.2.5)

There is, indeed, a great conspiracy within this same human nature, alive and rational. For although the will of each lies hidden to everyone else, there are yet some wills which everyone knows to be universal. And even though no one knows what another individual wills, in certain matters it is possible for anyone to know what all will. ... All will to be blessed, and not to be miserable. ... For whatever else anyone wills in the secrecy of one's heart, no one withdraws from this will, which is well known to everyone and well known to reside in everyone.

(De Trin., 13.3.6)

All see within their heart that they will to be blessed; and so great in this respect is the conspiracy of human nature that one may not be deceived in projecting this same will from one's own soul to another's. For we know that everyone wills this.

(De Trin., 13.20.25)

Knowledge and love of mind, then, are always present in that human being somehow searches for blessedness in whatever it pursues, in whatever it seeks to know and to love. However, the will for blessedness does not include explicit knowledge of that in which true blessedness, truly human life, consists.

It is a wonder that, although there is for all human beings a

single will to lay hold of and to possess blessedness, there exists so great a variety and diversity of wills concerning that blessedness itself. It is not that anyone does not will blessedness; rather, it is that not everyone has come to know it.

(De Trin., 13.4.7)

Again a question emerges regarding the peculiar knowledge implied in the will for blessedness. There cannot be thought to be will or desire apart from some knowledge of what is desired. Thus there can be no willing of blessedness without a certain knowing of it.

How is it, then, that all human beings love with the greatest fervor what not all know? Who can love the unknown? . . . Why, therefore, is blessedness loved by all, yet not known by all?

(De Trin., 13.4.7)

The knowledge referred to in this passage would seem to be positive, articulate knowledge, which leaves open the possibility of another form of knowledge available to all human beings and implied in the desire of all for true blessedness.

Augustine sees that the will for blessedness is most often negative in practice; most often it takes the form of a denial rather than an affirmation. The desire for blessedness finds expression in the will's itinerant restlessness, the will's refusal to embrace finally or wholly its world or any part of its world. Since the desire for blessedness is somehow present in every human desire, the finite objects of desire become unacceptable in the light of their final inadequacy.

Things are moved by their own weights and seek their own proper places. When things are less than perfectly ordered they are restless;

and, when they are in order, they are at rest. My weight is my love.
By love I am drawn to wherever I am drawn.

(Conf., 13.9)

For the mind to embrace someone or something with the whole of
its love is to place upon the object of that love the full, unqualified
demands of human being. Regardless of how little the person is
accustomed to asking of its loves, each person remains human and
cannot do other than ask everything in the end from the loves in
which it rests or rather seeks rest. This introduces still another
meaning of speech for Augustine—inquiry or interrogation—which
is closely related to speech as judgment. When the mind speaks,
when it looks upon anything or anyone with love, what it finally
asks of that person or thing is blessedness, fulfillment, or rest.
Human speech alone is able to interrogate the world, to ask of it
more than it offers, and to judge that world on terms that are not
its own. To human being, when it asks everything, when it voices
the full human question, creation speaks not of itself but of God
its creator.

Does not this sight of the world present itself to all who have the full
power of their senses? Why, then, does it not say the same things to
everyone? Animals great and small see it; but they are unable to
interrogate it. For in them, reason is not placed over the announce-
ments of the senses as their judge. But human beings are able to
interrogate the world with a view toward seeing the invisible things
of God made visible to the intellect by the things that are made.
Those things do not respond, however, unless those who bring
questions also make judgments. For those things do not alter their
own voice, that is the sight they present, when one person has only
vision, while another person both sees and interrogates. The result is
that this sight appears in one way to the one person and in another
way to the other. Still, it presents itself identically to both, although
it is silent to the one and speaks to the other. In the truest sense, of
course, it speaks to all. But they alone understand who receive its
voice outside the mind and then, deep within them, unite it with the
truth. For Truth says to me: Your God is not sky and earth, nor
every corporeal thing.

(Conf., 10.6)

The answer which each created person and thing gives to one who would know and love it is the response of its own inadequacy to the desire and the claims which human being cannot help but bring to their relationship. One who does not understand the refusal of the world fears total, unending rejection, while one whose quest is somehow conscious and articulate recognizes that one is being counseled to reject, at least finally, what one has come to know and to love.

What do I love when I love you [my God]? ... I questioned the earth and it answered "I am not God." And all earthly things made the same response. I questioned the sea and the deeps and creeping things and they responded: "We are not your God; inquire higher." And so I interrogated the airy world above; and the all-encompassing sky, with all that dwell therein answered me: "Anaximines is wrong; we are not God." I questioned heaven, sun, moon, and stars: "Neither are we," they said back, "the God whom you seek." And I said to all the things that surround the gateways of my flesh: "Since you are not my God, speak to me of him. Tell me something about my God." And with one great voice they exclaimed: "He himself made us." My question was my intending and the sight of these things was their response. I directed myself to myself and to myself I said, "You, who are you?" And I responded, "A human being."

(Conf., 10.6)

A person can know with certainty and sovereignty only what it has made from the beginning, only that for which it is solely responsible. And Augustine realizes that finally neither he nor his world are of his own making. The universe, the whole, has become a question to Augustine as he has become a question to himself.

The word and the work of divine creation whereby human nature comes to be what it is in each person is eternal and thus everpresent. Through the memory of what is essentially present, the mind has access to that relationship and love wherein the mind is fashioned after the image of God. So long as the mind is forgetful of this relationship and dwells apart from this love, the mind is deformed, which deformity is experienced as personal misery and restlessness. In this misery, one's question is one's quest for blessedness.

CHAPTER 5

WILL

Readings

• 1 •

If a course plotted by reason and the will itself would reach that port of philosophy from which already there is sole access to the region of the blessed life ... I don't know whether it would be rash for me to say that many fewer human beings would have been likely to reach that port, although now, too, as we see, they are surely few and rare who arrive there. For God or nature or necessity or our will or some combination of these or all together—this is, after all, an obscure matter, which we nevertheless take up now for you to shed light upon it—have cast us, as if with random disregard, into this world like an open sea in storm. This being the case, how many would understand where they should strive toward or to where they ought to return, unless at some point a storm should blast against our own willings and strivings, a storm which to the foolish appears adverse, and unless it should convey us, unknowing and errant, to that most hoped-for land?

(De beat. vit., 1.1)

142

• 2 •

And then I began again. "We wish to be happy," I said.

As soon as I had uttered this, with one voice and with one mind they concurred.

"Does it seem to you," I asked, "that we are blessed if we do not have what we want?"

"No," they answered.

"What? Are we always blessed when we have what we want?"

It was then my mother who responded. "If we want and have what is good, then we are blessed. If, however, what we want is evil, though we have it, we are miserable."

I smiled at her and said eagerly, "Mother, you have truly grasped the very center of philosophy. Undoubtedly you lacked the words to express yourself in the manner of Cicero whose ideas you have proposed. For, in his *Hortensius,* a book in praise and defense of philosophy, he says, 'Behold, not philosophers, but those inclined to debate are the ones who say that all those are blessed who live as they themselves want to live. This, indeed, is false; for to want what would be inappropriate is itself a very miserable thing. But it is not as miserable to fail to attain what you want as it is to want to attain what would not be proper. For depravity of will brings with it more evil than fortune brings good.' ". . .

"Therefore," I said, "whoever possesses God is blessed."

When they gladly and most freely accepted this, I said, "In my judgment our only inquiry should be into who it is that possesses God; for such a one will be perfectly blessed. How, I ask you, does this seem to you?"

Here Licentius commented, "One who lives rightly possesses God."

"The one who possesses God," added Trygetius, "is the one who does what God wants done."

Lartidianus yielded to this opinion.

However, that boy, the slightest of all (Adeodatus, Augustine's own son), said, "Whoever possesses a pure soul possesses God."

Mother approved of all that was said, but of this most of all. . . .

"If, therefore," I went on, "one who seeks God does what God wants, that one both lives rightly and possesses a pure soul. However, one who seeks God, does not yet possess God. Therefore, it does not follow that whoever either lives rightly or does what God wants or has a pure soul should be said to possess God. . . ."

"But no one," responded Mother, "can reach God without having first sought God."

"Very well," I said; "yet, one who is still seeking God and has not yet reached him, is also already living rightly. Therefore, not everyone who lives rightly possesses God. . . ."

"To possess God," added Mother, "is one thing, and not to be without God is another. . . . As far as my understanding reaches, this is my opinion. One who lives rightly possesses a God who is propitious. But one who lives wrongly possesses a God who is adverse. One, moreover, who is still seeking and who has not yet found him, possesses neither a propitious God nor an adverse God. Yet such a one is not without God. . . ."

Then I said, "Tell me, please, doesn't it seem to you that God is propitious to that one whom he favors? . . . It follows, then, that one who seeks God possesses a propitious God; and everyone who possesses a propitious God is blessed. Therefore, the blessed one is the one who seeks. One who is seeking, however, does not yet possess what one wants. Thus, one who does not possess what one wants is blessed."

Mother then broke in. "In no way," she said, "it seems to me, are we blessed if we do not possess what we want."

"Therefore," I responded, "not everyone who has a propitious God is blessed."

"If reason forces this conclusion," she said, "I cannot deny it."

"There will, then, be this distinction," I explained. "On the one hand, everyone who has already found God and possesses a propitious God is also blessed. On the other hand, moreover, everyone who is seeking God possesses a propitious God, but is not yet blessed. And, surely, whoever with vices and sins alienates oneself from God, is not only not blessed but does not even live with God's favor . . . then the question of who is blessed is most perfectly resolved. It will be that one who is without indigence. For, everyone who is not miserable is blessed. Therefore, blessed is the one who lacks indigence, if what we call indigence is the same as what constitutes misery. . . .

"Therefore, indigence of soul is nothing other than foolishness. For this is the contrary of wisdom, just as death is the contrary of life, and as the blessed life is the contrary of misery. There is no middle ground between them. For just as everyone who is not blessed is miserable, and as everyone who is not dead is alive, so it is manifestly the case that everyone who is not foolish is wise. . . . If everyone who lacks wisdom suffers a great indigence, and if everyone possessed of wisdom lacks nothing, it follows that foolishness is indigence. Moreover, just as every fool is miserable, so everyone who is miserable is a fool. Thus, just as all indigence is misery, so all misery is identical with indigence. . . .

"Whatever is either too little or too much, on account of its lacking measure, is subject to indigence. The measure of the soul is, therefore, wisdom. Indeed, wisdom is undeniably the contrary of foolishness; and foolishness is indigence. The contrary of indigence, moreover, is fullness. Therefore, wisdom is fullness. Whence the famous saying, deservedly regarded as the most useful principle in life: Nothing in excess.

"At the outset of our discussion today we had said that, if we found misery to be nothing other than indigence, we would admit that we are blessed if we lack nothing. And, indeed, we have found this. Therefore, to be blessed is nothing other than to lack nothing; and that is what it is to be wise. Moreover, if you inquire into the nature of wisdom . . . , it is nothing other than the measure of the soul, namely, that by which the soul maintains its balance, lest it digress into excess or reduce itself to less than its own proper fullness. Moreover, the soul's digressions are luxury, despotism, pride, and things of that sort which the souls of the immoderate and miserable suppose to be the equivalent of joy and power. On the other hand, the soul is reduced by meanness, fear, grief, lust, and other things, whatever they may be, with which the miserable confess their own misery.

"But when the soul finds and contemplates wisdom and . . . commits itself to wisdom—not to fraudulent likenesses whose embrace is a weight inclined to fall and sink away from God, an embrace excited by emptiness, an embrace which turns the soul around—[when the soul, then, commits itself to wisdom] it fears no immoderation, and thus no indigence, and therefore no misery. Therefore, whoever is blessed possesses one's measure, which is wisdom.

"But what ought wisdom to be called unless the wisdom of God? We accept, moreover, on divine authority, that the son of God is nothing other than the wisdom of God; and the son of God is truly God. Therefore, whoever is blessed possesses God, to which we all agreed earlier. . . . But what do you suppose wisdom to be, if not the truth? For this too has been said: I am the truth (Jn. 14.6). Truth, moreover, so that it might be, comes to be through another supreme measure; for if the supreme measure is a measure through the supreme measure, it is a measure through itself.

"But the supreme measure must, of necessity, also be the true measure. For as truth is engendered by measure, so measure is recognized in truth. Therefore, there has never been measure without truth.

"Who is the son of God? It has been said: Truth. Who is it that has no father? Who other than the supreme measure? Whoever, therefore, comes to the supreme measure through the truth, is blessed. What this is for souls is to possess God, which is to enjoy God. Other things do not possess God, although they are possessed by God.

"A certain admonition, moreover, emanating from the very font of truth to us, urges us to remember God, to seek him, and to thirst after him with every painful effort. This hidden sun floods our inner eyes with that beaming light. It is the same source of every truth which we speak, even when we hesitate to turn boldly and to behold wholly with eyes either not yet sound or only recently opened. This light appears to be nothing other than God, perfect, free of any flaw. For there is every whole and perfect thing; and, at the same time, there is God.

"And yet, so long as we are seeking, we are not yet satiated by that font and . . . by fullness and we should confess that we have not yet reached our measure. And, therefore, although God is now assisting us, we are not yet wise and blessed.

"This is, then, the full satisfaction of souls, this is the blessed life: piously and perfectly to understand the one who leads you to the truth, to understand what truth you enjoy, and to understand your relationship to the supreme measure.

(De beat. vit., 2.10.11.12; 3.19, 20, 21;
4.23, 28, 32, 33, 34, 35)

· 3 ·

It is a wonder that, although there is for all human beings a single will to lay hold of and possess blessedness, there exists so great a variety and diversity of wills concerning that blessedness itself. It is not that anyone does not will blessedness; rather, it is that not everyone has come to know it. For if all knew it, it would not be supposed by some to be excellence of soul, by others bodily pleasure, by others both: by some here, by others there. Thus, whatever has delighted them most, therein they have constituted the blessed life.

How is it, then, that all human beings love with the greatest fervor what not all know? Who can love the unknown? . . . Why, therefore, is blessedness loved by all, yet not known by all? Or is it perhaps that all know what blessedness itself is but do not know where it is; and from there arises the dispute? It is as if it were a matter of some place in this world where one who wills to live blessedly ought to will to live, so if in seeking what blessedness is there would be no question regarding where blessedness is. For surely if blessedness is in bodily pleasure, one is blessed if one enjoys bodily pleasure; and if blessedness is in excellence of soul, one is blessed if one enjoys excellence of soul; if blessedness is in both, one is blessed if one enjoys both.

Thus, when someone says that to live blessedly is to enjoy bodily pleasure and when, moreover, someone says that to live blessedly is to enjoy excellence of soul, is it not the case either that both are ignorant of what blessedness is or at least that not both of them know what blessedness is? Or is what we have set down as most true and most certain—that all human beings will to live blessedly—perhaps false? For if to will blessedly is, for example, to live in accord with excellence of soul, how does one will to live blessedly when one does not will this? Would we not more truly say: This human being does not will to live blessedly on account of not willing to live in accord with excellence, which alone is what it means to live blessedly? Not all, therefore, will to live blessedly, indeed few will this, if there is no way to live blessedly except by living in accord with excellence of soul, which many do not will.

Will that, then, be false which not even Cicero the Academician doubted, although the Academicians doubt everything? For, when he wished to begin his argument in the dialogue *Hortensius* from some certain point concerning which no one would have doubts, he said: Certainly we all will to be blessed. Far be it from us to say that this is false. What then? Should it be said that, even if to live blessedly is nothing else than to live in accord with excellence of soul, even one who does not will this nevertheless wills to live blessedly? This indeed appears to be too absurd. For this is as if we were to say: Even one who does not will to live blessedly wills to live blessedly. Who would listen to this contradiction; who would propose it? Regardless, this is where necessity thrusts us, if it is true both that all will to live blessedly and that not all will to live in the only way in which life may be blessedly lived.

Might we, perhaps, be brought out of these straits by what we have said—that all locate the blessed life in that which delights them the most, Epicurus in pleasure, Zeno in excellence, and another in another thing? And might we say that to live blessedly is nothing other than to live in accord with one's own pleasure and thus that it is not false that all will to live blessedly, since all will in such a way as delights each. . . .

But even Cicero, when he had proposed this position against his own, argued against it in such a way as to make those blush who maintain it. For he says: Behold, indeed not the philosophers, but rather those who are ready to dispute, say that all are blessed who live as they themselves would wish. This is what we have meant by saying: as delights each. But he thereupon suggests: This is surely false. For to will what is inappropriate is itself a most miserable thing; nor is it as miserable to fail to obtain what you will as it is to will to obtain what is not fitting. This is altogether most brilliant and most true. For who is so blinded in mind, so foreign to every glimmer of decency, so enveloped in the shadows of shame as to call that one blessed who lives wickedly and disgracefully, free of anyone's restraint or revenge, with no one daring to rebuke and, even more, with the praise of many—for as the divine scripture says: The sinner is praised in the desires of his or her soul and the worker of iniquity receives blessings (Ps. 9.3)—who, again, would call that one blessed who satisfied all of his or her most bewitching and infamous willings, on the grounds that such a one lives as he or she wills to live? Indeed, one would even be miserable, though less so, if one had been able to have none of those things wrongly willed. For everyone is rendered miserable by an evil will alone, but even more miserable by that power through which the desire of an evil will is satisfied.

Wherefore, since it is true that all human beings will to be blessed and desire that one thing with a most ardent love and on account of that one thing desire whatever else they desire, and since no one can love something while being wholly ignorant of what it is or of what sort it is—nor can one be ignorant of what one knows oneself to know—it follows that all know the blessed life. Moreover, all who are blessed have what they will, although not all those who have what they will are necessarily blessed. They are necessarily miserable, however, who either do not have what they will or have what they wrongly will. Therefore, no one is blessed without having one's every will fulfilled and without having willed in each case rightly.

Since, therefore, the blessed life consists of these two things, and is known to all and dear to all, what do we suppose to be the cause of this phenomenon: When human beings cannot have both of these, they choose to have everything they will rather than to will all things rightly even if they do not have them? Or is it the very depravity of humankind that, although it is not concealed from them, neither that one is blessed who has what he or she wills nor is that one blessed who has what he or she wills wrongly, but that one is blessed who both has whatever good things he or she wills and wills no evil things, yet when both of these things by which the blessed life is realized are not given, that one is chosen whereby one is removed all the more from the blessed life—for whoever obtains what was wrongly desired is further from the blessed life than one who does not obtain what was willed—whereas the right will ought to have been chosen and preferred, even when it has not obtained what it desires?

One is nearly blessed when one is right in willing whatever one wills and when one wills those things in the attainment of which one will be blessed. And surely they are not evil things but good things that make one blessed when they do so. And of those good things such a one has already something, namely the good will itself, a thing not to be lightly esteemed. . . .

(De Trin., 13.4.7÷13.6.9)

• 4 •

Seek your own good, O soul. For one thing is good to one creature and another to another. And all creatures have their own good, appropriate to the wholeness and the perfection of their nature. From creature to creature, what is required for its perfection differs. Seek your own good. No one is good except the one God (Mt. 19.17). The supreme good, this is your good. For there are also inferior goods, which are good for some or for others. . . . Raise your hope to the good of all goods. He himself, by whom you in your humanity have been made good, and by whom all things in their natures have been made good, will be your good.

(En. in Ps., 102.8)

· 5 ·

To follow after God constitutes the desire for blessedness; but to reach God is blessedness itself. We follow God by loving him. We reach him, in truth, not when we become altogether what he is, but rather when we become nearest to him, touching him in a marvelous and intelligible way, inwardly illumined and seized by his truth and holiness. He is the light itself; and it is granted to us to be illumined by him. The greatest commandment, therefore, which leads to the blessed life, and the first, is this: You shall love the lord your God with your whole heart, soul, and mind. Indeed, for those who love God all things work toward the good. Thus Paul, shortly after this, adds: I am certain that neither death, nor life, nor angels, nor virtues, nor things present, nor things future, nor height, nor depth, nor any other creature will be able to separate us from the love of God, which is in Christ Jesus our lord (Rm. 8.28, 38, 39).

If, then, for those who love God all things work toward the good, and if no one doubts that the supreme good, which is also called the highest good, not only should be loved but should be loved such that we are bound to love nothing more than we love it, then we find here sign and expression of what has been said: with the whole soul, heart, and mind. With these things established and most firmly believed, who, I ask, has doubted that the supreme good—toward the attainment of which we must, with all else put aside, hasten—is nothing other than God? And so, if nothing is able to separate us from his love, what can be not only better but also more certain than this?

But let us attend to each of these points briefly. No one separates us from the love of God by threatening us with death. For that whereby we love God cannot die, except insofar as it fails to love God, since it is death itself not to love God. And this is, simply, to love and to follow something else in preference to him. And no one separates us from the love of God by promising us life; for no one separates us from the fountain in promising us its water. No angel separates us; for, when we cling to God, no angel is more powerful than our mind. No virtue separates us; for, if what we are here calling virtue has any power in this world, the mind, when it clings to God, is wholly lifted up beyond the entire world. But if what we mean by virtue is the perfect uprightness of our soul, then, if it is someone else's virtue, it favors our union with God, and, if it is our virtue, it accomplishes our union with God. Present times of trouble do not separate us; for the more closely we cling to God, the lighter we find their burden by which they endeavor to separate us from him. Neither does the promise of future things separate us, for whatever good lies in the future is the more certain promise of God, who is indeed already well present to those who cling to him. And nothing is more good than God. Neither height nor depth separates us from God. For if, perhaps, these words refer to the height and depth of knowledge, I will not be so curious as to be severed from God. And no teaching, by which error is to be driven away, separates me from him; for no one errs unless one is separated from him. But if, by height and depth, is meant the highest and lowest things of this world, how could I be promised heaven so as to be severed from the maker of heaven? Or how could I be frightened by hell into deserting God, when I would know nothing of hell unless I would have deserted him? Finally, what place will tear me from the love of God, who would not be wholly everywhere, if he were contained in any one place?

He tells us that no other creature separates us. O man of highest mysteries! He was not content with saying "creature"; but he says "other creature," thus reminding us that whereby we love God, and that whereby we cling to God, namely, the soul and mind, is a creature. Therefore, the body is another creature. And if the soul is something intelligible, namely, something known only by intellectual understanding, the "other creature" comprises everthing sensible, namely, something which, as it were, offers itself to be known through the eyes, or ears, or smell, or taste, or touch. And this latter creature is necessarily inferior to what is grasped by intellectual understanding alone.

Therefore, since God too can be known by worthy souls only through intellectual understanding—although he is more excellent than that understanding by which he is understood, for he is its creator and author—there is reason for fear, lest the human soul, by being numbered among invisible and intelligible things, should judge itself to be of the same nature as he who created it. And so it would fall away through pride from him with whom it should be united in love. For the human soul becomes like God to the extent granted by its subjecting itself to God to be honored and enlightened. And if, in that subjection by which the soul becomes like God, it approaches very near to him, it is necessarily cast far from him in that audacity by which it wishes to be more like God. It is with this same audacity that the soul refuses to observe the laws of God while it desires to be of its own power, as God is.

The further, therefore, that the soul departs from God, not in space, but in its affection and in lust for things beneath it, the more it is filled with foolishness and misery. And thus the return of God is by love, a love which the soul strives to place itself in contention with God but beneath him. The more urgent and zealous the soul has been in doing this, the more blessed and sublime it will be. And its freedom will be perfect with God alone as its lord. Thus the soul must know that it is a creature. For it must believe what is true, that its creator remains always in the inviolable and unchanged nature of truth and wisdom; and it must, however, confess, especially in face of the errors from which it longs to escape, that it can fall into foolishness and falsehood. Yet, on the other hand, the soul must take care lest, by the love of another creature, namely, by the love of this sensible world, it be separated from the love of God which sanctifies it for an enduring and perfect blessedness.

(De mor., 1.11.18-21)

• 6 •

Let us, therefore, ask, according to reason, how human being ought to live. Certainly we all want to live blessedly. There is no human being who does not concur with that statement, even before it has been fully uttered. Moreover, in my judgment, we can never be called blessed unless we have what we want, whatever that might be. Neither can we be called blessed if we have what we want and if what we want is harmful. Nor can we be called blessed if we do not love what we have, even if it is the highest good. For when we seek what we cannot obtain, we are tormented; and when we have obtained what was not to be sought, we are mistaken. And when we do not seek what ought to be obtained, we ail. Moreover, none of these befall the mind without misery; and both blessedness and misery do not as a rule reside in the same human being at the same time. In none of these instances are we blessed. However, as I see it, there remains a fourth alternative, wherein the blessed life can be found: when we love and possess the highest human good. What else do we mean by enjoyment, except to have at hand what we love? No one is blessed except in the enjoyment of human being's highest good. Thus, if we have it in mind to live blessedly, our highest good must needs be at hand for us.

It follows that we should now ask what is human being's highest good, which surely cannot be less than the human being itself. For any time we follow after what is less than us, we ourselves become less. Moreover, every human being must follow what is highest. Therefore, human being's highest good is not less than human being. Perhaps, it will be something of the same sort as human being? Indeed, this is so, if there is nothing higher than human being which can be enjoyed. If, however, we find something which is both more excellent than human being and can be at hand for one who loves it, who will still have doubts that human being should strive after that something so as to be blessed and that it is manifestly more excellent than the one who strives after it? For if to be blessed is to have attained a good such as cannot be surpassed, which is, moreover, what we call the highest good, then how can one be included in that definition without having yet reached one's supreme good?

(De mor., 1.3.4-5)

• 7 •

In this life, however great one's knowledge may be, it is not yet a matter of perfect blessedness; for what is still unknown is by far uncomparably greater.

(Retr., 1.14.2)

• 8 •

But not even the saints and the faithful believers in the one true and highest God are safe from the trials and multiformed temptations of the demons. For in this place of weakness and in these evil days anxiety of this sort has its use in inspiring with fervent desire the search for that security in which lies the fullest and most certain peace. For there there will be gifts of nature, that is, all the things which the creator of all natures has bestowed on ours, not only good things, but eternal ones which affect not only the spirit, which is healed through wisdom, but also the body which is renewed through the resurrection. There there are virtues which do not struggle against any vices or evils but have the eternal reward of victory, a peace which no enemy will disturb. For this is the ultimate blessedness, the very ultimate perfection, which has no finite end. In this world we are considered blessed when we have peace—at least as much as a good life can have on this earth. But the blessedness on this earth is misery when compared to that blessedness which we call without end. So when human beings have whatever peace is available to us on this earth, then virtue uses well even the ills which human beings suffer. But true virtue exists when it refers itself, and all the goods which it makes beneficial use of, and whatever results from the use of goods and evils, to that end where we will have a complete peace which no other peace can supersede in quantity or quality.

(De civ. Dei, .19.10)

· 9 ·

Since the highest good of the city of God is an eternal and perfect peace—not the peace through which mortals pass in their birthing and dying but the peace in which immortals abide untouched by any suffering—who would deny either that that life is the most blessed or that the life we have now is most miserable in comparison, no matter how rich this life may be in spiritual, corporeal, and external goods? Yet if we always conduct our life in this world with the assumption that it is a means leading to that end which we ardently desire and faithfully hope for, it is not absurd to say that we can be blessed in this life, though through hope rather than in actuality. But blessedness in this life, unaccompanied by hope for that life, is a false blessedness and a great misery. Here we do not enjoy the soul's true blessing since the wisdom which does not direct its involvement in what it observes with prudence, does with fortitude, restrains with temperance and arranges with justice toward that end when God will be all in all, when there will be certain eternity and perfect peace, is not a true wisdom.

(De civ. Dei, 19.20)

· 10 ·

Why, then, is the soul admonished to know itself? This, I believe, is the reason: so that it might reflect upon itself and live in accord with its own nature. To live thus would mean for the soul to desire for itself that it be ordered in accord with its nature, beneath him to whom it is rightfully subject and over those things placed in its charge, again, beneath its proper ruler and over its proper subjects. For the soul does many things out of a perverse desire, as though it were forgetful of itself. For in that more excellent nature which is God, it sees certain intrinsically beautiful things. And, although it ought to stand fast to enjoy them, it wills to assign those things to itself and wills not to be like God by God's doing but by its own doing to be what God is. Thus the soul is turned from God, set in motion, and slips into less and less, which it supposes to be more and more. For it is not sufficient for itself, nor is anything sufficient for one who withdraws from him who alone suffices. Thereupon, in its need and difficulty, the soul becomes excessively intent upon its own actions and upon the restless pleasures which it gathers through them. Thus, by desiring to acquire knowledge from these things which lie beneath it, whose sort it knows and loves and fears can be lost unless clung to with lavish care, the soul loses its security. And the more secure it feels that it cannot lose itself, the less it thinks of itself.

(De Trin., 10.5.7)

· 11 ·

If we ask what answer the city of God would give to questions on these matters, and especially on its opinion about the limits of good and evil, it will answer that the highest good is an eternal life, and the highest evil a truly eternal death; and that we must live correctly in order to acquire the former and avoid the latter. For this reason it is written: A just person lives by faith (Hab. 2.4). For we do not now see our own good and so must seek it by believing; nor is it ours to live correctly on our own, except when he who has bestowed on us faith itself, through which we believe that we must have his help, helps us because we believe and pray. Those who have thought that the limits of good and evil exist in this life, locating the highest good either in the body or in the soul or in both—or, to put it more explicitly, either in pleasure or in virtue or in both; or in quiet or in virtue or both; or in pleasure and quiet simultaneously, or virtue, or in all of these; or in the first principles of nature or in virtue or both—those people have desired through an incredible vanity to be blessed in this world and to become blessed by themselves. Truth mocked these through the prophet who said: The lord knows the thoughts of human beings (Ps. 94.11) or, as the apostle Paul quotes this passage: The lord knows the thoughts of the wise, that they are vain (1 Co. 3.20).

What person, no matter how eloquent, is capable of unfolding the miseries of this life? To the farthest extent of his talent Cicero lamented the death of his daughter in his *Consolatio;* but how far did that talent reach? Indeed when, where, or how could those things called first principles of nature be so firmly held in this life that they do not shift in varying circumstances? What pain is not able to spoil the pleasure of one who is wise; what restlessness can not interrupt such a one's peace? Certainly amputation of the limbs or lameness overcomes soundness of body; as deformity does beauty, weakness health, lassitude energy, and torpor or sluggishness mobility. And which of these things might not invade the body of one who is wise? The condition and movement of the body are numbered among the first principles of nature when they are fit and proper. But what if some evil condition should shake the limbs with trembling? What if one's back is so bent that one's hands touch the ground and one walks on all fours like an animal? Will this condition not destroy all beauty and grace when the body moves and stands? What of the first principles of the soul which are considered good? The first two of these, because of their relationship to the comprehension and perception of truth, are sense and intellect. But what degree or quality of sense remains to a blind and deaf person, to name two of many ailments? Where will reason and intellect go, where will they sleep, if someone becomes delirious in sickness? When mad people say or do crazy things, which are different from, or even opposed to, their normal ways and habits, who of us can hold back tears on seeing, considering, and pondering these things? What should I say about these who suffer demonic possession? Where do they keep their own intelligence hidden or buried when an evil spirit uses their body and soul for his own will? And who has confidence that this misfortune cannot happen to the wise in their life? Then how clear and extensive is our perception of the truth while in this body, when, as we read in the true book of wisdom, the corruptible body weighs down the soul and habitation on this earth oppresses the mind while it thinks many things (Ws. 9.15).

Furthermore, the impetus or desire for action, if that is the correct translation of the Greek word *hormē*, is also considered one of the first principles of nature, but it is the very thing which causes those miserable movements and acts of the insane which we shudder at, when sense is perverted and reason sleeps. In addition, although it claims to be the highest of human goods, what does virtue itself do— it is not among the first principles of nature since it follows after them, introduced by learning—except wage constant war against vices, not external but internal ones, not other people's but our very own ones? This is especially true of temperance, which the Greeks call *sophrosunē*, for it controls carnal lusts so that they may not drag the mind, with its own consent, into wickedness. For it is not a small vice when, as the apostle says, the flesh has desires in opposition to the spirit. To this vice there is an opposing virtue when, as the same man says, the spirit has desires in opposition to the flesh. He says that these things are opposed to each other with the result that you cannot do what you wish. Yet what do we want to do when we strive to achieve the highest good other than cause the flesh not to have desires in opposition to the spirit and remove any vice in us in opposition to which the spirit strives? Since we cannot, in this life, achieve that goal, although we want to, at least with the help of God we do manage not to yield, with our spirit overcome, to the flesh which has desires in opposition to the spirit. We also manage not to be led into committing a sin wilfully. Let it be far, then, from our belief that we can, while we are still involved in this internal war, achieve blessedness at which we want to arrive by victory. Who is so wise that he need never fight against lusts?

What is that virtue which we call prudence? Surely all its vigilance goes to distinguish good things from evil, so that no error stealthily enters into the process of attaining good and avoiding evil. This virtue is itself witness to the fact that we exist among vices or that vices exist in us. For it teaches us that it is evil to consent to sin and it is good not to give consent to it. However, that evil to which prudence teaches us and temperance allows us not to consent, neither prudence nor temperance can remove from this life. What of justice, whose function it is to give to all human beings their due— and thereby it happens that there is a certain just order of nature in

every human being, such that the soul submits to God and the flesh
to the soul, and thus both soul and flesh submit to God? Is it not
clear that justice is still struggling with its work rather than resting at
the end of its job? The less the soul is occupied with God in its
thoughts the less it subjects itself to him; and the more the flesh has
desires against the spirit, the less the flesh submits to the soul. As
long as there is in us this weakness, this plague, this lassitude, how
will we dare to say that we are saved? And how, if we are not yet
saved, will we dare to say that we are blessed with that final
blessedness? Indeed even that virtue which is called fortitude is very
clear testimony to the ills of human existence which require patience
if we are to bear them, no matter how wise we are. The Stoic
philosophers astound me when they claim with boldness that these
are not ills, although they admit that if things become so bad that a
wise person cannot, or ought not to, bear them, that person is forced
to commit suicide and depart from this life. These people, who think
that the highest good is available to them in this life and that they
can become blessed by themselves, are so stupid because of their
price that their "wise" person—that is, someone they define with
incredible vanity as such—even if blind, deaf, dumb, lame, racked
with pain, or afflicted with any evil which can be named or thought
of, is not ashamed to call life blessed even when it is beset by such
ills. What a blessed life, which seeks the aid of death to finish it! If it
is so blessed let the wise person remain in it! In what way are these
things not ills which overcome the good of fortitude and force the
same fortitude not only to yield but also to claim deliriously that life
is blessed and at the same time argue that it must be abandoned?
Who is so blind as not to see that if life were so blessed one would
not have to abandon it? Yet they admit openly with the voice of
weakness that it must be abandoned. Why, then, can they not also
admit, with their proud necks bent, that life is miserable. Was it, I
would like to know, from patience or impatience that Cato killed
himself? He would not have done so unless he was unable to bear
the victory of Caesar with patience. Where, then, is his fortitude?
Without a doubt it yielded, succumbed, and, in fact, was so
overcome that it deserted, fled, and abandoned a blessed life. Or
perhaps that life was in the end not so happy? Then it was
miserable. How, then, were those things not ills which caused a life
to be miserable and then terminated?

And so those who confess that these are evils, like the Peripatetics
and the old Academicians, whose part Varro takes, have a more

tolerable point of view, although they also make the incredible
mistake of believing that in the face of these evils, even if these are
so bad that they must be escaped through suicide, life is nonetheless
blessed. Varro says: Bodily torture and torment are ills which grow
worse the greater they become, and which must be avoided by
abandoning life. What life, I would like to know? The one, he says,
which is burdened by such great afflictions. Then surely it is blessed
while in the midst of those very ills on account of which you say that
it must be abandoned?

Or do you claim that it is blessed precisely because it is possible
for you to escape these ills through death? Then what if you are held
among these ills by some divine judgement and are not allowed to
die or even to be without them. Then, surely, you would say that
such a life is miserable. It does not, therefore, become devoid of
misery because it can be left quickly, since if it were eternal then
even you would judge it miserable. So if life is brief it should not,
therefore, be considered without misery, since that is as absurd as
saying that if misery is brief it should be called blessedness. There is
great power in these ills which force even wise human beings to
deprive themselves of their being to fight against them, although
they claim, and claim rightly, that it is the first principle and greatest
maxim of nature that human beings become their own allies and so
naturally flee death and that they be so kind to themselves that they
strongly wish and strive to remain alive and exist in this conjunction
of body and soul. There is a great power in these ills by which that
understanding of nature is defeated, in which death is to be avoided
in every way and with all our power and persistence. And it is
defeated so thoroughly that what is to be avoided is wished for and
sought after, and, if it cannot be acquired by other means, inflicted
by human beings on themselves. There is great power in these ills
which make fortitude homicidal—if indeed we must call that thing
fortitude which is so overcome by these evils that it not only cannot
take care through patience of that human being whom it undertook,
like a virtue, to guard and rule but also is forced itself to destroy that
human being. It is true that a wise person ought to bear death
patiently, but a death which comes from elsewhere. However, if a
person is compelled to commit suicide to oppose those evils, then
they must admit that those are not only evils but intolerable evils
which force a person to do this. So a life which is oppressed by the
weight of such great or heavy evils, or which is surrounded by ill
fortune, would never have been called blessed, if the people who

called it this had designed to yield to the truth, just as they yield to unhappiness when, overcome by the weight of their ills, they commit suicide. Nor would they have made the mistake of thinking that they could enjoy the highest good in this life when the virtues themselves, than which nothing in life is more beneficial or useful to human beings, are all the more accurate testimony or useful to human beings, are all the more accurate testimony to life's miseries the more helpful they are against the power of danger, labor, and griefs. If the virtues, which cannot exist except in those who have true piety, are truthful, they will admit that they cannot entirely prevent the human beings in whom they exist from suffering miseries. True virtues are not deceitful, but they claim that human life, which is considered miserable because of the many great ills of this age, is blessed in the hope of a future age, just as it is also safe in that hope. How is something blessed which is not yet safe? For this reason the apostle Paul said of those who live according to true piety and have true virtues—but not of those who are imprudent, impatient, intemperate, and wicked: We are made safe by hope. Yet the hope which is seen is not hope. For why does someone hope for what is already seen? If we hope for what we do not see, we wait for it with patience (Rm. 8.24). Thus just as we are made safe by hope, so are we made blessed by hope; and blessedness, just like safey, we do not hold now, in the present, but we wait for them in the future with patience. For we are in the midst of evils which we must bear patiently until we reach those goods where all things will exist which we enjoy ineffably and nothing will exist which we must endure. Such salvation, which will come in a future age, will itself be the final blessedness. This blessedness some philosophers try to fabricate most artificially in this world, since they do not want to believe in what they do not see. And the prouder they are, the falser is their virtue.

(De civ. Dei, 19.4)

· 12 ·

The philosophers have said many things about friendship. But among them true piety is not to be found, that is honest worship of the true God, from which all duties of a good life should be drawn. The cause for this is, as far as I understand, nothing other than a desire on their part somehow to construct for themselves their own blessed life which they suppose is something to be done for oneself rather than done for one, even though there is no other giver of blessedness than God. No one makes human being blessed except he who made human being. For he who lavishes so many goods on his creatures, whether good or evil—that they exist, that they exist as human beings, that their senses are powerful and their bodies strong, and that they have abundant resources—will give himself to the good so that they may be blessed, because their very goodness is his gift. There are others who, in the midst of this laborious life, with bodies doomed to death and bent under the burden of corruptible flesh, have willed to author and establish their own would-be blessed lives, as if to seek and to secure them with their own resources. They neither beseech nor place their hopes in the wellspring of all resources; and they are utterly blind to how God resists their pride. . . .

In the last part of the fifth book of Cicero's *Tusculan Disputations* there is a passage which should be noted in connection with what I am saying. After he had affirmed, in his discussion on blindness, that a wise person even when blind could be blessed, he said that the pleasures which he could receive through his aural senses he could, if he became deaf, transfer to the eyes. But if, he said, a human being were deprived of both senses and became deaf and blind, he did not dare in this case to hold the same opinion and say that this person could be blessed. He added that there are other very severe illnesses of the body which, if not themselves fatal, would cause human beings to kill themselves and thus, freed by this act of courage, reach the safe habor of nonfeeling. So wise people yield to the worst of misfortunes and are so overwhelmed by them that they are forced to commit suicide. Whom would they spare the suffering of these ills, if they could not spare themselves? Of course, they are always blessed and of course they cannot lose the blessed life, which they have established by their own power, through the force of any calamity. And look at this! Either they have lost their blessedness in the midst of blindness and deafness and the most terrible bodily afflictions or, if their lives remain blessed in the midst of such afflictions, then there must somehow be, according to the arguments of the most learned men of this kind, a blessed life that a wise person cannot bear or, which is even more absurd, that a wise person ought not to bear but ought to flee, interrupt, reject, and withdraw from by inducing death voluntarily with a sword or poison or any other means. In this way a wise person may either reach a state of nonbeing or complete nonexistence, as the Epicureans and others of similar stupidity thought, or else may still be blessed, having been freed from that blessed life as if it were a plague. What unbelievably proud boasting! If the life of a wise person is blessed in the midst of bodily affliction, why not remain in it and enjoy it? If it is miserable why, I ask you, not admit it and pray to God and supplicate the just and merciful one who is able to remove evils from this life or soften them or arm us with fortitude to bear them or freedom to escape them and then bestow a truly blessed life, in which no evil is allowed and the highest good is never lost? Why, I ask you, if not from blinding and swollen pride?

This is the reward of the pious. In the hope of acquiring it we lead this temporal and mortal life not with enjoyment but with tolerance. We bear its ills bravely through good advice and divine help when we enjoy God's faithful promise of eternal good and our own trusting expectation. To encourage us to this the apostle said: Rejoice in hope and be patient in tribulation (Rm. 12.12). By putting "Rejoice in hope" first, he shows the reason for "patience in tribulation." I urge you on to this hope through Jesus Christ our lord. God himself taught it by hiding the majesty of his divinity and making clear the weakeness of flesh, not only through the oracle of his speech, but also through the example of his passion and resurrection. He taught us through the one what we should bear, and through the other what we should hope for. For this those people would have been grateful if they had not, in their swollen pride and exaltation, stupidly tried to create a blessed life for themselves. But God alone has promised that he will give to his true believers blessedness after this life. Cicero expresses a sounder opinion when he says: That life is death which I could lament if I found it pleasing. How, then, could it be thought blessed if it is fittingly lamented? Should it not rather be thought miserable, since it is fittingly lamented. So grow into the habit, I beg you, of being ble sed in hope so that you may be blessed in reality when your persistent piety is rewarded with eternal happiness.

(Epist., 155.2-4)

• 13 •

Humankind goes outside itself to follow what it creates, abandoning him within by whom it was created and destroying what it was made to be. But even for this I sing a hymn to you, my God and my glory, and I offer praise to my sacrificer. For the beautiful things which pass from the soul into skillful hands come from that beauty above our soul for which I sigh day and night. But the creators and followers of external beauty take from it criterion for judgment but not a guideline for the use of beautiful things. Yet, although they do not see it, it is there to prevent them from straying and to help them store their strength for you and not to waste it on delights which carry weariness with them.

(Conf., 10.35)

• 14 •

"Every tree produced from the earth" we take to mean every spiritual joy, namely, the soul's rising above the earth and not being entangled or buried in the snares of earthly lusts. Moreover, the tree of life planted in the middle of paradise signifies that wisdom by which the soul must understand itself to be ordered at a certain midrank of things so that, although it has every corporeal nature subject to it, it might nevertheless understand the nature of God to be above it and thus might turn aside neither to the right, by arrogating to itself what is not, nor to the left, by contemning, through negligence, what is. This, then, is what is meant by the tree of life planted in the middle of paradise.

By the tree of knowledge of good and evil, moreover, is signified that same middle position and ordered integrity of soul, for this tree is planted in the middle of paradise. And thus it is called the tree of discernment of good and evil, because, if the soul which ought to reach toward the things before it, namely, God, and to·forget the things behind it (Ph. 3.13), namely, corporeal pleasures, should desert God and turn to itself and will to enjoy its own person as though without God, the soul swells with pride, which is the beginning of every sin. And once punishment follows upon this sin, the soul learns through experience the difference between the good and the evil into which it fell. And this will mean that the soul has tasted of the tree of the discernment of good and evil.

(De Gen. c. Man., 2.9.12)

• 15 •

"And you shall be as gods, knowing good and evil" (Gn. 3.5). From these words we see that sin was made to prevail through pride ... they were unwilling to be under God but preferred to be in their own power without God, so that they would not observe his law, as though God himself were jealous lest they rule themselves, in no need of his interior light, but using instead a providence of their own, seemingly their own eyes, to discern good and evil, which he had prohibited. Therefore, they were persuaded of this, to love their own power to excess. And, since they wished to be the equals of God, they put to bad use that middle position, through which they had been subjected to God and had bodies subject to them. . . . Thus, they lost what they had received, while they wished to usurp what they had not received. For the nature of human being has not been given to be blessed through its own power apart from the rule of God; for it belongs to God alone to be blessed through his own power apart from the rule of any other.

They heard the voice of God and hid themselves from his sight. Who is it that hides from the sight of God unless one who, having deserted God, now begins to love what is one's own . . . moreover, one who speaks a lie, speaks of one's own . . . (Jn. 9.44). Whoever, therefore, is turned away from the truth and toward oneself, whoever rejoices not in the God who guides and illuminates but in one's own movements, as if they were free, that one is shadowed by a lie. For one who speaks a lie, speaks of one's own. . . . Hence, turned away from God and toward himself, confronted with the sight of his own nakedness, Adam was pained at having nothing of his own.

(De Gen. c. Man., 2.15.22; 2.16.24)

• 16 •

The love, therefore, of acting contrary to the mounting passions of one's body turns the soul away from the contemplation of eternal things ... the love, too, of working with bodies distracts and disquiets the soul. ... Truly, the general love of action, which turns the soul away from what is true, proceeds from pride, the vice by which the soul prefers to imitate God rather than serve him. Thus it is rightly written in the holy scriptures: The beginning of human pride is the apostasy from God; and: The beginning of every sin is pride. Moreover, there could be no better way of showing what pride is than in what has been written there in scripture: Why does earth and ashes take pride, for in its life it has spewed forth its insides? (Si. 10.9-14).

(De mus., 6.13.39; 6.13.40)

• 17 •

Likewise, as sin or iniquity is not the desiring of evil natures but the abandoning of better things, so it is found to be written in the scriptures that: Every creature of God is good. And, on this account, every tree too, which god has planted in paradise, is surely good. Human being did not, therefore, desire an evil nature in touching the forbidden tree. Rather, in abandoning what was better, human being itself committed an evil deed. For the creator is better than any creature which he established. His command should not have been abandoned so that what was prohibited, although good, might be touched; for when the better thing was abandoned, the good of the creature was desired, a good touched contrary to the creator's command. Thus, God had not planted in paradise an evil tree. But he who prohibited its being touched was better.

For he had also made this prohibition to show that the nature of the rational soul ought not to reside in its own power but, rather, ought to be made subject to God, and to show that this nature guards the order of its own salvation by obedience and corrupts that order by disobedience. Hence, he also called that tree, which he forbade to be touched, the tree of discernment of good and evil (Gn. 2.9); for when one would have touched it contrary to the prohibition, one would experience the penalty of sin and would thereby discern the difference between the good of obedience and the evil of disobedience.

For who would be such a fool as to suppose that a creature of God, especially one planted in paradise, should be censured, when, indeed, not even thorns and thistles—which the earth brought forth to contend with the sinner's labor in accord with the willed judgment of God—are rightly censured? For even such herbs have a measure, form, and order of their own, which anyone, who has considered them carefully, will find should be praised. But those things are evil for that nature, which due to sin must be restrained. Therefore, as I have said, sin is not the desiring of an evil nature but the deserting of a better. And so the deed itself is evil rather than that nature which the sinner uses evilly. For it is evil to use a good thing evilly. Whence the apostle reproaches those damned by the divine judgment: who have worshipped and served the creature rather than the creator (Rm. 1.25). He does not reproach the creator—to do this is to do injury to the creator—but them who have deserted the better and made evil use of the good.

Accordingly, if all natures would observe their own proper measure, form, and order, there would be no evil. If, on the other hand, anyone would wish to make evil use of these good things, the will of God is not thereby overturned. For God knows how to order justly even the unjust, so that if they through perversity of will were to misuse God's good things, then God, through the power of his own justice would use well their evils, rightly assigning to punishments those who perversely assigned themselves to sins.

(De nat. boni, 34-37)

• 18 •

You punish the crimes which people commit against themselves, because even when they sin against you, they do wrong to their souls and their iniquity deceives itself. This they do either by corrupting and perverting their own nature, which you made and composed; or by making excessive use of what is permitted; or by burning to make unnatural use of what is not permitted; or they are found guilty of raging against you in their souls and in their words and rebelling against your goad; or they delight at the disruption of the boundaries created by human society, boldly making private pacts and schisms in accordance with their private likes and dislikes.

This happens when you are forsaken, fountain of life, who are the sole true creator and ruler of the universe; through personal arrogance, a thing which is a part is falsely loved as a whole. And so with humble devotion we must return to you. You cleanse us of our bad habits and show mercy to those who confess to you their sins;

you hear the groan of those who are enchained and you loosen the bonds which we make for ourselves, as long as we stop shaking our fist at you from a sense of false liberty; this we have because of a love for our own good stronger than our love for you who are the good of all.

(Conf., 3.8)

• 19 •

Peace of the body consists in the ordered proportioning of its parts, while peace of the irrational soul consists in the ordered calming of the passions and peace of the rational soul may be defined as consistency of thought and action. Peace of the body and soul brings an ordered life and health to the human being. Peace between human beings and God comes from ordered obedience in faith to the eternal law, while peace between human beings is ordered harmony. Peace in the home means an ordered harmony between those among the inhabitants who give orders and those who obey, while civic peace means harmony between the citizens who command and the citizens who obey. Peace in the heavenly city is created by the most ordered and harmonious society of those who enjoy God and each other in God. Peace of all things is the tranquility of order.

Order is the distribution in its proper place of each thing, equal or unequal. So miserable people lack the tranquility of order where there is no unrest because, in as much as they are miserable, they have no peace; but, on the other hand, because they are deservedly and justly miserable, they are in their very misery not outside the realm of order. They are not connected with the blessed but they are severed from them by the law of order. And when people are not immediately troubled they are fitted to their circumstances with a certain amount of harmony; thus there exists in them a modicum of tranquility and of peace. Yet they are miserable because even though they sometimes exist in security without suffering, they are nonetheless not in that place where they need not suffer as well as be secure. However, they would be more miserable if they did not have the peace from that law by which the normal order is enforced. When they suffer, disorder arises out of peace in the part in which they are suffering. But there is still peace in the part which does not burn with suffering and whose unity is not dissolved. Thus there can be life without suffering, although there can never be suffering without life. In the same way there can be peace without war but no war without peace. This is not because of what war is but because of the nature of those who wage it. These people could not exist if they were not allowed some peace.

There is a nature in which there is no evil, nor even the possibility of evil. However, there cannot be a nature in which there is no good. And so not even the nature of the devil, insofar as it exists, is evil. But perversity makes it evil. And so the devil did not stand fast in the truth but neither did he evade the judgment of truth. He did not rest in the tranquility of order but, on the other hand, he did not escape the power of order. The good of the lord which he has in his nature did not allow him to be removed from God's justice which found order in his punishment. Nor did God reproach the good which he had created. It was the evil which the devil had committed which he reproached. He did not remove completely the nature which he had given but he took away part of it and left another part, so that the devil might come to feel pain at the loss of the part he had removed. This pain is itself evidence for the removal of one part and the leaving of another. For if some good had not been left he would not have been able to feel pain at the loss of good. Sinners are made worse if they rejoice in the loss of righteousness. Those who are in pain at least suffer at the loss of health, even if they do not acquire any good from it. Since righteousness and health are both goods, and since the loss of a good is to be mourned rather than enjoyed—unless there is the compensation of a greater good; for instance, righteousness of the soul is a greater good than health of the body—then it is more suitable for a wicked person to feel pain at being punished than joy in having committed a crime. Thus just as joy in the loss of a good through sinning is evidence of an evil will, so grief at a good lost in punishment bears witness to a good nature. Whenever human beings grieve at their nature's loss of peace, they do so because they have within them some remaining peace which makes their nature friendly to itself. It is right that in the final punishment the unjust and impious should weep at the loss of their natural goods, knowing that they have been taken from them by a most just God, a most kind benefactor, whom they despised.

So God is the wisest provider and the most just regulator of all natures. He established the human race as the earth's greatest ornament and he gave to human life certain goods suitable to it;

that is, whatever temporal peace there can be in life from health and safety and the society of fellow human beings and whatever is necessary for the keeping or recovering of that peace, like those things which are properly fitted to our senses: light and night, breathable air and drinkable water, and whatever else is suitable for the feeding and sheltering, caring for and embellishing of the body.

And these things are given to us with the most just understanding that the human beings who make proper use of such goods as are created for their peace, may receive greater and better goods, namely the very peace of immortality which also brings glory and honor to a life spent eternally in the enjoyment of God and of one another in God. But those who use them wrongly receive no more goods but lose those which they have.

Therefore all use of temporal things relates to the reward of earthly peace in the earthly city. But in the heavenly city it relates to the reward of eternal peace. So if we were irrational beings we would seek nothing beyond the ordered proportioning of the parts of the body and the quieting of our passions; nothing, that is to say, but rest for our flesh and an abundance of pleasures, so that the peace of our bodies might create peace in our souls. If bodily peace is lacking then the peace of the irrational soul is hindered, because it cannot achieve a quieting of the passions. Both contribute to that peace which the soul and the body have between them, the peace of an ordered life and of health. Just as animals show that they love peace of body when they avoid pain and peace of the soul when they pursue pleasure to fill the needs of the appetites, so they also indicate by fleeing death how much they love the peace by which their soul and body are brought into harmony.

But because human beings have rational souls all that they have in common with beasts is subordinated to the peace of the rational soul, so that the mind may be free to contemplate and to act in accordance with its contemplations, and so that there may be an ordered agreement of thought and action, which is how we have defined peace of the rational soul. For this purpose a human being wishes not to be molested by pain or upset by desires or obliterated by death, so that a useful knowledge may be gained to unite life, thought, and habit. But human beings, because of the weakness of the human mind, have need of a divine teacher in order to be able to avoid disastrous error while striving for understanding. A divine teacher they may obey with certainty and a divine helper they may obey with freedom. Because human beings stray from God as long as they have their mortal bodies, they walk in faith, not with sight.

And so all bodily and/or spiritual peace is related to that peace which human beings have with the immortal God in order to bring into order their faithful obedience under an eternal law. God the teacher gives us two major precepts: the love of God and the love of our neighbor, through which we find three things to love: God, ourselves, and our neighbors. Thus when we love God we do not err in loving ourselves, and, in addition, we advise our neighbor, whom we are ordered to love as ourselves, to love God. And we would want our neighbor—be it wife, son, servant, or whoever is able—to do the same for us if we are in need. In this way we will be at peace, as far as we are capable, with all people. This is the harmony whose order is, first of all, never to harm anyone and, secondly, to aid whomever we can. Our first duty is to our family.

We have greater opportunity and easier access to helping them because of the order of nature or of human society itself. Therefore the apostle says: Whoever does not provide well for family and servants goes against faith and is worse than the unfaithful (1 Tm. 5.8). From this arises domestic peace, that is the ordered harmony among the people in a family who command and those who obey. Those command who care for the rest, like a husband in relation to his wife, parent to child, master to slave. Those who are cared for obey, like wives to their husbands, children to parents and servants to masters. But in the house where people live firstly out of faith and yet are still wandering far from the heavenly city, those who command serve those whom they seem to command. For they do not command out of a desire for power but out of a duty to care for others; not out of pride in their position but out of mercy which comes from caring for others.

The natural order prescribes this and in this way God created humankind. He said: Let them rule over the fish of the sea and the birds of the air and all the things which crawl over the earth (Gn. 9.25). He did not wish rational beings made in his image to rule over anything but irrational beings not human beings over human beings, but human beings over cattle. And so the first just men were shepherds ruling cattle rather than kings ruling over other people. In this way God indicated what the order of creatures demands and what recompense is required of sinners. The condition of slavery is understood to be imposed justly on the sinner. Never in the scriptures do we read the word "slave" until with justice Noah brandished the sin of his son with this name. So guilt deserved this name, but not nature.

(De civ. Dei, 19.13-15)

• **20** •

Whoever seeks the path by which to arrive at the blessed life seeks nothing other than the path to the end of good; that is, the path where the highest good for humankind is established not through distorted or rash opinion but by incontrovertible truth. Where this good is established cannot be discovered except in the body, or in the soul, or in God, or in any two of these, or, indeed, in all of them. If you have been taught that neither the highest good nor any part of it exists in the body, two possibilities remain: the soul and God, in one of which, or in both, it may be.

However, if you have been taught, in addition, that what is true of the body is also true of the soul, what will be available as that in which the highest good for humankind is to be found, except God? Not that there are no other goods, but I am speaking of the highest one to which all others are referred. Enjoying it brings blessedness and because of it other goods are desired, although it is desired not for any other good but for itself. So it is called an end because in it there is no running back and forth but only rest from seeking, security in happiness, and the most tranquil joy in the finest will.

Give me, then, the people who quickly understand that the body is not the good of the soul but rather that the soul is the good of the body. For then we need no longer inquire whether that highest good or some part of it exists in the body. It is stupid to deny that the soul is better than the body. Likewise it is stupid to deny that that which bestows the blessed life or some part of it is better than that which receives it. Therefore, the soul does not receive the highest good, or any part of it, from the body. Those who do not see this, because they are blinded by the sweetness of carnal pleasures, which they do not see as coming from weakness in the soundness of the body—but perfect soundness of body will be the final immortality of the whole person; God gave the soul such a strong nature so that from its fullest blessedness, which is promised in the end of time to the holy, there will flow into the weaker nature of the body not blessedness, which belongs to enjoyment and understanding, but perfect soundness, that is, the strength of incorruptibility—as I was saying, those who do not see this fight restless battles as violently as each is able, and they excite seditious turmoil in the passions. . . .

Give me those, too, who see that the soul is not blessed by its own good, when it is blessed, since then it would never be miserable. Then we need no longer ask whether that highest and most blessed good lies in the soul, or at least some part of it. For when the soul rejoices in itself as its own good, it is proud. When it perceives itself as mutable at least in this one thing, that it moves from stupidity to wisdom, and when it sees wisdom as unchangeable, it should then also see that wisdom is above its own nature and that by participation in it and by its enlightenment the soul rejoices more fully and surely than by itself. By stopping its boasting and by deflating its swollenness it strives to cling to God and to be remade and reformed by him who is unchangeable. It understands then that not only all species of all things come from him, whether they are perceived by the mind's intelligence or bodily senses, but also that the very capacity for creation, which exists before creation—since something is called unformed which can be formed—comes from him. And so it senses itself to be that much less stable the less it clings to God who is the highest. And it understands that he is the highest because he neither progresses nor regresses through change. But the soul understands that it profits from the change by which it progresses toward being able to cling perf ctly to him; that change toward regression is a failing; and that all regression leads to destruction. Whether anything arrives at final destruction may not be apparent; yet it is apparent that regression infects everything with destruction so that nothing remains as it was. Hence it follows that nothing regresses or can regress for any other reason than it is made out of nothing. That there is anything which remains and even in the face of deficiencies is arranged to connect with the totality of things is due to the goodness and omnipotence of God who is highest and who is so powerful a creator that he makes out of nothing not just something, but something great. The soul understands that the first sin, that is, the first failing of will, was to rejoice in its own power. For that is to rejoice in something less than if one rejoiced in the power of God which is far greater. . . .

You will find two errors colliding head on, one which places the highest good in the body, the other in the soul. And you will find that the reasoning of truth, by which God is understood to be our highest good, opposes both errors but does not teach truth before destroying mistakes. . . .

But Platonists were not able to play the part of true reason as fully as those others played the part of their errors. They lacked the example of divine humility which was brought to light at the most opportune time by our Lord Jesus Christ. To this one example the pride of all fiercely arrogant souls yields and is broken and dies. But the Platonists were not able through the strength of this authority to lead the masses, blinded by the love of earthly things, to invisible faith, when they saw them moved by the arguments of Epicureans not only to drink deeply of the pleasures of the body, which they did willingly, but also to defend this as the highest good of humankind. And they saw at the same time that those who were moved by praise of virtue to oppose these pleasures were able to contemplate virtue with less difficulty in the souls of people, from which arise good deeds which they could to some extent judge. But if they tried to introduce to these people the idea that there is a divine being, unchangeable over all, which cannot be reached by our bodily senses but must be understood by the mind whose nature, nevertheless, it far exceeds and that this being is God who is offered to the human soul for its enjoyment when it has been cleansed of all stain of human lusts and in whom alone we satisfy our appetite for blessedness and find the end of all goods, they saw that the people would not understand and would hand the palm of victory to the Stoics or Epicureans far more readily than to them. The result would be, they saw, that the true and saving belief would sink into disrepute through the contempt of the untaught masses, a result most dangerous to the human race. . . .

It is evident that Platonic philosophers, after changing their belief slightly to meet the demands of Christian doctrine, might bow their heads piously to the one invincible king, Jesus Christ, and might understand the word made flesh of God, who commands and is believed, the word which they feared even to utter.

I would wish you to submit to him with complete piety and to build for yourself no other path to the grasping and holding of truth than the one provided by God who saw the infirmity of our steps. This is in the first place humility, and in the second, and in the third; and however often you might ask, I would say the same, not that there are no other precepts to mention. But unless humility precedes, accompanies, and follows after whatever good we do, unless it is placed before us to view and next to us to cling to, and on top of us to hold us in check, pride may wrench from our hands any good deed in the midst of our enjoyment of it. There are, of course, other vices besides pride, but pride must be feared especially in the doing of good deeds lest what has been admirably done be lost through desire for that very admiration. Just as that greatest orator is said to have answered "pronunciation" when asked what he thought should be considered the first rule of eloquence, and, when asked what the second rule should be, answered "pronunciation," and gave the same answer for the third rule, so no matter how often you might ask me about those precepts of the Christian religion, I would tend in each case to answer humility, unless necessity should force me to name others.

(Epist., 118.13-17, 21-22)

• 21 •

Those, moreover, who have been converted to God, let go of those things which in this world they used to embrace dearly. For they rejoice not in those things in which they used to rejoice. And until a love of eternal things comes to be in them, they are not without grief's wounds. . . .

Where there is no contention, there is perfect peace. Therefore the sons of God are peacemakers; for in nothing do they resist God. Indeed, sons are to bear the likeness of their father. Moreover, all those who order and subject the movements of their soul to reason, namely, to mind and spirit, and who have tamed thoroughly their carnal lusts, are within themselves peacemakers and become the kingdom of God, wherein all things are so ordered that that which is peculiar and preeminent in human being has unquestioned command over all else which we have in common with beasts. And yet that particular excellence of human being, namely, mind and reason, is itself subject to what is still greater, truth itself, the only begotten son of God. For human being is unable to command over lesser beings, unless it subjects itself to the higher being. And this is the peace which is given on earth to human beings of good will (Lk. 2.14). This is the life of one who is perfectly and consummately wise.

(De serm. Don., 1.2.5,9)

• 22 •

These virtues are great goods. But you must remember that not only great goods but even the least goods depend for their existence upon him from whom all good things come, namely, God. . . . Those virtues, therefore, by which one lives rightly are great goods; while all forms whatever of bodies, without which it is quite possible to live rightly, are the least goods. The powers of the souls, moreover, without which it is not possible to live rightly, are intermediate goods. No one puts virtues to bad use, since it is precisely the work of virtue to put to good use those things which we can also put to bad use. No one, moreover, puts something to bad use by putting it to good use.

Wherefore, God's great and abundant goodness is responsible for the existence not only of great goods but also of intermediate and least goods. His goodness is to be praised more in great goods than in intermediate goods, and more in intermediate goods than in least goods. But his goodness is to be praised more in all things than if he had not granted existence to them all. . . .

Reason itself is known by reason. Or have you forgotten that, when we were asking what things are known by reason, you admitted that reason too is known by reason? Don't be surprised, therefore, that, if we use other things through free will, we can also use free will through itself. For, as the will, which uses other things, uses itself, so reason, which knows other things, knows itself. Memory, too, encompasses not only all else which we remember, but also, because we do not forget that we have a memory, memory somehow retains itself in us. It remembers not only other things but itself too, or, rather, through memory we remember ourselves, other things, and memory itself.

When the will, therefore, which is an intermediate good, clings to the unchangeable good, which is common and not privately one's own—such as truth, concerning which we have spoken much, but nothing worthy of it—then human being possesses the blessed life. This blessed life itself, namely, the soul's state in clinging to the unchangeable good, is human being's first and proper good. In that good too are all virtues, which no one is able to put to bad use. For, although these virtues are great and principal human goods, it is sufficiently understood that they are nonetheless the property of individual human beings and are not common at all.

All human beings are made wise and blessed by clinging to truth and wisdom which are common to all. But one individual is not made blessed by another's blessedness. For even when one imitates the blessed with a view toward being blessed oneself, one's desire to be made blessed is directed toward that common and unchangeable truth by which we see others to have been made blessed. Neither is anyone made prudent by another's prudence, nor courageous by another's courage, nor temperate by another's temperance, nor just by anyone else's justice, but, rather, by conforming the soul to the virtues' unchangeable rules and illuminations, which live beyond corruption in truth itself and in common wisdom. Those who have conformed their soul to this truth and wisdom and fixed their soul upon them are endowed with these virtures and are held up for imitation.

The will, therefore, by adhering to the common and unchangeable good, attains the principal and great human goods, although the will itself is an intermediate good. The will, moreover, sins whenever it turns from the unchangeable and common good and turns to its own private good or to something exterior to it or beneath it. The will turns to its own private good when it wills to exist of its own power. It turns to an exterior good when it strives to know what belongs privately to others or whatever does not pertain to it. And it turns to an inferior good when it loves the pleasure of the body. Thus, one who becomes proud, and curious, and sensuous is caught up in another life which, compared to the higher life, is a death. And yet such a life is ruled over by the governance of divine providence which arranges all things in their appropriate places and which gives to each thing its due.

And so it happens that neither those goods desired by sinners nor free will itself, which we have found is to be counted among the intermediate goods, are in any way evil. Rather, what is evil is the will's turning away from the unchangeable good and its turning to changeable goods. And yet these turnings, since they are voluntary and not forced, are deservedly and jointly followed by the punishment of misery.

But you are perhaps about to ask whence the will's movement comes to be; for the will is, indeed, moved when it turns from the unchangeable good to a changeable good. That movement is truly evil, even though the will, without which life cannot be lived rightly, is to be numbered among things that are good. . . . Yet since this defect (the defective movement of the will) is voluntary it lies within our power. If you fear it, you must not will it; and if you do not will it, it will not be. What, therefore, is more secure than to be in that life wherein nothing can happen to you against your will? But, since human being cannot rise up as it fell, by the mere assertion of its will, let us grasp with a firm faith the right hand of God, namely, our lord Jesus Christ, extended to us from on high. Let us await him with a certain hope, and long for him with an ardent love.

(De lib. arb., 2.19.50-2.20.54)

• 23 •

Deformed and evil is the life lived according to the trinity of the outer human being; for that trinity, which, admittedly, imagines within, nevertheless imagines external things. And that trinity is begotten for the purpose of using sensible and corporeal things, which no one could use, especially use well, unless they were retained by the memory in an image of sensory things, and unless the greatest part of the will should dwell amidst higher and more inward things, and unless that same will, which is accustomed, whether to bodies outside or to images within, refers whatever it seizes in them to a better and truer life, and rests in that end, which the will gazes upon and in that light judges that these things are to be done. What else do we do but what the apostle forbids us to do when he says: "Be not conformed to this age"? (Rm. 12.12).

Therefore, that trinity is not the image of God; in fact, it comes to be in the soul itself through the sense of the body, from the lowest, namely corporeal, creature, to which the soul is superior. Yet it is not altogether dissimilar; for what does not have resemblance to God proportionate to its kind and measure, since God made all things exceedingly good (Si. 39.2), for no other reason than that he is the supreme good? A thing is good, therefore, insofar as it is. Thus, however greatly distant a thing may be from the supreme good, it still has some resemblance to the supreme good. If it bears a natural likeness, then it is right and well ordered; but if a corrupt likeness, then it is shameful and perverse. For, even in their sins, souls pursue only a certain likeness to God, with their proud, inverted, and, I would say, servile liberty. Thus our first parents could not have been persuaded to sin if they had not been told: You shall be like gods (Gn. 3.5). Surely not everything which in creatures is in some way similar to God should also be called God's image, but only that to which God above us is himself superior. For what proceeds from God wholly as his expression is that nature which has no other nature placed between itself and God.

Perhaps we can speak rightly of vision as the end and the repose of the will at least insofar as this one thing (the body to be seen) is concerned. For it does not then follow that the will stops willing anything else because it sees something which it willed. Thus this is not wholly the will itself of human being whose only end is blessedness. Rather, it is a passing will which has no other end than to see that one thing, whether it refers what it sees to something else or not. For if it does not refer its vision to something else but only wishes to see, there is no need to debate how the end of the will may be shown to vision, which is manifest. If, however, it does refer its vision to something else, then it surely wills something else. And there will not be merely a will to see, or if a will to see, not a will to see merely this thing. . . . All these and other such wills have their own proper ends. These ends are, in turn, referred to the end of that will by which we will both to live blessedly and to attain that life which is referred to nothing else. For that life suffices in itself for one who loves it.

(De Trin., 11.5.8; 11.6)

• 24 •

That part of us which is occupied by the activity of handling things corporeal and temporal in a way not common to us and beasts is indeed rational, but is, on the one hand, drawn, as it were, from that insubstantial rationality of our mind by which we reach up and cleave to the intelligible and immutable truth and is, on the other hand, assigned to govern inferior things. For just as there was not found among all the beasts a help for human being like unto itself, unless this were taken from human being itself, and formed into a consort, so too for our mind, by which we consult superior and inner truth, there is in our intercourse with corporeal things, inasmuch as human nature requires this, similarly no help from those parts of the soul which we have in common with the beasts.

And so a certain part of our reason, not set off as a sunderance of unity, but, as it were, derived as an aid to fellowship, is sent off to perform its own proper work. And just as with male and female one flesh belongs to both, so the mind's own nature embraces intellect and action, or counsel and operation, or reason and rational appetite, or whatever other formulations might convey the same distinction in a more significant manner. Thus, just as it has been said of these two (male and female): The two shall become one flesh (Gn. 2.24), so it could be said of these two (parts of reason): The two shall become one mind.

When, therefore, we discuss the nature of the human mind, we are discussing one specific thing, which I do not double into these things which I have mentioned unless we speak of it in terms of its two works. And so we seek a trinity in it, we seek in it as a whole, without separating rational action amidst temporal things from the contemplation of eternal things such that we then seek some third thing with which the trinity might be filled out. Rather, it is for us to disclose a trinity in the whole nature of the mind so that if there is no action upon temporal things—for which work assistance is a necessity which is why a part of the mind is set apart for the administering of these inferior things—a trinity may still be found in a mind that is one and is nowhere dispersed. And once this distribution has been made, there may be found in that part alone which has to do with the contemplation of eternal things, not only a trinity but also an image of God. In that part, however, which is set apart for action upon temporal things, even if a trinity can be found, there cannot be found an image of God.

Let one accustom oneself so to find in corporeal things the traces of spiritual things that, having begun to ascend upward from them with reason as guide, one may reach the unchangeable truth itself through which these things have been made, without dragging along to the highest things what one despises in the lowest things.

We have said of the nature of the human mind that, if it as a whole contemplates the truth, it is an image of God; and, when something is divided from the mind and by a certain intention set apart for action upon temporal things, that part of the mind which consults the visible truth is in no way less an image of God, while that part of the mind which is inclined toward the doing of lesser things, is not an image of God. And the more the mind has extended itself toward that which is eternal, the more it is thereby formed after the image of God. . . .

For, as not only most true reason but also the authority of the apostle himself declares, human being has been made after the image of God not according to its bodily form but according to its rational mind. . . . Moreover, does not this same blessed apostle say:

Be renewed in the spirit of your mind and put on the new human being, that which is created according to God (Ep. 6.23-24); and elsewhere more clearly: Leaving behind the old human being and its actors, he says, put on the new, which is renewed unto the knowledge of God according to the image of one who created it (Col. 3.9-10)? If, therefore, we are renewed in the spirit of the mind and it is the new human being itself which is renewed unto the knowledge of God according to the image of the one who created it, no one can doubt that human being has been made in the image of the one who created it, not according to the body, nor according to any part of the soul, but according to the rational mind where there can be the knowledge of God. . . .

But since they are renewed unto the image of God there wherein there is no sex, human being is made unto the image of God there where there is no sex, that is, in the spirit of its mind . . . the image of God dwells only in that part wherein the human mind clings to the considering and the consulting of the eternal reasons. And it is manifest that not only masculine human beings but also feminine human beings possess that part of the mind.

Therefore, in their (men's and women's) minds, a common nature is recognized; but in their bodies the division of this one mind is figured. As we ascend, then, inwardly in the stepwise path of our consideration through the parts of the soul, reason begins from that point where there enters something unique to us, no longer in common with the beasts. It is there that the human being can now be recognized. But if this inner human being itself, through that reason delegated to the administration of temporal things, slips too far into exterior things in a movement of immoderacy and if its head (the reason delegated to the contemplation of external things) gives consent, namely, if that which presides in the watchtower of counsel, what is figured as the masculine portion, does not prohibit it and hold it back, then it grows old among its enemies . . . and the vision of eternal things is taken away even from the head itself, which with its spouse eats of what is forbidden, so that the light of its eyes is no longer with it.

For the soul, loving its own power, slips from what is whole and common to what is partial and private. And, although it could have been most excellently governed by the laws of God, if it had followed God as its ruler in the created universe, the soul in that apostatizing pride which is called the beginning of sin (Qo. 10.15), desiring something more than the universe and struggling to govern it by the soul's own law, is pressed into caring for a part, since there is nothing more than the universe. And so, by desiring something more, it has become less, whence it is also said that avarice is called the root of all evils (Tm. 6.10). The soul conducts everything through its own body, which it only partially possesses, when it struggles to assert something of its own over against the laws with which the universe is administered. So, having delighted in corporeal forms and movements, which it cannot have within itself with itself, the soul is wrapped in their images, which it has fixed in memory, and is perverted and disgraced by the fornication of fantasy. It strives for a standard above other souls giving over to bodily senses, or it is immersed in the muddy whirlpool of carnal pleasure.

When, in fact, the soul does anything for the sake of obtaining things sensed through the body on account of its lust for experiencing or excelling or handling, so that it places in them the end of its own good, it does to its disgrace whatever it does. It commits a sin of fornication against its own body. It seizes inwardly the deceptive appearances of corporeal things and arranges them with its vain reflection so that to it nothing seems divine unless it be of such a sort. Privately avaricious, it is prolific in errors; and privately extravagant, it is emptied of its powers. Yet it would not begin by leaping in a single instant to such disgraceful and miserable fornication; but, as it is written: One who despises moderate things, shall fall little by little (Si. 19.1).

For just as a serpent slithers not with evident steps but with the most minute treadings of its scales, so the slippery movement of falling away takes over the negligent in minute degrees. And, beginning from a perverse desire for likeness to God, human being arrives in the end at likeness to the beasts. For this reason, stripped of their first clothing, they [Adam and Eve] merited by their mortality garments of skin (Gn. 3.21). For the true honor of human being is the image and likeness of God which is kept only in relation to the one by whom it is impressed. And so one clings to God all the more insofar as one loves what is one's own all the less.

Driven by the passion of putting its own power to the test, human being, with a nod from itself, rushes toward its own self as though to a middle ground. Thus, when human being wills to be as God is, beneath no one, it is hurled in punishment from its own proper middle place to the lowest place where the beasts delight to be. And so, human being's peculiar disgrace is its likeness to the beasts, since its peculiar honor is its likeness to God. Human being did not understand when it was placed in honor; it is compared to the witless beasts and is become like them (Ps. 48.13).

By what path, then could human being travel so long a distance from the highest to the lowest, unless through itself as a medium. For when it neglects the love of wisdom which remains always the same, and lusts after that science which proceeds from experimentation with changeable, temporal things, human being is puffed up but does not edify (1 Co. 8.1). Thus the soul, overburdened, is dragged away from blessedness as if by its own weight. And through that trying out of human being as its own center, it learns from its punishment what lies between the good it has abandoned and the evil it has committed. Nor can human being, its powers dissipated and profligate, return without the grace of its creator who calls to penance and remits sins. For who will deliver the hapless soul from the body of its death if not the grace of God through Jesus Christ our Lord? (Rm. 7.24).

As much as the lord's assistance enables us, then, let us bring to completion the consideration which we have undertaken of that part of reason to which belongs science, namely the understanding of temporal and changeable things which is necessary for carrying out the actions of this life. For, in that manifest marriage of the first two human beings to be made, the serpent did not eat of the forbidden tree but only persuaded that it should be eaten. Moreover, the woman did not eat alone but gave of the tree to her man; and they ate together, even though she alone spoke with the serpent and she alone was seduced by it. (Gn. 3.1-6). It is just so, in this marriage too which is made and discerned in one human being, the secret and hidden wedding of the flesh or, as I should say, the sensual movement of the soul which is directed to the senses of the body and which is common to us and to the beasts, set apart from the reason of wisdom.

For corporeal things are sensed by the sense of the body, while eternal and unchangeable spiritual things are understood by reason of wisdom. Yet appetite is near to the reason of science, since that which is called the science of action reasons concerning corporeal things themselves which are sensed by the sense of the body: if it reasons well, with a view toward referring its knowledge to the end of the supreme good; and if badly, with a view toward delighting, as it were, in goods such as those on which it might rest with a false blessedness.

When, therefore, that carnal or animal sense presses upon this intention of the mind—which is set into motion by the enduring liveliness of reasoning amidst temporal and corporeal things for the sake of the function of action—a certain allurement to enjoy itself as some private good all its own rather than as a public and common, namely, unchangeable good, then it is as though the serpent addresses the woman. To consent to this allurement, moreover, is to eat from the forbidden tree. But if that consent is satisfied with only the pleasure of thought, in which case the members of the body are indeed held back by the authority of the higher counsel such that they are not offered for sin as the weapons of evil (Rm. 6.13), then, I think, it is to be regarded as if the woman alone ate the forbidden food. If, however, in the consenting to use badly those things sensed through the sense of the body, it is so decided that the sin, whatever it may be, should be completed also in the body, if there is the power to do so, then that woman should be understood to have given to her man the forbidden food so that he might eat with her. For it cannot be decided by the mind that a sin is not only to be thought about with pleasure but also to be carried out in action, unless also that the intention of the mind, which possesses the highest power of setting the members of the body into operation or of holding them back from operation, yields to and serves the wicked action.

When the mind is pleased with merely thinking of illicit things, and in fact decides that they are not to be done, and yet it retains and pleasantly turns over those things which it ought to have refused as soon as they touched the soul, clearly it is not to be denied that there is sin, but a sin much less than if a decision were made to complete it in deed. And, therefore, we should beg forgiveness for such thoughts, and we should strike our breast and say: Forgive us our debts. And then what follows must be done and joined in the prayer: as we too forgive our debtors (Mt. 6.12).

It is not the same as with those first two human beings each of whom bore its own person, in which case, if the woman were the only one to have eaten the illicit fruit, she would also be the only one to be punished with the penalty of death. Thus, it cannot be said, in the case of one human being that—if thought alone is pleasantly fed with illicit delights from which it ought to turn away at once, even if it decides that the evils are not to be done but only delightfully retained in remembrance—the woman, so to speak, can be damned without the man. May we be far from believing this. For this is one person, one human being, and it is damned as a whole, unless those things which are thought to be sins of thought alone— without the will of putting them into operation but still with the will of delighting the soul with such things—are forgiven through the grace of the Mediator.

And so in this discussion we have sought in the mind of each individual human being a certain rational marriage of contemplation and action, inasmuch as the functions of mind are divided between these two, while in both the unity of the mind is preserved. Likewise, the history of that truth is intact, a history handed down by divine authority concerning the first two human beings, specifically a man and his wife, who propagated the human race. Yet it only need be listened to as it helps us to understand that the apostle, in attributing the image of God only to the man and not to the woman, wanted to signify something which is sought in one human being, although in the figure of the different sex of two human beings.

It has not escaped my notice that certain ones who were before us outstanding defenders of Catholic faith and interpreters of divine speech—when they sought out these two in one human being whose soul, good and whole, they considered to be a kind of paradise— spoke of the man as the mind and of the woman as the sense of the body. And, according to this division by which the man is put forth as the mind and the woman is put forth as the sense of the body, all things seem to come together appropriately, if they are treated reflectively, except that it has been written that there was not found for the man a help like him and then the woman from his side was made for him (Gn. 2.20-22). On this account, I have not thought that the sense of the body should be put forth for the woman; for we see that sense is common to us and to the beasts. I have wanted something, instead, which the beasts do not have. And I have judged that the sense of the body should, in fact, be understood for the serpent, who, it is written, is wiser than all the animals of the earth (Gn. 3.1). Indeed, among those natural goods, which we see to be common to us and the irrational animals, sense excels with certain liveliness . . . that fivefold sense in the body by which corporeal form and movement are sensed, not only by us but also, in truth, by the beasts.

But whether what the apostle said—that man is the image and glory of God and that woman, moreover, is the glory of man (1 Co. 11.7)—is to be taken in this way, or that way, or in some other way, it is still apparent, when we live according to God, that our mind, intent upon his invisible things, ought to be formed continuously from his eternity, truth and charity, and also that a certain part of our rational intention, that is, of our mind. must be directed toward the use of changeable and corporeal things, without which this life cannot be managed. This is not however so that we might conform to this age (Rm. 12.2) by constituting our end in good things of this sort and by distorting the desire for blessedness and forcing it toward them; but, rather, so that, whatever we do reasonably in our use of temporal things, we might do while contemplating upon those eternal things which must be attained, passing through the temporal things and clinging to the ete nal.

For science too has its own good measure, if that in it which puffs up or is accustomed to puff up, is overcome by the love of eternal things, which does not puff up, but, as we know, edifies (1 Co. 8.1). Indeed, without science the very virtues, by which life is rightly lived, cannot be had, these virtues by which this miserable life is so governed that it might attain to that eternal life which is truly blessed.

There is a difference, however, between the contemplation of eternal things and the action by which we use temporal things well; the former is deputed to wisdom, the latter to science. For, although what is wisdom [sapientia] can also be called science [scientia]—as even the apostle speaks of it when he says: Now I know [scio] in part; then, however, I shall know even as I have been known (1 Co. 13.12); whereby he clearly wants us to understand the science of the contemplation of God, which will be the supreme reward of the saints—yet, wherein the apostle says: To one is given the utterance of wisdom [sapientia] through the spirit, to another is given the utterance of science [scientia] according to the same spirit (1 Co. 12.8), he is certainly without a doubt distinguishing between these two, even though he does not therein explain how they differ and whence each can be distinguished from the other.

Having searched into the manifold abundance of the holy scriptures, I come upon this written in the Book of Job, where that same holy man is speaking: Behold piety is wisdom; moreover, to refrain from evils is science (Jb. 28.28). In this distinction it is to be understood that wisdom belongs to contemplation, knowledge to action. In this passage he put down piety for the worship of God . . . but to refrain from evil things, which Job called science, refers, beyond a doubt, to temporal things.

If, then, this is a right distinction between wisdom and science—
that to wisdom belongs the intellectual knowledge of eternal things,
while to science belongs the rational knowledge of temporal things—
it is not difficult to judge which is to be put before or to be put after
the other. Moreover, if another discrimination is to be applied by
which these two may be told apart, the apostle teaches us without a
doubt how they differ when he says: To one is given the utterance of
wisdom through spirit, to another is given the utterance of science
according to the same spirit. Still, the distinction between these two
which we have drawn is most evident: that the one is the intellectual
knowledge of eternal things and that the other is the rational
knowledge of temporal things and that no one doubts that the
former is to be preferred to the latter.

Thus, as we quit those things which belong to the outer human
being and, from those things which we have in common with the
beasts, desire to ascend inwardly, before we come to the knowledge
of the intelligible and supreme things which are eternal, the rational
understanding of temporal things comes to the mind. If we can,
therefore, let us find therein some manner of trinity—as we did in
the senses of the body and in those things which through the senses
entered imaginatively into our soul or spirit—so that, beyond the
corporeal things which, placed outside us, we touched with sense,
we might within us have the likeness of bodies impressed upon the
me ory, from which thinking might be formed, while the will, as a
third, joins the other two together—just as the sight of the eyes was
formed from without when th will, so that vision might occur,
applied the eye's sight to the visible thing and joined the two
together, while the will added itself thereto as a third.

(De Trin., 12.4.4; 12.5.5; 12.7.10; 12.7.12; 12.14.22; 12.15.25)

• 25 •

We enjoy the things which we have come to know wherein the
will, delighted in them for their own sake, finds rest. But we use
these things which we refer to another thing which is to be enjoyed.
Indeed, human life is not vicious nor culpable in any other way than
in one's using inappropriately and in one's enjoying inappropriately.

(De Trin., 10.10.16)

• 26 •

Therefore, of all these things, only those are to be enjoyed which we have recounted as eternal and unchangeable. The rest, moreover, are to be used with a view toward our being able to attain to the full enjoyment of the former. And we who enjoy and use other things are ourselves things. For human being is a great thing made after the image and likeness of God, not insofar as it is enclosed in a mortal body, but insofar as it surpasses the beasts, distinguished as it is by its rational soul. And so it is a great question whether human beings ought to enjoy themselves, or use themselves, or both. For we have been instructed to love one another. But the question remains whether human beings ought to be loved by one another on their own account, or on some other account. If on their own account, then we enjoy them; if on account of something else, then we use them. It seems, moreover, to me that human beings are to be loved on account of something else. For the blessed life resides in that which is to be loved on its own account. And this is not yet realized, although the present hope of it now consoles us. Moreover, they are cursed who place their hope in human being (Jr. 17.5).

None of us are to enjoy ourselves, if you perceive clearly, because we ought not to love ourselves for our own sakes, but rather for the sake of him who is to be enjoyed. For human beings are truly best then when their whole lives strain toward unchangeable life, and when, with all their affection, they cling to him. If, however, they love themselves for their own sakes, they do not refer themselves to God. Instead, they are turned to themselves and thus not to something unchangeable. Wherefore they enjoy themselves imperfectly, because they are better when they cling wholly, and are bound, to the unchangeable good, than they are when they are slackened from it or inclined toward themselves.

If, therefore, you ought not to love yourself for your own sake but for the sake of him who is the most fitting end for your love, then no other human beings should be incensed if you love them for the sake of God. For this rule of love has been divinely established; for he said: Love your neighbor as yourself; and love God with your whole heart, your whole soul, and your whole mind (Lv. 19.18; Dt. 6.5; Mt. 22.37,39). Consequently, you are to direct all your thoughts, and your whole life, and your whole intellect to him from whom you have those very things which you direct. Moreover, when he said "with your whole heart, your whole soul, and your whole mind," he left no part of our life which could properly be empty and, as it were, give place to a wish to enjoy any other thing. But whatever else presents itself to the soul to be loved is to be taken up to that place to which the whole force of our love rushes. Therefore, they who love rightly their neighbors ought to love them in such a way as for them too to love God with all their heart, all their soul, and all their mind. For in so loving them as themselves, they refer both their love of themselves and their love of their neighbors to that love of God which allows no trickle to be diverted from it and so to lessen it.

We are not to love, moreover, all things which are to be used, but only those things either which by a certain association with us are referred to God, such as a human being or an angel, or which, in relation to us, need the beneficence of God through us, such as our body. For surely the martyrs had no love for the wickedness of those who persecuted them; and yet they used it to win God.

There are, therefore, four kinds of things to be loved: first, things above us; second, ourselves; third, things equal to us; fourth, things below us. Concerning the second and fourth, no instructions need be given. For however far human beings fall away from the truth, there remains in them the love of self and the love of one's body. Indeed, when the soul flees from the unchangeable light, the ruler of all things, it does so in order that it might rule over itself and its own body; hence, it cannot but love itself and its own body.

Moreover, the soul supposed that it has attained to something great if it has been able to lord it over its associates, namely, other human beings. For it is characteristic of a vicious soul to desire more and to claim as its due what is properly due to God alone. Such love of self is better called self-hatred. For it is iniquitous to want to be served by what is below oneself, while one is oneself unwilling to serve what is above. Most rightly has it been said: To love iniquity is to hate one's own soul (Ps. 10.6). And in this way the soul grows weak and is tormented by the mortal body. For of necessity the soul loves the body and is weighted down by its corruption. Immortality and incorruption of the body arise, moreover, from health of soul. And health of soul consists in clinging most firmly to something more powerful, namely, to the unchangeable God. In truth, even when the soul strains to lord it over those who are naturally its equals, namely, human beings, its pride is altogether intolerable.

(De doctr. chr., 1.22.20-23)

• 27 •

One book of Solomon, called Ecclesiastes, at very great length
brings all earthly things into the highest contempt. It begins thus:
Vanity of the vain, said Ecclestiastes, vanity of the vain; and all is
vanity. What profit is there for one in all one's labor, in all that one
labors under the sun? (Qo. 1.2;3). . . . The vain are those who are
deceived by things of this sort (transient, earthly things). Moreover,
that which deceives them he calls vanity, not that God did not
create those things, but because human beings, through their sins,
wish to subject themselves to those things which by divine law are
subjected to them through right conduct. For, when you consider
things which are less than oneself as things to be marveled at and
sought after, are you not simply being toyed with and deceived by
false goods? The man, therefore, who is temperate in mortal and
transient things of this sort has a rule of life supported by both
testaments: that he should love none of them, that he should not
regard any of them as something to be sought after for its own sake,
but, rather, that he should make sufficient use of them so far as is
necessary for the duties of this life, provided that he does so with the
moderation of a user and not with the affection of a lover.

(De mor. 1.21.39)

• 28 •

The soul which serves God properly commands the body; and in
that soul reason, which submits correctly to the lord God, commands lust and other vices. Therefore when humankind does not
serve God, why should it be thought to contain justice? For the soul
can never justly rule the body, nor reason the vices, when they do
not serve God. . . .
Even when the soul seems admirably to rule the body and reason
the vices, yet if soul and reason do not serve God, they cannot
correctly rule the body and the vices. What kind of a master over
the body and the vices can that mind be which is ignorant of the
true God, since it does not submit to his rule but prostitutes itself to
the most sinful and corrupting demons? It follows that the virtues
which the mind seems to have, and through which it commands the
body and the vices, are not, in fact, virtues but are vices when the

mind refers its acquiring and maintaining to anything except God. Certain people claim that virtues are true and honest when they have reference only to themselves and do not seek anything outside of themselves. But then they are inflated and proud, and therefore they must not be judged virtues but vices. Just as that which is not of flesh but above it gives flesh life, so what makes human life blessed is not from humankind but above it. This is true not just of humankind but of any power or celestial virtue.

(De civ. Dei, 19.21,25)

· 29 ·

If we are delighted with wondrous spectacles and with beauty, let us long to see that wisdom which directs our steps with strength from one end to another and with sweetness arranges all things. For what is more marvelous than incorporeal force fashioning and ruling over the corporeal world? What is more beautiful than i s ordering and adorning thereof?

(De ver. rel., 51.100)

· 30 ·

Let our God be our hope. He who made all things is better than all things. He who made beautiful things, is more beautiful than all things. He who made what is mighty, is mightier; and he who made what is great, is greater. Whatever you will have loved, he will be that for you. Learn to love the creator in the creature, the maker in what is made, lest you grasp what he has made and lose him by whom you too have been made.

(En. in Ps., 39.8)

· 31 ·

Reason.—There is one prescription I can make to you. I know no other. We must take flight entirely from things of sense. So long as we bear this body, we must take great care lest our wings be held

back with the birdlime of those things. We need whole and perfect
wings to fly from darkness to that light, which does not deign even
to show itself to those shut up in this cave, unless they are such that
they can escape what is broken and dissolute and reach their proper
heights. And so, when you have become such that nothing earthly
gives you the least delight, in that moment, believe me, at that
precise point in time, you will see what you desire. *A.*—When will
that be, I pray you? For I do not think I can ever possibly hold
earthly things in the highest contempt until I will have seen that in
comparison with which they become sordid.

(Solil., 1.14.24)

• 32 •

Therefore, whoever either is truly blessed or desires to be so wills
to be immortal. One does not live blessedly, moreover, to whom
what is willed is not present. Consequently, there is no way for a life
to be truly blessed if it is not everlasting. . . .

So if the son of God by nature became the son of man by mercy
for the sake of the sons of human beings—for this is the meaning of:
The word was made flesh, and dwelt among us human beings—how
much more credible is it that the sons of human beings become the
sons of God by the grace of God and dwell in God, in whom alone
and from whom alone the blessed can be participants in his
accomplished immortality? And so that we might be persuaded of
this, the son of God became a participant in our own mortality. . . .

Let a human being be prudent, brave, temperate, just, and—so
that these things might be truly possible—let a human being wish
wholly for power and seek to be powerful in oneself and, strangely,
to be against oneself for one's own sake. And as for those other
things which one rightly wills, and yet cannot obtain, such as
immortality, and true, full felicity, let a human being desire them
without ceasing and await them patiently. . . .

Now let us see what this extended decision has accomplished,
what it has gathered together, and where it has reached. It belongs
to all human beings to will to be oneself blessed; yet that faith, by
which the heart is cleansed and brought to blessedness, does not
belong to all human beings. And so it happens that, through that
faith which not all will, one must strive toward that blessedness

which no one who exists cannot will. All see within their heart that
they will to be blessed; and so great in this respect is the conspiracy
of human nature that one may not be deceived in projecting this
same will from one's own mind to another's. For we know that
everyone wills this.

Many despair, however, of being able to be immortal, although
what all will, namely, to be blessed, is not possible otherwise. Still,
all will to be immortal, if they could be so. But in not believing that
they can be immortal, they do not live so far as for it to be possible.
Faith is, therefore, necessary for our reaching blessedness in all the
good things of human nature, that is, of soul and body. Moreover,
this same faith holds that this faith is defined in Christ who has risen
in the flesh from the dead never to die again and that no one is
delivered from the domination of the devil through the forgiveness
of sins except through him, and that in the domains of the devil life
must necessarily be miserable, unendingly so, and should be called
death rather than life.

(De Trin., 13.8.11; 13.9.12; 13.13.17; 13.20.25)

How Great Can the Power of Mortals Be?

Augustine frequently lists the conditions for human blessedness. And always the two formal requirements for attaining
blessedness are these: to will rightly and to possess what one wills.
"No one is blessed," he points out, "without having one's every
will fulfilled and without having willed in each case rightly" *(De
Trin.,* 13.5.8).

In my judgment, we can never be called blessed unless we have
what we want, whatever that might be. Neither can we be called
blessed if we have what we want and if what we want is harmful.
Nor can we be called blessed if we do not love what we have, even if
it is the highest good. For when we seek what we cannot obtain, we
are tormented; and when we have obtained what was not to be
sought, we are mistaken. And when we do not seek what ought to be
obtained, we ail. Moreover, none of these befall the mind without
misery; and both blessedness and misery do not as a rule reside in
the same human being at the same time. In none of these instances
are we blessed. However, as I see it, there remains a fourth

alternative, wherein the blessed life can be found: when we love and possess the highest human good. What else do we mean by enjoyment, except to have at hand what we love? No one is blessed except in the enjoyment of human being's highest good. Thus, if we have it in mind to live blessedly, our highest good must needs be at hand for us. *(De mor.,* 1.3.4)

The essential elements of human blessedness, according to Augustine, are, then, wisdom and possession.

Augustine had once thought that the blessed life was available to human beings in time and that he and others could reasonably hope for human blessedness as the fruit of leisure, virtue, and reflection. Thus, in the opening passage of his dialogue *On the Blessed Life* Augustine made significant use of the image of a ship reaching port, while a more characteristic image throughout his later writings is the pilgrim's path, the way, which defines the whole of one's lifetime. Partly through the dissolution of his dreams for a life of contemplation among fellow contemplatives and his subsequent round of consuming ecclesiastical responsibilities, partly through disillusionment over the fragmentary character of his own conversion, partly through his own growth in age and wisdom, Augustine was led to qualify his hopes for blessedness and place them beyond his expectations from earthly life.[1] Augustine, who once said of the blessed life that "we must assume that we who hasten toward it can attain it with a well-founded faith, a lively hope, and a burning love" *(De beat. vit.,* 4.35), spoke years later of "the mindless pride of those who in this life imagine themselves as having the final good and as becoming blessed from their own resources" *(De civ. Dei.,* 19.4). Given the fact that human beings die and meantime are not happy, it is clear that no one may reasonably hope to satisfy, within lifetime, both formal conditions for blessedness. For reasons of which we will later attempt to offer some account, Augustine argues that human misery demands that one choose between the requirements for blessedness, a choice quite unevenly weighted from the outset.

---

1. cf. *De beat. vit.,* 1.5, 4.35; *C. Acad.,* 2.2.4; *De util. cred.,* 11.25.

With considerable inconsistency of formulation, Augustine distinguishes between the two general functions of the mind: the one he often calls wisdom *(sapientia)* and the other science or knowledge *(scientia)*. "Wisdom belongs to contemplation, knowledge to action" *(De Trin., 12.14.22)*. Knowledge is "the action by which we make right use of things temporal," while wisdom refers to "the contemplation of things eternal" *(De Trin., 12.14.22)*. Once again, wisdom represents "that part of reason with which the human mind cleaves to the beholding or the consulting of the eternal reasons," whereas knowledge represents "that part of reason which is diverted to the governing of temporal things" *(De Trin., 12.7.12)*. These two diverse powers or faculties of mind seem to correspond closely and in every respect to the diverse concerns of nature and person. Both person and knowledge have to do with events and actions which occur in time and which depend upon the agency of human beings for their accomplishment. The person is concerned with beginnings, progressions, and outcomes; and knowledge represents quite generally one's capacity for sensing and living and acting in a world whose changes are matters of personal concern. On the other hand, nature is concerned with what is beyond change, without beginning and without end, with what simply is; and wisdom represents generally one's capacity for searching out, glimpsing, and gazing upon the eternal things in the contemplation of which human being finds its own proper blessedness.

A critical distinction between wisdom and knowledge is made in the context of a distinction which Augustine draws between the love of temporal, carnal things and the love of eternal, spiritual things.

In the love of spiritual things, the word born and the word conceived are the same. Not so in the love of carnal things. The word conceived and the word born are, however, the very same, when the will finds rest in the very act of knowing, if one knows justice perfectly and perfectly loves it, that one is already just even if there is no necessity to act on it outwardly through the members of one's body. But in the love of carnal and temporal things, as in the offspring of animals, the conception of the word is one thing and the bringing forth of the word quite another. For here, conceiving is a matter of desire and giving birth is a matter of attainment. For greed is not satisfied with knowing and loving gold but must also have it. Neither is it enough, in the case of eating or of lying with another, to know about and love these things, unless one also does them. In fact, all such things, even if they are attained, are insufficient. "For one who drinks of this water," he says, "will thirst again" *(Jn., 4.13). (De Trin., 9.9.14)*

The mind's spiritual word is perfectly one with its object. For the mind to know and to love the eternal is for the mind to possess the eternal. However, the mind's carnal, temporal word is quite apart from its object. For the mind to look upon temporal things with love is for the mind to desire and perhaps to anticipate possession of what is foreign to it. Attainment is another and further consideration and concern; and attainment involves management, arrangement, control of temporal and material affairs, or simply, power. Practical reason, as distinct from theoretical reason, knowledge as distinct from wisdom, involves action or kinetic activity, which in turn involves the employment of force, the medium of exchange in a world of occurrence and event. The mind's word regarding temporal things, which most comprehensively means the life of the person, must be vindicated once spoken, and once vindicated, vindicated again and again.

When Augustine surely implies (cf., e.g., *De Trin.,* 13.6.9) that one must choose between the formal requirements for attaining blessedness, that one must choose either wisdom or possession, he seems to mean that one must rank wisdom and possession in one's life, somehow subordinating one to the other. What clearly follows from these two alternatives is an altogether Augustinian distinction between two fundamental possibilities available to human being; we may call them the life of wisdom and the life of power. For the person, in time, the pursuit of wisdom and the pursuit of power or attainment diverge and exclude one another; for each is wholly consuming and demanding of the energies and concerns of a lifetime. It seems that one may either strive to want the right thing, or strive to have what one wants. The search for wisdom somehow involves the renunciation of power, the renunciation of possession, while the search for power somehow involves the renunciation of wisdom, since it presupposes the appropriateness of what it is striving to attain. The life of power is founded upon a single insight, a limited conception of what would please and of what would be a worthy object of one's energies, while the life of wisdom is founded upon insight itself and thus upon an awareness of the passing and inadequate character of any single conception of what would be good or right for human being. Each of these two lives has its own peculiar threat or risk. The life of wisdom is threatened by final resourcelessness, by the possibility that in the end one will possess no more than one does in the course of one's life. The life of power, on the other hand, is threatened by final foolishness, by the possibility that in the end one will find one's attainment futile or even bitter. Briefly, one who above all wants to desire the right thing may in the end never have what is most desired, while one who above all wants to have what is most desired may in the end realize that all along one desired the wrong thing. Now, after having simply sketched the profiles of these two possible ways of life, it would be well to consider each in depth.

The life of power is founded upon the desire to attain or to possess within the horizon of one's own lifetime some person or thing, whose goodness is perceived as compellingly desirable. This desire for possession is, in turn, somehow conditioned by a sense of personal mortality, an awareness of the failing character of one's energies and the fleeting, contingent character of one's joys. In the face of such intransigent limits, it seems appropriate to respond by limiting the scope of one's desires to prudently calculated proportions, proportions scaled to one's own energies and resources. One despairs of true human blessedness, of a fully human life, and confesses misery to be the inescapable lot of human beings. Augustine suggests the appropriateness of Terence's remark that "Since you cannot become what you will, will what you can become," and comments that this is "advice given to the miserable, lest one be more miserable" *(De Trin.,* 13.7.10). Even the miserable may reasonably hope for a limited blessedness of their own design and attainment. Regardless of what would make all human beings truly blessed, one may decide all but arbitrarily upon some possession or accomplishment from which one could at least expect to receive some satisfaction and pleasure.

> Philosophers have, indeed, made for themselves, as each found pleasing, their own would-be blessed lives, so that they might be able, by virtue of some excellence peculiar to them, to do what they could not do by virtue of the common condition of mortals—namely, to live in accord with their own will. *(De Trin.,* 13.7.10)

> There are others who, in the midst of this laborious life, with bodies doomed to death, and bent under the burden of corruptible flesh, have willed to author and to establish their own would-be blessed lives, as if to seek and to secure them with their own resources. They neither beseech nor place their hopes in the wellspring of all resources; and they are utterly blind to how God resists their pride. *(Epist.,* 155.2)

When the person, according to its own unique ambitions and resources, attempts to redeem itself from human being's common misery, the person reduces its expectations from the desire for human being's supreme good to the desire for one's own peculiar good. "For the soul, loving its own power, slips from what is whole and common to what is partial and private" *(De Trin.,* 12.9.14). The soul attempts to govern and administer the whole according to laws of its own making, "although it could have been most excellently governed by the laws of God, if it had followed God as its ruler in the created universe" *(De Trin.,* 12.9.14). When a person decides what things are to be sought above all else, it reorders the whole in the person's own unique image and lives as if the whole were somehow of the person's own making and thus particularly responsible to it. Any such personal rendering of the whole must be forced and reinforced upon the whole, which means that power replaces wisdom as definitive of human being's posture toward the whole. And "when, whether from the passion to experience, or to excel, or to handle, the soul does anything for the sake of attaining those things which are sensed through the body, in order that it may place in them its final good" *(De Trin.,* 12.10.15), the soul virtually re-creates human being; for human being is defined by its end, its final good. The mind, so far from being inspired by a glimpse of the eternal, "is perverted and disgraced by the fornication of fantasy" *(De Trin.,* 12.9.14) when it places its end in objects of its choice, thereby "distorting the desire for blessedness and forcing it toward them" *(De Trin.,* 12.13.21) so that it might repose in them with a false blessedness (cf. *De Trin.,* 12.12.17). Once the person recognizes no limits upon itself except those general limitations within which it conceives of and pursues its own quite limited objectives, the person sees itself as, in principle, absolutely powerful with only extrinsic, practical limits upon its inventiveness.

Within the context of a life of power, the mind's word is purely creative, creative of a would-be whole and of a particular life within that whole, both of which are uniquely one's own. One's word is answerable to the mind as its creation and is without support apart from whatever temporal reality the person is capable of conferring upon it and of sustaining in it. Such a project, according to Augustine, "beginning from a perverse desire for likeness to God, arrives in the end at likeness to the beasts" *(De Trin.,* 12.11.16). Clearly, personal re-creation of the whole, a reordering of all created goods according to their probable attainability by one's efforts rather than according to their intrinsic claims upon one's desires, implies a denial of divine creation, and represents a convergence of pride and covetousness, the twin matrices of all evil, according to Augustine (cf. *De Trin.,* 12.19.14).

> Driven by the passion of putting its own power to the test, human being, with a nod from itself, rushes toward its own self as though to a middle ground. Thus, when human being wills to be as God is, beneath no one, it is hurled in punishment from its own proper middle place to the lowest place where the beasts delight to be. And so, human being's peculiar disgrace is its likeness to the beasts, since its peculiar honor is its likeness to God. *(De Trin.,* 12.11.16)

A frequent theme of Augustine's is that human being cannot escape service (i.e., its own proper place in the other of things) and that all of its attempts at mastery merely alter the conditions of its servitude. Ironically, perhaps, human being is never without its lord. Human being never itself becomes sovereign. When human beings rebel against their God, they never escape their lord; rather, they only encounter the nether side of the lord of creation, God's dark and wrathful countenance. When human beings rebel against creation and struggle to rearrange it in their exclusive favor, they suffer the revenge of a violated creation. Would-be masters

> become the slaves of mortal things while they incompetently desire to be lords. *(De Mor.,* 1.23.42)

> When mind deserts the God above it, at whose side alone it might be able to preserve its own strength and enjoy its own light, ... mind is rendered so weak and shadowed that it begins to fall more miserably away even from itself and to fall in with those things which are not what it is and whose place is beneath mind. This fall of mind is on account of loves which it does not have the strength to conquer and deceptions from which it sees no return. *(De Trin.,* 14.14.18)

We may notice the reversal of metaphors in this passage. When counted by itself, human strength is simply weakness and human brilliance simply darkness. To possess perversely is to be possessed perversely.

At the center of the life of power is the will, reduced in its focus, intent upon what one can know, control, and possess within the horizon of personal mortality. The most basic and common form of the life of power would be a life in which one collects, hoards, and defends material possessions and prerogatives. However, a more subtle and refined form of the life of power would be a life in which one grasps and demands certainty of understanding, in which case one's possessions would simply be one's personal doctrines. In either case there is a proud reliance on one's own authority and resources, whether they be physical might, civil prestige, economic influence, or mental capacity. Regarding the latter, Augustine remarks:

> There are those who gaze with admiration upon the powers of the human mind, upon the great beauty of its words and deeds.

Ashamed to place the supreme good in the body, they have yet
placed it in the mind itself. In doing so, they have indeed placed the
highest good lower than it should be placed by reason that is
perfectly pure. *(Epist.,* 118.15)

Those who have chosen to live a life of power may never boast
of blessedness or of a fully human life, the despair of which is the
root of their project; rather, their only claim may be to have
succeeded in a calculated undertaking in which they may take
pride and find some cause and place for repose. They possess,
however, no measure by which to judge the work of their
accomplishment, which lack is a merciful one in their favor. And
they possess no common language by which to communicate and
share their accomplishments, which are finally altogether private
in their conception as well as in their fruition.

I do not know whether one should show ridicule or compassion for
what is finally the blessedness of proud mortals who glory in living
in accord with their own wills. It comes to this: they bear willingly
and patiently what they do not wish to be their lot. Thus they say
that Terence spoke wisely when he said: Since you cannot become
what you will, will what you can become. Who denies that there is a
certain aptness to this saying? But it is advice given to the miserable,
lest one become more miserable. But to the blessed, which is what
all wish themselves to be, there is no rightness and truth in saying:
What you want cannot come to be. *(De Trin.,* 13.7.10)

It seems faithful to Augustine to broaden the specific Stoic
reference of this critique to include all attempts to embrace and
construe the whole of one's life according to personal will. The
most a person is able to claim on its own is that its life is its
ownmost word, free and creative, that one's life is the product of
one's own decisions, which on the one hand speaks a truism and
on the other hand tells of arbitrarily impoverished origins. Such a
word cannot be spoken in public. Such a life has no public or
communal significance. It is a word spoken in a silence into which
the threatened mortal steals himself or herself to create what
cannot be taken easily away. But taken away it always is.

Even the qualified misery of the successful life of power is, after all, misery. And Augustine questions the significance of those qualifications which human beings are able to effect through their own designs and resources. A life of power may fail in one or both of two ways: one may never attain what one set out after, and one may find that what one set out after was not worth one's efforts toward its attainment. Regardless of the first, Augustine considers the second failure to be inevitable and decisive. In fact, such failure is confirmed by the "success" of attainment. Augustine wonders whether mortals may reasonably speak at all of power; for as mortals they have no final power over life and death.

> What creature's power is comparable to the power of the creator? ... For how great can the power of mortals be? Therefore, let mortals hold fast to justice; power will be given to immortals. Compare this with the power of those called mighty on this earth and the latter proves to be sheer laughable weakness. *(De Trin.,* 13.13.17)

The life of wisdom or, more properly, a life in pursuit of wisdom is defined by the inherent primacy of the desire to will the right thing, to love the supreme good. And since the person's knowing and willing of the supreme good are, within lifetime, most often negative in practice, the life of wisdom comes to mean the person's restless refusal of temporal, created goods. Such a life knows no final repose, no final certainties. And so long as human being's proper end remains unknown and in question, then human being itself remains in question. And this, Augustine admits, becomes one's weakness and infirmity. The mind's word is one of inquiry; and the whole of one's life and activities has a certain halting character, lacking in self-assurance. All of one's joys are fleeting, and

> yet if something is pleasing such that the will rests in it with a certain delight, it is nevertheless not yet that toward which the will is inclined to strive. Rather, this something is referred beyond itself so that it might be regarded, not as a homeland for the citizen but as a place of renewal, or even as a place of lodging for the traveler. *(De Trin.,* 11.6.10)

The life of wisdom is a journey in which one has no permanent city or land. As will be made clear, the life of wisdom is, for Augustine, most properly the Christian life; and for the Christian not even the church provides a lasting dwelling. The Christian's only true city, according to Augustine, is the city of God, the heavenly city, which does not belong to time. In contrast, the life of power represents, on the scale of the individual life, the life of a city. To suggest briefly several parallels, the founding of a city involves the encircling of a limited area of land, which a people may reasonably hope to wall in, to cultivate and defend, just as the founding of a life of power involves a quite iimited conception or project which one hopes to make prosper.

The city belongs to its citizens and has a primarily inward focus, just as the life of the powerful human being is focused upon some altogether private good. Pagan cities had their own gods, laws, and myths, just as the life of power has its own understanding of itself, its own work, which Augustine regards as fantastic, idolatrous, and perverse. The claims of cities, like the claims of human beings must be carved out of rock, established by force, sustained and defended by force. The founding of one's own life as well as the founding of cities, both altogether prideful and private, set person against person, and thus brother against brother, sister against sister. And finally, cities are mortal as are their inhabitants and the glory of both passes without lasting flourish; both turn to dust. These brief remarks are meant to suggest the ppropriateness of this discussion of the life of power and the life of wisdom to the theme of the two cities in *The City of God,* although any fuller analysis of *The City of God* lies beyond the scope of these reflections. Clearly, the life of power belongs to the city of human beings, the earthly city; and the life of wisdom belongs to the city of God, the heavenly city, in its earthly sojourn.

If you have a house of your own, you are poor; if you have the house of God, you are rich. In your own house you will fear thieves; in God's house God himself is the wall. Blessed, then, are they who dwell in your house. They possess the heavenly Jerusalem, without distress, without pressure, without diverse and divided boundaries.

All possess it; and each singly possesses the whole. *(En. in Ps.*, 83.8)

The human being who lives a life in pursuit of wisdom is always uncertain what it means to be a human being, and for that reason can neither achieve nor afford any certainty regarding the meaning of personal life, what it means to be this particular human being. One's experiences furnish examples of what one is not and of things in which one may not properly find rest, things which are not finally enough; and it is given to a few human beings to catch a glimpse of the truth, the supreme good, and the meaning of human being.

> To attain to the intelligible things themselves with the keen vision of mind belongs to few human beings. And when the mind, insofar as this can happen, reaches those things, it does not dwell in their midst. Rather, the mind is sent away, as if the eye itself were driven back. And so there comes to be a passing reflection of what does not pass. This passing reflection is, moreover, committed to memory by virtue of those disciplines in which the mind is learned, so that the mind might be able to return to that from which it is compelled to pass or.... What the passing glance of mind once seized it stored within memory, as if it were swallowing something into its stomach. By recalling this passing reflection, the mind is able, in a certain manner, to ruminate over it; and what the mind so learns it can convey into the discipline of thought. *(De Trin.*, 12.14.23) [2]

Regardless of the particular privileges of a few human beings, Augustine regards the life of wisdom as generally commendable to all.

> One is nearly blessed when one is right in willing whatever one wills and when one wills those things in the attainment of which one will be blessed ... [such a one] longs to rejoice in those good things for which human nature is well-suited ... [such a one] strives with a prudent, temperate, courageous mind after such good things as are possible even in this present misery and takes to one's own however much is given, so that even amidst evils one may be good, and so

---

2. See references to Augustine's own similar experiences recorded in his *Confessions:* 7.10; 7.17; 10.40.

that when all evil things have come to nothing and all good things have come to fullness one may be blessed. *(De Trin.*, 13.6.9)

What is arbitrary, according to Augustine, and perversely gratuitous, is not the desire for blessedness and a life faithful to the claims of that desire, but rather the denial of the desire for blessedness and the calculated reduction of one's expectations to what "reasonable" mortals may devise and accomplish.

Apart from its foundation in the nature of human being, the life of wisdom is given new warrant by revelation and, in particular, by the life of Christ. The life of wisdom is finally the expansion of the will to embrace revelation in faith. Satan, the father of lies, promised to human beings a knowledge by which they would become as gods. However, Augustine points out that:

> ... it had been said in the gospel that Jesus has given the power of becoming God's children to those who received him. And what it means to have received him had been explained briefly in these words: to those believing in his name. *(De Trin.*, 13.9.12)

According to Augustine, the life of Jesus serves as both an example and an assurance to those who would live lives of wisdom.

> He postponed what he could have done so that he might do first what was fitting. Therefore it was necessary for him to be both human and divine. For unless he were a human being, he could not die. And unless he were God, we would not believe that he had declined to do what he could have done, instead of his having been unable to do what he wanted. Neither would we suppose that he had preferred justice to power, instead of his having been devoid of power . . . and so, by the death of one so powerful, justice has been commended and power has been promised. For he accomplished one of these by dying and the other by rising again. . . . He conquered the devil first with justice and afterwards with power. *(De Trin.*, 13.15.19)

What Augustine insists upon, then, is that this "order must be preserved . . . let mortals hold fast to justice; power will be given to immortals" *(De Trin.,* 13.13.17). Knowledge, human being's capacity for the material and the temporal, is to be restrained and governed by wisdom, human being's capacity for the spiritual and the eternal, without, however, questioning or impairing the legitimacy and unity of both. The person is properly the mind's word spoken in time; person is properly born of nature as Eve was drawn from the flesh of Adam.[3]

> That part of us which is occupied by the activity of handling things corporeal and temporal ... is indeed rational ... on the one hand, drawn, as it were, from that substantial rationality of our mind by which we reach up and cleave to the intelligible and immutable truth and, on the other hand, assigned to handle and to govern inferior things. For just as there was not found among all the beasts a help for human being like unto itself, unless this were taken from human being itself and formed into a consort, so too for our mind, by which we consult supernal and inner truth, there is in our intercourse with corporeal things, inasmuch as human nature requires this, similarly no help from those parts of the soul which we have in common with the beasts. And so a certain part of our reason, not set off as a sunderance of unity but, as it were, derived as an aid to fellowship, is sent off to perform its own proper work. And just as with male and female one flesh belongs to both, so the mind's own nature embraces intellect and action, or counsel and operation, or reason and rational appetite, or whatever other formulations might convey the same distinction in a more significant manner. Thus, just as it has been said of those two (male and female): The two shall become one flesh (Gen., 2.24), so it could be said of these two parts of reason: The two shall become one mind. *(De Trin.,* 12.3.3)

The person, its concerns and its loves, are not to be altogether denied or disdained; rather, according to Augustine, there is an order of things to be loved. Every created thing is good and "can

---

3. In Augustine's discussion of Adam and Eve in the *De Trinitate,* Adam represents the masculine principle and Eve the feminine principle; both are present within human being. Augustine does not suggest that the masculine principle is dominant in men or that the feminine principle is dominant in women.

be loved both rightly and evilly: it is loved rightly when its place in the order of things is preserved; evilly when that order is disturbed" *(De civ. Dei,* 15.22).

> Thus it seems to me that this is a brief and true definition of virtue: It is the order of love. On this account, in the holy Canticle of Canticles, the spouse of Christ, the city of God, sings: Order love within me. *(De civ. Dei,* 15.22)

There is a love proper to each thing: and in this context Augustine distinguished between use and enjoyment. Use belongs to knowledge and defines the posture of the person toward creation, while enjoyment belongs to wisdom and defines the posture of the mind toward its creator.

> It is a matter of inordinate desire, when a creature is loved for its own sake. Then, instead of aiding one who uses it, the creature corrupts one who would enjoy it. For when a creature's place is equal to our own, it is to be enjoyed, but enjoyed in God; and when a creature's place is beneath us, that creature is to be used for the sake of God. *(De Trin.,* 9.8.13)

> Justice, then, shall provide this rule of life ... that one willingly serve God, whom one loves, that is, the supreme good, supreme wisdom, supreme peace and that one rule over that portion of all else which is already subject to oneself and anticipate one's rule over that portion which remains to be subjected to oneself. This norm for living is supported by the authority of both Testaments. *(De mor.,* 1.24.44)

There is a sense, then, in which Augustine sees the person to be defined by its highest characteristic expectation, which means by one's personal image and understanding of blessedness. Human being cannot but act and its actions necessarily change the changeable. Yet every human act possesses theoretical foundations and implications, however unconscious and inarticulate these may be. A person's life is accounted for and finally judged by that conception of the good which informs it and which thus provides the horizon for action and for the consequent unfolding of personal life.

> All these and other such wills have their own proper ends. Those ends are, in turn, referred to the end of that will by which we will both to live blessedly and to attain that life which is referred to nothing else. For that life suffices in itself for one who loves it. . . . All wills bound together are, moreover, right if that one will is good to which each of the others is referred. If, however, that final will is depraved, then all the other wills referred to it are depraved. And thus, in the unity of right wills, those who ascend to blessedness have a kind of path, made, as it were, of quite sure steps. The entanglement of depraved and distorted wills is, moreover, a chain by which one who acts in this way is bound so as to be cast into the outer darkness. *(De Trin., 11.6.10)*

The central concern of the life of wisdom is that one live truthfully, that the mind's word, the whole of one's life, be the expression, the confession of truth beheld or believed.

> For necessarily, when we speak truth, that is, when we speak what we know, from that very knowledge, which we retain in memory, there is born a word which is altogether of the same sort as that knowledge from which it is born. For the reflection which is from that thing which we know is the word which we speak in the heart. *(De Trin. 15.10.19)*

Wisdom and understanding are properly prior to speech. One's word, one's life and its loves are to be born of sight. "When, therefore, that is in word which is in knowledge, then there is a true word" *(De Trin., 15.11.20)* However, no lasting vision of the good, no full wisdom is available to human being. There is only the privileged glimpse of the contemplative and the faith of the believer, neither of which confer wisdom and blessedness upon the person in time. Only the word of God spoken in time is wise and perfect—"This word is truly truth" *(De Trin., 15.14.23)*. This word, the divine word incarnate in time, is word governed wholly by vision, time in the pure service of eternity. Thus, for Augustine, this text is decisive: The son can do nothing of himself but what he sees the Father do (Jn. 5.19). This vision and this service does not belong to human being in time. And so it is for the person who would live in pursuit of truth to make of its life, its word, one of humble inquiry rather than proud creation.

> Interrogate creation. If it is of itself, dwell in it. If, however, it is from him, it is pernicious to one who loves it on this account alone, that it is preferred to the creator. *(En. in Ps.,* 79.14)

The whole of the life of wisdom is a desire for blessedness, free of wilfullness because it is not directed toward any created good of one's choosing, and free of presumption because it is grounded in faith and hope rather than in one's own strength. "The whole life of a good Christian is an holy desire" *(Tr. in Joann. ep.* 4.6).

> What you now long for, you do not yet see. But by your longing you are made capable, so that, when what you would see is come, you might be filled. It is as if you would fill some enclosure, the opening of the bag, or whatever else. You know how much you would put into it and see that the enclosure is narrow. By extending it you make it capable of holding more. So too, God, by deferring our hope, extends our desire, and by our desiring extends the mind, and by extending the mind makes it more capacious. Let us, therefore, desire, brothers, because we are to be made full. . . . Our life is this: that by our longing we are to be exercised. *(Tr. in Joann. ep.,* 4.6)

The personal quest for blessedness is seen to be futile in the realization that one must choose one essential element of blessedness to the virtual exclusion of the other. Only with the convergence of power and wisdom does blessedness become imaginable—an image which human being is helpless to construct and, even more, to realize. Such an image must be the work and the word of God, to be beheld and loved only by faith.

CHAPTER 6

FAITH

Readings

• 1 •

You are great, lord, and intensely to be praised. Great is your strength; there is no limit to your wisdom (Ps. 147.5). And human beings want to praise you, human beings who are but a part of your creation and who carry with them their mortality, carry the evidence of their sin and the evidence that you oppose the proud (Jm. 4.6). Yet human beings, a part o your creation, want to praise you. And you encourage us to delight in praising you, because you made us for yourself. Our heart is restless until it finds quiet in you. Allow me, lord, to know and to understand whether I should praise you or pray to you first; whether I should pray to you or know your first. But who could pray to you without knowing you? An unknowing person might mistake one thing for another in prayer. Or is it rather through addressing you in prayer that we know you? But how will they believe without a preacher? (Rm. 10-14). They will praise the lord who seek him. For in seeking him they find him, and finding him, they will praise him. (Mt. 7.7). May I seek you, lord, in prayer and, believing in you, may I pray to you? For you have been preached to us. My faith, which you have given me, which you have inspired through the incarnation of your son and the ministry of your preacher, prays to you.

(Conf., 1.1)

· 2 ·

Lord, in the poverty of my life my heart is busy, driven on by the
words of your holy scripture. Therefore the poverty of human
intelligence is often involved in lengthy discussions because questions require more words than answers; searching is a longer process
than obtaining; and the hand which knocks is busier than the hand
which receives. We hold a promise; who will falsify it? If God is on
our side, who is against us? (Rm. 8.31). Ask and you will receive;
seek and you will find; knock and it will be opened for you (Mt.
7.7). These are your promises; who would fear deception when truth
promises?

(Conf., 10.34)

· 3 ·

I call my conscience to witness, I call God who dwells in pure
souls to witness that I judge nothing to be more prudent, more
chaste, more religious than all those scriptures which the Catholic
Church retains under the name of the Old Testament. I know that
you wonder at this. For I cannot pretend that I did not used to be of
a far different persuasion. But there is surely nothing more rash, and
as a boy I used to be rash, than to abandon the expositors of those
books, which they profess themselves to hold and to be able to hand
on to their disciples, and to ask for opinion of these books from
those who, for no reason I can think of, have declared a most bitter
war on the establishers and authors of those books. For who even
supposed that the recondite and obscure books of Aristotle should
be expounded to one by an enemy of Aristotle, to speak of studies in
which a reader may stumble upon sacrilege? Finally, who ever
wished to read or to learn the geometrical writings of Archimedes
with Epicurus for one's teacher, who, so far as I can judge,
understood nothing of them and yet wrote with great pertinacy in
opposition to them.

Are those scriptures of the law so very self-evident, against which
they [the Manichaeans] lodge their vain, foolish attack, as if the
scriptures lay open to vulgar understanding? They seem to me to be
like that little woman whom they themselves are accustomed to
deride. That woman was angered by another woman, a Manichaean

quite simple in her religion, who praised the sun and commended it as a thing to be worshipped. The first woman, in her excitement, leapt up and beat the ground repeatedly with her foot in that spot upon which the sun had shone through the window. "Behold I put my heel to your god the sun," she began shouting. Utterly foolish and just like a woman. Who denies it? But don't they [the Manichaeans] seem to you to be like this? With a violent assault of oratory and maledictions, they lash out at books they don't understand, books whose purpose and character they know nothing of, books which, although they appear quite everyday, are nevertheless subtle and divine to those who understand them. And because the ignorant applaud them, they rate themselves as having accomplished something.

Believe me, whatever is in those scriptures is lofty and divine. Truth is wholly in them, and learning most suited to the remaking and renewal of souls, but plainly measured so that no one is unable to draw therefrom what suffices, provided that one come near to draw forth in devotion and piety, such as true religion requires. To prove this to you would require many reasons and a long discourse. The first thing to be done with you is to have you not hate those authors and then to have you love them. And in what other way is this to be done than by expounding their ideas and their writings? Therefore, if we hated Vergil, indeed, if we did not rather love him, on the basis of our elders' recommendations, before we ourselves understood him, we would never derive satisfaction from those innumerable Vergilian questions by which teachers of literature are wont to be stirred and troubled. . . .

Surely we should extend a similar good will to those through whom the holy spirit has spoken, as long-standing posterity has established. But, as such very intelligent youths, marvelous explorers of reasons, without so much as opening these books or questioning these teachers, without the slightest accusation of our own slowness of understanding, and finally yielding nothing of our mediocre heart to those who have wished writings of this sort to be read, guarded, and studied throughout the whole world for so long a time, we supposed that nothing of what they say is to be believed. In this, we were prompted by the voice of their hostile enemies, in whose company, with a false promise of reason, we were compelled to believe and to cherish an unheard-of number of tales.

But now, if I am able, I will go on with what I have set forth to do . . . to urge those who care for their souls to examine the great mysteries of the Catholic faith; and I shall show to them the hope of divine fruit and of the discovery of truth.

(De util. cred., 6.13-7.14)

· 4 ·

Let truth, light of my heart, and not the shadows within me speak to me! I slid down into that state and was in darkness, but even from there I loved you. I strayed and yet I remembered you. I heard your voice behind me, telling me to return, but I heard only faintly because of the uproar of the restless. And now I am returning, sweaty and out of breath, to your fountain. Let no one get in my way. I will drink this and I will live it. May I not be my life; I have lived badly on my own. I was my own death. I revive in you. Speak to me; discuss with me. I have believed your books and their words are full of mystery.

(Conf., 12.10)

· 5 ·

You have already told me, lord, loudly in my inner ear, that you are eternal and also have immortality, since you never change in form or through motion; nor is your will modified in time since a will which is sometimes one thing and sometimes another is not immortal. This is clear to me in your sight; may it become clearer and clearer, I beg you; and through its manifestation let me continue to live in moderation under the protection of your wings. Also you have told me with your strong voice in my inner ear all natures and all substances, which are not what you are but nonetheless exist, you created. Only that which does not exist is not from you. And you have said that the movement of the will away from you, who are, toward that which is less is a wrongdoing and a sin; you have said that the sin of a human being does not harm you or disturb the order of your rule in first or last matters. In your sight this is clear to me; may it become clearer and clearer, I beg of you, and through its manifestation let me continue to live in moderation under the protection of your wings.

You have also said to me with a loud voice in my inner ear that your creation for whom you are the sole pleasure, is not eternal along with you; but it drinks you in with the most persistent chastity and never shows at any point its own mutability. In your eternal presence, to which it clings with complete affection, without a future to wait for or a past into which to project memories, your creation does not alter through change nor disperse itself in time. Oh, it is blessed, if anything is, because it clings to your blessedness; it is blessed in you who are its eternal inhabitant and enlightener. I can discover nothing I would call the heaven of heavens which is the lord's more freely than your house which exists for the contemplation of enjoyment in you without any distraction: a pure mind unified most strongly through the steadfast peace of the holy spirits, those citizens of your city in the heavenly regions beyond the heavens we see.

(Conf., 12.11)

• 6 •

After hearing these things and grasping them so far as my weakness, which I confess to you, my God who knows, allows, I see the possibility of two kinds of disagreement when something is related through symbols by honest reporters; the first disagreement concerns the truth of the report, the second the intention of the person who is reporting. For sometimes we ask what the true circumstances of the creation were and sometimes we ask what Moses, an outstanding minister of your faith, wanted the reader or listener to understand through his words. In the first case I reject everyone who claims to know things which are false; in the second case I reject those who think that Moses said things which are false. Let me join and rejoice in you with those, lord, who are nourished by your truth in the midst of love's largeness. Let us approach together the words of your book and seek in them your will through the will of your servant by whose pen you have given them to us.

But there are so many truths which occur to those who seek, depending on whether the words are understood in this way or that. Which of us, then, could say that Moses meant this or wished to convey that in that particular passage as confidently as he would say that this is true, whatever Moses meant? Behold, lord, I am your servant who vowed to you the sacrifice of a confession in this book; I pray that through your mercy I may fulfill my vow to you. Look how confidently I affirm that you have created in your immutable word all things, visible and invisible. But do I say as confidently that Moses meant this and nothing else when he said: In the beginning God created heaven and earth? I do not see what specific thing he was thinking when he wrote this in the same way that I see this to be a certain thing in your truth. He could have meant "at the start of creation" when he said "in the beginning." By "heaven and earth" he could have meant to refer not to an already formed and perfected nature, either spiritual or corporeal, but to two as yet unformed and incomplete natures. I understand that either of these possible interpretations of his meaning might be true. But which of them he intended in his words I do not see clearly. However, whether he had in mind one of the possibilities I have mentioned or something else which I have not, I have no doubt that, being the great man he was, he saw the truth and expressed it properly.

I hope no one can now annoy me by saying: Moses did not mean this, as you say, but that, as I say. If that person were to say to me: How do you know that Moses meant by his words what you claim?, I should endure it calmly and perhaps give the same answer I gave above, or an even fuller one, if the questioner were more stubborn. But when someone says: He did not mean what you claim he meant but what I claim, and when that same person does not deny that both of us could be right, then I beg you, my God, life of the poor, in whose heart argument does not exist, drench my heart with soothing balm, that I may bear such people with patience. They do not say this to me because they are divinely inspired and have looked into the heart of your servant for their words. They say this because they are proud and know nothing of Moses' thought but love their own—not because it is true but because it is theirs. If this were not so they would love another's truth equally, just as I love what they say when it is true—not because it is theirs, but because it is true. For if it is truth, then it is not theirs, precisely because it is true. If they love it because it is truth, then it is both theirs and mine, since it is the common property of all lovers of truth.

However, when they claim their interpretation of Moses to be the right one and mine to be wrong, I reject them; I do not love them. For such a statement comes not from the boldness of knowledge but from brashness; it is born not from vision but from a swollen head. And so, lord, your opinions are awesome because your truth is neither mine nor anyone else's but belongs to us all, whom you call publicly to share in it. You warn us terribly not to want to have it for ourselves, so that we may not deprive ourselves of it. For when a person claims as private property what you have provided for the delight of all humankind and wants to possess individually that which is the possession of all, that person is driven from the common property to the private—that is, from truth to falsehood. For when humankind tells a lie, it tells it on its own (Jn. 8.44).

Hear, best judge, God, truth itself; hear what I say to the person who contradicts me. I say it openly to you and openly to my brothers who use the law correctly to the end of charity. Hear and see if what I say to that person pleases you. I answer with this brotherly and peaceful tone: If we both see the truth in what you say and the truth in what I say, where, I ask, do we see it? I do not see it in you; you do not see it in me. But we both see it in the unchangeable truth which exists above our minds. Since we do not disagree about that light of our lord God, why do we disagree about the opinion of the person next to us. We cannot see this opinion in the same way the unchangeable truth is seen. For example, if Moses himself had appeared to us and said: I thought this, we would not see what he said exactly but we would believe him. So let us not, each one of us, be puffed up in favor of some and opposed to others beyond what is written (1 Co. 4.6). Let us love our lord God with all our heart, all our soul, all our mind (Dt. 6.5); and let us love the person next to us as we love ourselves (Mt. 22.37). If we do not believe that Moses' intention, whatever he meant in those books, was in accordance with these two precepts of love, we will make God into a liar, by holding an opinion of his servant's soul different from what he has taught us. Look how idiotic it is to insist boldly on one interpretation of Moses' thought as most likely when there is such a wealth of very true thoughts which could be extracted from his words; how silly it is to offend by hurtful arguments that very love for which he said everything and whose words we try to explain.

Yet, my God—height of my humility and rest of my work, you who hear my confessions and forgive my sins—since you order me to love the person next to me as I love myself, I cannot believe that you would have given less to your most faithful servant, Moses, than I would wish for and want from you for myself, if I had lived in his time and if you had placed me in his position: to disperse through my heart and tongue, your slaves, those writings which would for so

long in the future benefit all peoples, and would from the height of
their authority overpower the words of all false and proud teachings
throughout the world. I would want, if I had been Moses then—for
we all come from the same lump and what is humankind, except
that you are mindful of it?—so, if I had been what he was, and had
been bound by you to write the Book of Genesis, I would want to
have been given a talent for eloquence and a power of expression
such that those who were not yet able to understand how God
creates would not reject my words as beyond their power of
understanding and such that your servants who already understand
this would not find whatever true opinion they had reached in their
thought skimmed over in a few words. And if someone had seen
something else in the light of truth, the words should not lack the
possibility of bearing that interpretation.

(Conf., 12.23-26)

• 7 •

Among a diversity of true opinions may the truth itself create
harmony: may our God be merciful to us, so that we use the law
properly, the end of the commandment, pure love. And so if anyone
asks me: Which of these interpretations is the true meaning of
Moses, your servant?, these are not the record of my confessions if I
do not reply: I do not know. Yet I do know that these are true
opinions with the exception of the carnal ones; about them
whatever I have thought, I have spoken. These little ones of good
hope are not frightened by the words of your book, words which are
so exalted in their humility and so plentiful in their brevity.

But let all of us who, I confess, see and speak true things in these
words, love each other in turn; and let us love you, our God, the
source of truth, if we thirst for truth and not meaningless things. Let
us so honor your servant, the disseminator of this Scripture, who
was full of your spirit, that we believe that, when he wrote these
things, he was guided by your revelation to strive for the meaning
which excels in the light shed from its truth and in the profit gained
from its utilization.

So when one person says: The meaning is what I claim, and
another says: No, it is what I claim; I think my response would be

more reverent: Why not consider rather that he meant both, if both
are true? And if a third and a fourth interpretation be found, or
indeed if anyone finds any other truth in these words, why should
we not believe that all these things were meant by the author,
through whom the one God has tempered the holy scriptures to the
minds of many people who will see various truths in them?
Certainly if I—and I make this statement fearlessly from my heart—
were to write something which carried such authority, I would
prefer to write in such a way that my words resonated with whatever
truth each person might be able to extract from these matters and
not to set out one true opinion so plainly that I excluded others
which could not offend me as they are not false. I do not want, my
God, to be so rash as to disbelieve that that man had been granted
this capacity by you. He understood and considered, as he wrote his
words, whatever truth we have been able to find in them. And
whatever we have not been able to find, or not yet, can nonetheless
be found there.

Finally, lord, who are God and not flesh and blood, if a person
sees less, surely your good spirit, which will lead me into the law of
righteousness, could have missed none of the things which you
would reveal with these words to future readers, even if he, through
whom these things were spoken, perhaps understood only one of the
many meanings? If this be so, then let the meaning which he
understood be higher than the others and may you, lord, reveal to
us this same truth or any other you please, so that whether you
reveal to us the same truth you revealed to Moses or another
through the medium of the same words, still you feed us and error
does not deceive us. Look, lord God, I beg you, how many words,
how very many, I have written about these few ones! Where is the
strength and the time which would be sufficient for a discussion of
all your books with the same thoroughness? Allow me to confess to
you about them more briefly and to choose the truth which you
have inspired, a sure and good one, even if many occur to me when
there is the possibility of many interpretations. With this faith I
make my confessions, that, if I say what your minister meant, that is
proper and good, because that is what I ought to try for. But if I do
not achieve it, I will nonetheless say what your truth through his
words intended for me to say, your truth which also said to Moses
what it wanted.

(Conf., 12.30-32)

· 8 ·

Who but you, our God, has made for us in your divine scripture a firmament of authority stretched above us? For heaven will be folded like a book but now it is spread out over us like a skin. Your divine scripture is of higher authority now, when those mortals through whom you dispersed it among us have died. You know, lord, you know how you clothed humankind with skin when it had become mortal through sin. And you spread the firmament of your writing like a skin, your words which fit together so well, which through the service of mortals you placed above us. The authority of your words is solidified by the death of those who brought them to us and is spread high above everything which is beneath. When they lived on earth, it did not stretch so high. You had not yet stretched heaven like a skin; you had not yet spread everywhere the story of their death.

Let us look, lord, at the skies, the work of your hands. Take away from our eyes the cloud with which you have covered them. Here is your testimony which provides wisdom to the little one: My God, make perfect your praise in the mouths of infants and babies. We know no other book so destructive to the proud, to the hostile, and to those who resist reconciliation with you by defending their own sins. I know nothing, lord, nothing so purely stated which can move me so powerfully to confession, can ease my neck into your yoke, and lead me to your service for nothing. Let me understand your words, good father; allow this to me who am placed beneath them because you created them firmly for those beneath.

Above this firmament there are, I believe, other waters, immortal, spared earthly corruption. Let them praise your name; let the multitude of your angels who dwell above the heavens, praise you. They have no need of looking up to this firmament and of coming to know your word by reading what is written there. For they see your face always, and they read therein without the syllables of time the will of your eternal will! They read, they choose, they love. They read always and what they read never passes away. They read, by choosing and by loving, the very immutability of your counsel. Their book is never closed, nor is their scroll ever furled. For you yourself are their text and you are forever. You have placed them in an order above this firmament which you have set over the weakness of lesser people. Here below those people gaze upwards and come to know your mercy as it announces in time you who are the maker of time. For in the heavens, lord, are your mercy and your truth, reaching into the clouds. The clouds pass by, but the heavens remain. The preachers of your words pass away from this life into another one. But your scripture is indeed stretched over the peoples of the world even to the end of this present age. Heaven and earth shall both pass away; but your words shall not pass away. For the scroll will be rolled together, and the grass over which it was spread will, with all its own brilliance, wither; but your word endures forever. Your word now presents itself to us in a riddle of clouds and through the mirror of the heavens, not as it is. For, although we are the beloved of your son, what we shall be has not yet dawned on us. Through the latticed net of flesh he attended to us, caressed us, inflamed us; and we are fast upon his scent. Moreover, when he appears we shall be like him, for we shall see him as he is. It is ours, lord, to see him as he is, but our moment is not yet come.

(Conf., 13.15)

• 9 •

Most wisely, you our God, discuss these things with us in your book, your firmament; so that we may perceive all things through wonderful contemplation, though still through signs and in the passage of time, in days and in years.

(Conf., 13.18)

• 10 •

Since we were incapable of seizing eternal things, and since we were weighed down by the vileness of our sins, contracted by our love of temporal things and growing in us as if naturally from the shoot of our mortality, we needed to be cleansed. But it was only through temporal things that we could be cleansed so as to be ruled with eternal things. For it was with temporal things that we already had been ruled and were held fast. For nothing is further from sickness than is health. And unless the process of healing, which lies between these two, is suited to the sickness, it does not lead to health. Useless temporal things deceive the sick, whereas useful temporal things support those who need to be healed and, once they are healed, convey them to eternal things.

Moreover, even as the reasonable mind, once cleansed, owes its contemplation to eternal things, so the mind, when it requires cleansing, owes its faith to temporal things. A certain one of those whom the Greeks used to call wise said: Truth prevails over faith as eternity prevails over what has a beginning in time. And that is indeed a truthful saying. For what we say to be temporal is what he meant by something which has a beginning. We too belong to that same order of things not because we have bodies but because our minds are changeable. For nothing may properly be called eternal which is in any part changed. Therefore, insofar as we are mutable, so far are we removed from eternity.

Eternal life is, however, promised us through the truth; and, again, our faith is as far removed from the clear sight of the truth as is our mortality removed from eternity. Now, then, we put our faith in those things accomplished in time for our sake; and through this very faith we are cleansed, so that, when we have arrived at sight, as truth follows faith, eternity may likewise follow mortality. For this reason our faith will become truth, when we shall have come to that which is promised us who believe. Moreover, that which is promised to us is eternal life. And truth has said: This, moreover, is eternal life, that they may know you the one, true God and Jesus Christ whom you have sent (Jn. 17.3). When our faith shall, by seeing, become truth, then eternity shall hold fast our transformed mortality. But until this shall come to pass and in order that it may come to pass—since we accommodate our credulous faith to things which have a beginning, just as we place our hope for the truth of contemplation in things which are eternal, lest the faith of mortal life conflict with the truth of eternal life—truth itself, coeternal with the father, has had its beginning from the earth (Ps. 84.12), when the son of God came as that he might become the son of man and that he might take to himself our faith, thereby to lead us to his truth. He assumed our mortality in such a way as not to lose his own eternity. Truth prevails over faith as eternity prevails over what has a beginning.

We thus had to be cleansed, so that there might occur for us that beginning which would remain eternally, lest there be for us one beginning in faith and another in truth. Nor would we be capable of passing to eternal things from the condition of having a beginning, if we were not brought over to his eternity by way of an eternal fellowship with us through our beginning. Accordingly, our faith has now in some measure followed him to that place where we believe he has ascended, having been born, having died, having risen, and having been taken up.

Of these four we were acquainted with the first two in ourselves; for we know that human beings both are born and die. Concerning the other two, to rise and to be taken up, we rightly hope for these things for ourselves in the future; for we believe that in him they have been already accomplished. So, because in him that which also had a beginning has passed into eternity, so also is ours to make the same passage, once faith has arrived at the truth. For in order that they who already believe might stand fast in the word of faith and might be led from there to the truth and thereby be led to eternity and delivered from death he speaks as follows to them: If you remain in my word, you will truly be my disciples. And if they had asked what the fruit of this might be, he adds: And you shall know the truth. And, again, as if they had been asked of what profit the truth might be to mortals, he says: And the truth shall make you free. (Jn. 8.31,32). Free from what, if not from death, corruption, and changeableness? The truth indeed remains immortal, incorrupt, and unchangeable. Moreover, eternity itself is true immortality, true incorruptibility, true unchangeableness.

(De Trin., 4.18.24)

• 11 •

Of all that has been said from the beginning of our treatment of these matters, this is the culmination—that the fullness and end of the divine law and of all the divine scriptures should be understood to be love (Rm. 13.10; 1 Tm. 1.5), the love of a thing to be enjoyed, a thing which can enjoy with us the same thing. For we need not be commanded to love ourselves. Indeed, the whole temporal dispensation was constructed for our salvation y divine providence so that we might know and be able to act upon this truth.

(De doct. chr., 1.35.39)

· 12 ·

Do you, Dioscorus, or does anyone gifted with a sharp mind, doubt that humankind could have been advised to seek the truth in any better way than through the man who was born from the truth itself ineffably and miraculously and who, in performing his part on earth, persuaded us through his good teachings and divine deeds to have a saving belief in what could not yet be prudently understood? It is his glory we serve, and he is the one we urge you to believe in unswervingly and constantly. Through him it happens that, not a minority, but great masses of people who cannot judge with reason mock faith until, supported by his saving teaching, they emerge from their doubts into the air of the purest and most sincere truth. To his authority we ought to submit all the more devotedly the more we see that no mistaken doctrine dares to extol itself in order to draw to it the untaught masses without taking on the name of Christianity as cover. The only beliefs among the ancient ones to last, besides Christianity, with even greater attendance at their conventicles, are those who have writings in which they pretend to see and understand predictions of the coming of Jesus Christ. Further, those who glory in the name of Christianity although they are not part of its unity and catholic communion, are forced to oppose true believers and dare to attract the untaught with false reason since the lord has come with that greatest of medicines to command the faith of the people. But they are forced to do this, as I say, because they feel that they rate so badly in comparison with Catholic authority. So they try to overcome the stablest authority of the firmest church through false reason and promises. Such is usually the boldness of all heretics.

(Epist., 118.4.32)

· 13 ·

From where shall I make my beginning? From authority, or from reason? Whenever we learn anything, there is a natural order in which authority precedes reason. For a reason can appear quite weak when, once it has been offered, it afterwards takes up authority to make itself more secure. But since human minds—

darkened by having grown accustomed to shadows, which veil those minds in the night of sin and vice—are unable to direct themselves to a sight appropriate to the keenness and purity of reason, it has been most advantageously provided for, that authority ... should lead wavering human insight into the light of truth.

(De mor., 1.2.3)

• 14 •

But how do we follow him whom we do not see? or, how do we see him, we who are not only human, but foolish as well? For, although he is perceived not with the eyes but with the mind, then what mind, clouded over with foolishness, can be found fit and able to drink in that light, or even to try to do so. We must, therefore, fly to the instructions of those who, it is likely, were worse. This is as far as reason can bring us. For reason was employed in human affairs, not because it is more certain than truth but because it is more secure than custom. But when it comes to divine things, reason turns away. It cannot behold, it trembles, it grows inflamed, it gapes with love, it is driven back from the light of truth and is turned toward the familiarity of its own shadows, not by choice, but out of weariness. How much fear and trembling should be ours lest the soul contract still greater helplessness whence in its exhaustion it seeks rest! Therefore, when we desire to take refuge in shadows, may that shade of authority come to our assistance through the dispensation of ineffable wisdom; and may it charm us with its wondrous substance and with the voices which sound in its pages and which are, as it were, more modest and shaded signs of the truth.

What more could have been done for our salvation? What can be said to be more kind or generous than divine providence, which did not altogether abandon human being, fallen from the divine laws and propagating a mortal race, in just and deserved accord with its lust for mortal things? For that most just of powers has—in marvelous and incomprehensible ways, through perfectly concealed series of things which it created and which are in its service—both harsh punishment and merciful acquittal. Indeed, we shall never be able to understand how beautiful, how great, how worthy of God, and, finally, how true is what we are seeking unless, beginning with human things, nearest at hand to us, preserving the faith and precepts of true religion, we have not deserted the way which God has laid for us by the singling out of the patriarchs, by the bond of the law, by the presage of the prophets, by the sacrament of the men taken up, by the witness of the apostles, by the blood of the martyrs, and by the seizing of the gentiles. Why this order of succession? Let no one seek my opinion. Rather, let us listen to the oracles and submit our poor accounts to the divine pronouncements.

(De mor., 1.7.11-12)

• 15 •

What more should I discuss concerning right conduct? For if God is human being's supreme good, which you cannot deny, it clearly follows, since to seek after the supreme good is to live rightly, that to live rightly is nothing other than to love God with one's whole heart, with one's whole soul, and with one's whole mind. And from this it arises that this love must be preserved incorrupt and whole, which is the work of temperance; and that this love must not be broken by any hardships, which is the work of fortitude; and that this love must serve no other, which is the work of justice; and that this love must be vigilant in its discerning of things, lest deceit of fraud gradually creep in, which is the work of prudence.

This is human being's one perfection, by which alone it attains to the enjoyment of the purity of truth. This is sung by both Testaments in concert. This is commended to us from this and from that side alike. Why do you still contrive against the scriptures, of which you are ignorant? Are you unaware of the magnitude of your ignorance in attacking those books which are faulted only by those who do not understand them, and which only those who fault them fail to understand? For no enemy of the Scriptures is permitted to understand them, nor can one be other than their friend once they are understood.

Therefore, let us, whichever of us have resolved to attain to eternal life, love God with our whole heart, our whole soul, and our whole mind. For eternal life constitutes the entire reward, in the promise of which we rejoice. Nor can the reward precede one's merits; for it cannot be given before one is worthy of it. Indeed, what is more unjust than this; and what is more just than God? Let us not, then, demand the reward before we deserve to receive it.

At this point it is perhaps appropriate to ask what is eternal life. This, he says, is eternal life, that they should know you, the true God, and Jesus Christ, whom you have sent (1 Jn. 17.3). Eternal life, then, is the very knowledge of truth.

Therefore, see how perverse and preposterous are they who suppose that they hand on the knowledge of God to make us perfect, although this knowledge is itself the reward of those who are perfect. What, then, I ask, are we to do except first to love with our full love him who we will to know? Whence arises what we have insisted on from the beginning, that in the Catholic Church nothing more wholesome happens than authority's preceding reason.

(De mor., 1.25.46-47)

• 16 •

The next step for me to discuss is how those earnest people who are determined to live as described ought to be taught. There are two necessary means by which we are led to learning: authority and reason. In time, authority is the more important factor; but, for the thing itself, reason is the more important. For the factor which has primary importance in the actual doing and that which is thought to be most important in the seeking are not the same. So although the authority of the good may seem to be more beneficial to the untrained masses, reason is in truth more fitting for those who have been taught. Yet because no human being becomes skilled without first being unskilled, and because unskilled human beings do not know in what state to present themselves to teachers or through what kind of life they may become teachable, it turns out that it is authority alone which can open the door to those who wish to learn great and sacred goods. Once they have entered through the door without hesitation they pursue the precepts of the best life. It is through these precepts that they finally learn, when they have become teachable, with what powerful reason those very things are acquired which they pursued before reason. And they learn what that reason is w .ich they search for and comprehend steadfastly and capably after they have left the cradle of authority; they learn what that intellect is in which the universe exists—or rather which is itself the universe; and what, besides the universe of universes, is the beginning. Few arrive at this knowledge in the course of this life, and no one, even after death, can progress beyond it.

(De ord., 2.9.26)

• 17 •

The faith of believers appears to be something of slight account. You have no balance on which to weigh it. Hear, then, where it reaches; and learn how great a thing it is. . . .

We believe so that we might come to know; we do not come to know so that we might believe. What we shall come to know, neither eye has seen, nor ear heard, nor has it entered into the human heart (1 Co. 2.9). For what is faith other than believing what you do not see? Faith, therefore, is to believe what you do not see; and truth is to see what you have believed. . . . The lord, then, walked the earth, in the first place, for the creation of faith. . . .

If you remain in that which is believed, you attain to that which is seen. Thus John, the holy evangelist, says in his epistle: Dearly beloved, we are the sons of God, but it has not yet appeared what we shall be (1 Jn. 3.2). We are already, and we shall be something. What shall we be beyond what we are? Listen: It has not yet appeared what we shall be. We know that, when he has appeared, we shall be like him. How? For we shall see him as he is (1 Jn. 3.2). A great promise; but it is faith's reward. You seek the reward; so let the work precede it. If you believe, demand faith's reward.

(In Joann. ev., 40.8.9)

• 18 •

*Reason.—*It is well to be affected as you are. For reason promises what it says to you, that God will present himself to your mind as the sun is presented to the eyes. The mind has, as it were, its own eyes, senses of the soul. Moreover, the most certain truths of the learned disciplines are like things which the sun illumines so that they might be visible, such as the earth and all earthly things. And it is God himself who casts this light. I Reason, am in minds just as the power of looking is in eyes. For to have eyes is not the same thing as to look; and to look is not the same as to see. Thus the soul has need of three things: eyes which it can already use well, looking, and seeing. The eyes are healthy when the mind is pure of every bodily disgrace, namely, when it has been set off from and purged of inordinate desires for mortal things. And this is what faith alone first exhibits. For it is not yet possible to show this to a mind sick with vices and unreasonableness. Only a healthy mind is able to see. And if the mind does not believe that in this way alone it will come to sight, then it fails to work at its own health. But even if it believes this to be the case and thus believes that, if it has been able to see, only in this way will it come to sight and yet despairs of the possibility of its being healed, does not this mind utterly degrade itself and despair and refuse to observe the physician's instructions? *A.*—Precisely so, especially since the sickness necessarily experiences these instructions as harsh. *R.*—Therefore hope must be added to faith. *A.*—I believe it to be so. *R.*—What, then, if the mind believes all this to be so and has hope in the possibility of its own being healed, and yet does not love that very light which is promised, does not long for it, but supposes that meanwhile it ought to be content with its own darkness, already congenial through habit, does not that mind nonetheless spurn the physician? *A.*—Yes, entirely. *R.*—Therefore, a third is necessary, love. *A.*—Nothing could be so wholly necessary. *R.*—Without these three, then, no soul is healed so as to be able to see, that is, know its God.

When, therefore the soul's eyes are healed, what remains? *A.*—That it should look. *R.*—Reason is the soul's looking. But it does not follow that everyone who looks sees. And so, right and perfect looking, which is followed by vision, we call virtue; for virtue is right and perfect reason. But even the soul's looking cannot turn eyes, although already healed, to the light unless these three things endure: faith, to believe that the soul's looking is to be directed toward what is believed so that, when it is seen, it might make that looking blessed; hope, to presume that it will see, once it has looked rightly; and love, to desire to see and to enjoy. Looking is followed by the very vision of God, which is the end of looking, not in the sense that it does not now exist but in the sense that it has nothing further to strive for. This is truly perfect virtue, reason reaching its own end, which is the blessed life. Moreover, this vision is within the soul, the understanding composed of that which understands and of that which is understood, just as in the eyes what we call vision consists of the sense itself and of the sensible object; for, if either is lacking, nothing can be seen.

Now, let us see whether these three continue to be necessary for the soul, when it has attained the vision, that is, the understanding of God. Why should faith be necessary, though the soul already sees? And hope no less, when its object is already held. Yet, as for love, it will surely not be diminished; rather, it will be most fully increased. For when the soul has seen that unique and true beauty, it will love all the more. And unless the soul has fixed its eye thereon with an immense love and never turn away from this gazing, it will not be able to remain in that most blessed vision. But while the soul is in this body, even if its vision, namely, its understanding of God is perfectly full, because the bodily senses exercise their own proper function, they have the power to make us uncertain, even if they do not have the power to lead us into error. Faith can thus be said to resist the senses and to believe, instead, what is true. Again, in this life, although the soul may already be blessed in the understanding of God, still, because it bears the many troubles of the body, it must hope that none of those disadvantages will accompany it past death. Therefore, while the soul is in this life, hope does not quit the soul. But, after this life, when the soul has bound itself wholly to God, love remains to hold it fast. For there cannot be said to be faith concerning the truth of things when the soul is no longer disturbed by deceiving interruptions. And nothing remains for the soul to hope for, when it is secure in the possession of every hoped-for thing. These three, therefore, belong to the soul: to be healed, to look, and to see. Then too, there are these three: faith, hope and love, which are always necessary for the soul to be healed and to look, and, in this life, to see. But, after this life, love is the sole necessity.

(Solil., 1.6.12-1.7.14)

• 19 •

And when they see that intelligent human life has hitherto been subject to change, they are forced to place above it a certain unchangeable life, that life, indeed, which is not at one time foolish and at another time wise, but which is, indeed, wisdom itself. For the wise mind, namely, the mind which has attained to wisdom did not, prior to that attainment, used to be wise. But surely there can never be a time when wisdom itself was foolish; nor can it ever be foolish. And, if one were not to see this wisdom, one would never trustfully prefer the unchangeably wise life to the changeable life. Surely one sees the very rule of truth, by which one declares the former to be better. Indeed, unless one's vision extends above and beyond one's own nature, one never sees that rule, since one sees in oneself something changeable.

Now no one is so shamelessly foolish as to ask how one knows that the unchangeably wise life is to be preferred to the changeable life. For precisely that question—how one knows—is present at hand to everyone to be commonly and unchangeably contemplated. And one who fails to see this is like someone who is blind, standing in the sun and profiting not at all from the brilliant infusion of light so dazzling and so immediate to one's eyes. Moreover, one who sees and shrinks back brings a mental vision made weak by its accommodation to carnal shadows. And thus we are driven back from our homeland by the contrary winds of depraved habits. We follow what is lower and less rather than what we confess to be better and more excellent.

Wherefore, since that truth is to be enjoyed which lives without change, and since God the trinity, who made and established the universe, looks to the interests of those things which he has established, the soul must be purified so that it might be strong enough to perceive that truth and to cleave to it, once perceived. Let us, then, think of our purification as a kind of trek or voyage to our homeland. For it is not by a change of place that we move toward him who is present everywhere, but rather by desiring and living in accord with what is good.

But this is not something we could do, unless wisdom itself deigned to reach down to our great weakness and to provide us with a pattern for living, and to do so in a human life, for we too live human lives. When we come to that wisdom, we act wisely; and, consequently, when wisdom itself came to us, it was thought by the prideful to have acted foolishly. In coming to that wisdom we begin to recover our strength; consequently, when wisdom itself came to us it was deemed weak. But God's foolishness is wiser than human wisdom; and God's weakness is stronger than human strength (1 Co. 1.25). Therefore, though wisdom itself is our homeland, it made itself for our sakes the way home.

And although it is everywhere present to the inner eye that is sound and pure, it has deigned to appear even to the bodily eyes of those whose inner eye is weak and impure. For, since the world could not in the wisdom of God recognize God through wisdom, it has pleased God to save through the foolishness of preaching those who believe (1 Co. 1.21).

Wisdom is said to have come to us, therefore, not by traversing space but by appearing to mortals in mortal flesh. For it came to where it was, since it was in this world and the world was made through it (Jn. 1.10). But since human beings had become conformed to this world and were most appropriately called by the name of the world by virtue of their lust for enjoying reatures in preference to the creator himself, they failed to recognize wisdom, as the evangelist said: And the world knew him not (Jn 1.10). Thus, the world could not in the wisdom of God recognize God through wisdom. Why, therefore, has wisdom come although it was here, unless because it has pleased God to save through the foolishness of preaching those who believe.

(De doct. chr., 1.8.8-1.12.12)

• 20 •

But now, you will say, consider whether we ought to believe in religion. For even if we grant that to believe is one thing and to be credulous is another, it does not follow that one is free of blame in believing in religious things. Why? Perhaps to believe and to be credulous are both vicious, like getting drunk and being a drunk. But if one judges that to be certainly the case, it seems to me that one can never have a friend. For if to believe is something perverse, either one acts perversely in believing a friend, or one never believes a friend, in which case I fail to see how one could call oneself or the other a friend. You might say at this point: I grant that there are times when one should believe something; but explain how in religion it is not perverse to believe before knowing. I shall do this, if I can.

In this regard, I ask you, which do you consider to be the graver fault: To hand on religion to one who is unworthy of it, or to believe what they say who hand it on? If you do not understand whom I might call unworthy, I mean one who comes to religion with a false heart. I think you admit that it is more blameworthy to lay open holy secrets to such a one than to believe religious men when they affirm something concerning religion. It would not be fitting for you to respond in any other way. Now, suppose you are in the presence of one who is going to hand on religion to you, how are you going to assure him that you approach with a truthful soul and that there is in you no fraud or deceit regarding this religion? You will say with a good conscience that you feign nothing. You will assert this same thing with all the words at your command, and yet only with words; for as a human being you cannot open to another human being the hidden resources of your soul so as to be known in your depths. But suppose that the other one said: Behold, I believe you; but isn't it fair that you too should believe me, since, if I possess anything true, you are going to receive a benefit and I am going to give one? What shall we respond except that that one should be believed?

But, you say, would it not have been better for that one to have given me a reason so that without any rashness I could follow wherever I would be led? Perhaps so. But since it is so great a thing that you should know God by reason, do you think that all—or many, or few—are well-suited to perceive the reasons which lead the human mind to divine understanding? I think a few, you say. Do you believe yourself to be among the number? You reply that it is not for you to answer thus. Do you suppose that it belongs to that one (your teacher in religion) to believe this of you, which, indeed, that one does? Only remember, then, that that one has twice believed you as you spoke uncertain things, whereas you were unwilling to believe even one time as you were being religiously admonished. Suppose it is thus true that you approach to receive religion with a truthful soul and that you are among the few human beings who are able to grasp the reasons by which that divine power is brought to a sure knowledge. So what? Do you suppose that religion is to be denied to the others who are not endowed with such a clear genius? Or are they to be led to those highest realms step by step? You see clearly what is the religious response. For it cannot seem to you that any human being should in any way be abandoned or rejected in the desire for so great a thing. But don't you think that one will not obtain those things which are purely true otherwise than, first, by believing that one will arrive at that which one has resolved upon and then by offering a suppliant mind, and finally by becoming pure by a certain activity of life in obedience to certain great and necessary precepts? Surely this is what you think.

But what of those—I believe you to be in this category—who with the greatest of ease are able to grasp divine secrets with a sure reason? Does it do them any harm to come by that way followed by those who first of all believe? I don't think so. Yet you ask, why

must they tarry? For even if they do no harm to themselves by what
they do, they harm others by their example. For rarely is one's
opinion of oneself in accord with one's capacity. One who underesti-
mates oneself must be provoked, and one who overestimates oneself
must be restrained, lest the one be broken with despair and the
other be plunged headlong by boldness. This is easily accomplished
even if those who are able to fly are for a little while compelled to
walk where it is safe even for the others, lest the former represent
for anyone a perilous incitement. This is the providence of true
religion, divinely commanded, handed down by our blessed elders,
and preserved to our own day. To wish to disturb and prevent this is
nothing other than to seek a sacrilegious path to true religion. Those
who do this, not even if what they want is granted to them, can
reach where they intend to go. . . .

When we seek after religion, God alone is able to come to our
assistance in this vast difficulty. Indeed, we ought not to be seeking
true religion unless we believe that God exists and aids human
minds. For what do we desire to investigate with such great
exertion? What do we hope to attain? Where do we long to reach?
Something whose existence or pertinence to us we disbelieve?
Nothing is more perverse than such a state of mind. You would not
dare seek a favor of me, or you would do so with clear impudence, if
you did not believe that I, the one to give you the favor, existed; and
yet you come demanding the discovery or religion when you
suppose either that God does not exist, or, if he does, that he does
not care for us. What if religion is so great a thing that it cannot be
found unless it is sought zealously with all our powers? What if this
most difficult discovery exercises the mind of the seeker for the
grasping and making known of what shall be found? For what is
more pleasing and familiar to our eyes than this light? And yet after
a longtime darkness, our eyes cannot tolerate and endure the light.
What is better suited for a body exhausted by illness than food and
drink? Yet we see that convalescents are restrained and prevented
lest they dare to give themselves over to a satiety proper to those
who are strong, and thus by eating return themselves to that sickness
on account of which they were refusing to eat. Why do I speak of
convalescents? Don't we urge the ailing to eat something? In the
face of their so great disgust for food would they comply with our
urging unless they believed they would recover from their sickness?
When, therefore, will you give yourself over to a most painstaking
and laborious inquiry? When will you dare to impose upon yourself

an occupation and a care as great as religion itself warrants, when you don't believe that what you are seeking exists? It is, therefore, rightly ordaine by the majesty of Catholic discipline that before all else faith be prevailed upon those who approach religion. . . .

I judge that to believe before reasoning, since one is not suited to perceive reason, and by faith to ready one's soul to receive the seeds of truth, is not only most healthy but utterly the only way for health to return to sick souls. . . . Finally I confess that I have come to believe in Christ and to have resolved for my soul that what he said is true, even if no reason supports it.

We see how Christ himself . . . before all else and beyond all else wanted to be believed, since those with whom he was dealing were not yet fit to perceive their way to the divine secrets. For what else did so many and such great miracles accomplish—even Christ himself said that they were done for no other reason—than that he would be believed? He led the foolish with faith; you lead with reason. He cried out for belief, you cry out against it. He praised believers; you chide them. Would he change water to wine, to mention only one such marvel, if human beings could follow him, although he did nothing of this sort but merely taught? Or is this voice not to be listened to: You believe in God, believe also in me (Jn. 14.1)? Is that one to be blamed for rashness who did not want him to come to his house, believing that at Christ's mere command his boy's illness would pass? (Mt. 8.8). Christ, therefore, brought a medicine which would heal the most corrupt ways. By his miracles he gained authority, by his authority he deserved faith, by faith he drew together the multitude, with the multitude he possessed posterity, and with posterity he made religion firm. . . .

Wherefore, even though I have no capacity to teach, still I do not cease from giving this admonishment. Many wish to appear wise; and it is not easy to discern whether they are wise or foolish. With full attention, with all your vows, with groans and, finally, even with tears, if that can happen, pray to God that he might deliver you from the evil of error, if your heart is fixed upon the blessed life. And this will come about more readily, if you would freely observe his precepts, which he has willed to make firm by the so great authority of the Catholic Church.

For one who is wise is so closely joined in mind to God that nothing may come between to separate them. God is truth; and no one is in any way wise without touching the truth in one's mind. Wherefore, we cannot deny that, between human foolishness and

the most pure truth of God, there is placed, as a kind of inter-
mediacy, human wisdom. For one who is wise, so far as it is given to
one, imitates God. Moreover, nothing is closer by for the foolish
human being to imitate wholesomely than is the wise human being.
It is not easy, however, as has been said, to understand the wise
human being with reason. Thus it is necessary that certain miracles
be presented to the eyes, which fools use much more agreeably than
they do the mind, so that the life and ways of human beings moved
by authority might first be purified and thus might be made able to
accept reason.

Since, therefore, a human being had to be imitated and yet hope
could not be placed in human being, what could happen that would
be more divinely merciful and generous than that God's pure,
eternal, unchangeable wisdom itself, to which we must cling, should
see fit to take up human being? Not only did he accomplish those
wonders with which we might be incited to follow God, but he also
suffered those things by which we are discouraged from following
God. Now no one can obtain the most certain and supreme good
without having loved it with a full and perfect love; and that is not
possible so long as one dreads bodily evils and accidents. He,
moreover, by his wondrous faith and works, won our love; and by
dying and rising he banished our fear. And truly in all else that he
did, of which the account is long, he proved himself to be such that
we could have some sense of how far the divine clemency can reach
and of how high human infirmity can be lifted up.

This is, believe me, most wholesome authority. This is a prelimi-
nary raising of our mind above its earthly habitation. This is
conversion from the love of this world to the true God. Authority
alone moves the foolish to hasten toward wisdom. So long as we
cannot understand pure things, it is miserable, indeed, to be
deceived by authority; but it is certainly more miserable to be
unmoved thereby. For if the providence of God does not preside
over human affairs, religion should be paid no heed. But if both the
appearance of all things, which surely must be believed to emanate
from a font of true beauty, and some inward conscience exhort, as it
were both publicly and privately, the better souls to seek God and to
serve him, then we should not despair of this same God's himself
having established an authority for our support, like a secure stair,
in rising to God. Moreover, reason aside, this authority is, as we
have often said, most difficult for the foolish to understand in its
purity and yet it moves us in two ways, partly by miracles and partly

by the multitude of those who follow it. Neither of these is a
necessity for one who is wise, as no one would deny. But now it is a
matter of our being able to be wise, namely, of our being able to
cleave to the truth. And this is surely not possible for the unclean
soul. The more one is purified of those uncleannesses, the more
readily does one behold what is true. Therefore, to wish to see what
is true so as thereby to purify one's soul is certainly perverse and
preposterous, since the soul is purified so as thereby to see what is
true. Authority is thus at hand for one who is unable to behold the
truth so that one may become fit for that and may allow oneself to
be purified.

(De util. cred., 10.23-24; 13.29;
14.31; 14.32; 15.33; 16.34)

• 21 •

What, therefore, do we do when we are intent on being wise
except with all possible dispatch somehow to give over our whole
soul to what we touch with our mind, to station our soul there and
to keep it lastingly fixed thereon? What do we do except to rejoice
no longer in what is privately ours, and which ensnares us in things
that pass. What do we do except to strip ourselves of all the
affections of times and places and apprehend what is one and the
same always?

For just as the soul is the whole life of the body, so God is the
blessed life of the soul. So long as we do this, until we bring it to
completion, we are en route. And consider the fact that we are given
to rejoice in these true and certain goods which shine so brightly
even now in this shadowed journey. See whether this is what
scripture means when it describes how wisdom deals with its lovers
when they come seeking it. For it is written: In their journeys it
appears to bring them joy and with all-embracing providence meets
them along the way (Ws. 6.7).

(De lib. arb., 2.16.41)

• 22 •

Seek his face always (Ps. 104.4). What is the face of God, except
the presence of God? . . . But what does this mean: Seek his face

always? I know, indeed, that it is good for me to cling to God (P 72.28). But if God is always sought, when is he found? When he said "always" did he mean for the whole of this life which we now live, whence we come to know what we ought to do when he who is to be sought is also found? In fact, faith has already found him; but hope is yet seeking him. Love, moreover, has both found him through faith and seeks to possess him through sight, where he will then be found so as to satisfy us and to be sought no more. For unless faith found him in this life, it would not be said: Seek the lord. . . . And if, once found by faith, he were not still to be sought, it would not be said: If we hope for what we do not see, we wait with patience for it (Rm. 8.25).

And truly this is what is meant by: Seek his face always—that finding him should not bring an end to this seeking by which love is testified, but, as love grows, the seeking of him who has been found should also grow.

(En. in Ps., 104.3)

• 23 •

What, then, are we? We have already been born of him. But because we exist in hope, he says: Most beloved, we are now sons of God (1 Jn. 3.1). Now already? What, therefore, is it that we look for, if already we are sons of God? To this he says: It has not yet been revealed what we shall be (1 Jn. 3.2). But what else shall we be than the sons of God? Listen to what follows: We know that when he has appeared we shall be like him; for we shall see him as he is (ibid.). Now, attend to what is said "to be." You know that what is not merely said "to be" but which truly "is" is unchangeable. It remains always, knows no change, and in no respect is corruptible. It does not improve in that it is perfect; and never fails in that it is eternal.

And what is this? In the beginning was the word, and the word was with God. And the word was God (Jn. 1.1). And what is this? He who was in the form of God, did not think it thievery to be in the form of God (Ph. 2.6). The wicked are unable to see Christ in this way, in the form of God, the word of God, only begotten of the father, equal to the father. But according as the word has become flesh, the wicked shall be able to see him, since surely on the day of judgment they too shall see him. For he will come to judge even as he came to be judged. In form human, yet God; for accursed are all those who have put their hope in human being (Jr. 17.5).

As a human being he came to be judged; and as a human being he will come to judge. And if he will not be seen, what does it mean when it is written in scripture that: They will look upon him whom they have pierced? (Jn. 19.37). For of the impious it is written that they will see and will be confounded. How will the impious not see when he sets some on the right and others on the left? To those placed on the right he will say: Come, blessed of my father, receive the kingdom; and to those on the left: Go into eternal fire (Mt. 25.34,41). They shall see, but only the form of a servant; the form of God they shall not see. Why? Because they are impious; and the lord himself says: Blessed are the pure of heart, for they shall see God (Mt. 5.8).

Therefore, brethren, we are to see a certain vision, which eye has not seen, nor ear heard, nor has it entered into the human heart (1 Co. 2.9), a certain vision excellent beyond all earthly beauty, that of gold and silver, of groves and fields, beyond the beauty of sea and sky, beyond the beauty of sun and moon, beyond the beauty of stars and the angels, surpassing all things.

What, therefore, shall we be, when we shall see this? What has been promised to us? We shall be like him; for we shall see him as he is (1 Jn. 3.2). The tongue has done what it could do, it has sounded the words. The rest is left to the thoughts of the heart.

(Tr. in Joann ep., 4.5-6)

• 24 •

John the evangelist has begun his gospel in this way: In the beginning was the word, and the word was with God; and the word was God. The word was in the beginning with God. All things have been made through him; and without him nothing which has been made has been made. In him was life and the life was the light of human beings; and the darkness grasped it not. There was a human being sent out from God, whose name was John. He came for the sake of witness, to bear witness to the light, so that all might believe through him. He was not the light, but came to bear witness to the light. It was the true light which illumines everyone coming into this world. He was in the world, and the world was made through him, and the world knew him not. He came unto his own, and his own received him not. To as many as received him, however, he gave the power of becoming sons of God, to those who believe in his name, who are not born of blood, nor of the will of the flesh, nor of the will of human being, but of God. And the word was made flesh, and dwelt among us. And we have seen his glory, glory as the only begotten of the father, full of grace and of truth (Jn. 1.1-14). This whole passage, which I have cited from the gospel, has to do in its first sections with what is unchangeable and eternal, the contemplation of which makes us blessed; and, in its later sections, eternal things are called to mind mixed with temporal things. And, in this way, some things there pertain to science and other things to wisdom. ... For in the beginning was the word, and the word was with God; and the word was God. The word was in the beginning with God. All things have been made through him; and without him nothing which has been made has been made. In him was life and the life was the light of human beings; and the darkness grasped it not. These words require a contemplative life and must be discerned with the intellectual mind. And, in this, the more one advances, the more wise one doubtlessly becomes.

But on account of his saying: The light shines in the darkness and the darkness grasped it not, there was need by faith too, by which that which was not seen might be believed. For by darkness he wanted us to understand the hearts of mortals turned away from light of this sort and less well suited to behold it. On this account, he goes on to say: There was a human being sent form God, whose name was John. He came for the sake of witness, to bear witness to the light, so that all might believe through him. This is already accomplished in time, and pertains to science, which is comprised of historical knowledge. We think of John the human being, however, in terms of a fantasy impressed upon our memory from our knowledge of human nature. And they think in this same manner, whether they do not believe these words or whether they do. For it is known to both what human being is, whose exterior part, namely, the body, they have learned through the body's lights [eyes]. As for the interior part, namely, the soul, they possess it known because they are themselves human beings and converse with human beings; and so they are able to think what is said herein: There was a human being whose name was John. For they know names both from speaking them and from hearing them. But what is said therein: sent from God, those who possess it, possess it in faith. And those who do not possess it in faith, either waver in doubt or deride it in their unfaith. Both, moreover—unless they are among those utter fools who say in their heart: There is no God (Ps. 13.1)—when they hear these words think two things: what God is and what it is to be sent from God. And if they do not possess these things themselves as they really are, they surely come as close as they are able.

Furthermore, the faith itself, which anyone sees to exist in one's heart, if one believes, or which one sees not to exist in one's heart, if one does not believe—that faith we know in a different way. We do not know it as we know bodies which we see with our bodily eyes and which we retain in our memory through their images and even think of, though absent. Nor do we know it as we know these things, which we have not seen and yet which we somehow form in thought from things we have seen and commend to memory whither we may not return when we wish to discern them similarly in remembrance, or rather to discern their images such as we have tried to fix them there. Nor do we know it as we do a living human being, whose soul, even though we do not see it, we conjecture from our own, and from whose bodily movements we gaze upon in our thinking the living human being as we have learned to do from our seeing. Not in this way is faith seen in the heart wherein it is and by the one whose faith it is. Rather, a most certain science grasps it and conscience proclaims it.

Although we are not, then, commanded to believe on account of our being unable to see what we are commanded to believe, yet, when that very faith is in us, we see it in us. For the faith of absent things is present and the faith of outside things is within, and the faith of unseen things is seen; and still this faith itself comes to be in time in the hearts of human beings. And, if believers become unbelievers, faith perishes from them. At times, moreover, faith is accommodated even to things that are false; for we are thus accustomed to saying: Faith was placed in him and he was deceiving. Such faith, if indeed it should be spoken of as faith, perishes from hearts without fault, when the truth is found out and drives out faith. Moreover, as is to be desired, the faith of true things passes over into the things themselves. We should not, then, speak of "perishing," when those things which were believed are seen. For it is still to be called faith, even though faith has been defined in the Epistle to the Hebrews and said to be the conviction of things which are not seen (Heb. 11.1).

What follows is, as we have called it, a temporal action: He came for the sake of witness, to bear witness to the light, so that all might believe through him. For witness is borne in time even concerning an eternal thing, which is the intelligible light. To bear witness to this light, John came, who was not the light, but came to bear witness to the light. For it goes on: It was the true light which illumines everyone coming into this world. He was in the world, and the world was made through him, and the world know him not. He came into his own, and his own received him not. Those who knew the Latin language understand all of these words from those things which they have come to know already. Some of those things, more-over, have become known to us through the senses of the body, such as human being, such as the world itself, whose so evident greatness we discern, and such as the sounds of these very words; for hearing too is a sense of the body. But others of those things have become known through the soul's reason, such as that which was said in saying: And his own received him not. For by this saying it is understood that: They did not believe him. And what this is [i.e., what it is for them not to have believed] we have come to know, not by any sense of the body but by the reason of the soul.

We have learned the meaning, and not only the sounds, of those words themselves, partly through the sense of the body, and partly through the reason of the soul. Nor have we heard those words now for the first time; but we had already heard them. We had come to know and retained in memory not only the words themselves but also what they signified; and we recognized them here. For when this two-syllable word—*mundus* [world]—is spoken, as it is a sound, surely a corporeal thing has become known through the body, that is, through the eyes of the flesh. Indeed, the world, inasmuch as it is known, is known to see-ers. But this four-syllable word—*crediderunt* [they believed]—by its sound, for it is a body, reaches us through the ear of the flesh. What it signifies, moreover, is known through no sense of the body but through the reason of the soul. For unless we knew through the body what *crediderunt* is, we would not under-stand what they did not do, concerning whom it has been said: And his own received him not. Therefore, the sound of the word sounds in upon the ears of the body from without and strikes the sense called hearing.

The specific appearance, too, of human being is known to us in ourselves and, from without, is present to the senses of the body in others: to the eyes when seen, to the ears when heard, to touch, when held and touched. For this specific appearance also has in our memory its own image, indeed incorporeal, but yet like a body. Finally, the marvelous beauty of the world itself is from without present both to our sight and to that sense called touch, if we touch any part of it. It too has within us in our memory its own image, to which we return, when we think of it, whether we are behind seven walls or in the midst of darkness. But about these images of corporeal things, which are indeed incorporeal yet possessing the likenesses of bodies and pertaining to the life of the outer human being, we have already spoken sufficiently in book eleven.

We treat now, however, of the inner human being and of its science, that which belongs to temporal and changeable things. When, in the inner human being's intending, something is taken up, even concerning those things which pertain to the outer human being, it must be taken up for this reason, that something might therein be learned to serve rational science. And through this, the rational use of things which we have in common with the irrational animals pertains to the inner human being; nor can this use rightly be said to be common to us and to the irrational animals.

Those who have faith are called faithful; and those who do not have it, unfaithful, such as those who did not receive the son of God when he came unto his own. Although faith comes to be in us from hearing, it still does not belong to that sense of the body which is called hearing; for it is not a sound. Nor does faith belong to the eyes of this flesh; for it is not color or bodily form. Nor does it belong to that sense called touch; for it has nothing of flesh. Nor does it belong to any sense whatever of the body; for faith is a thing of the heart and not of the body. Nor is it outside of us, but rather in our inmost being. No human being sees faith in another; but each one sees faith within one's own self. Finally, it can be feigned by pretense and thus can be supposed to be in someone in whom it is not. Therefore, each one sees one's faith within oneself. One, moreover, believes but does not see it to exist in another; and this belief becomes all the more firm, the more one recognizes the fruits of that faith, fruits which faith is accustomed to bringing about through love (Ga. 5.6).

Wherefore, this faith is common to all those concerning whom the evangelist then goes on to say: To as many as received him, however, he gave the power of becoming sons of God, to those who believe in his name, who are born not of blood, nor of the will of the flesh, nor of the will of man, but of God. This faith is not common as is some bodily form to be seen by the eyes of all to whom it is present; for in some manner the gaze of all who look upon it is in some way informed by that very one object. Rather, faith is common as the human countenance is said to be common to all human beings; for this is said in such a way that individuals still have their very own countenances.

We say with the greatest truth that faith is indeed impressed from one doctrine upon the hearts of individual believers who believe this one same thing. Yet, those things which are believed are one thing; but the faith by which they are believed is another thing. The former are amidst those things of which it is said either that they are or that they have been or that they will be. The latter, however, is in the soul of one who believes and is visible to that one alone where it is; although it is in others, it is not this very faith, but a similar faith. For it is one, not numerically, but generically. Yet, on account of its similarity and lack of diversity, we speak of there being one faith rather than many faiths. For even when we see two human beings very much alike we wonder at this and say that they have one face between them. . . . And yet he who says: O woman, great is your faith (Mt. 15.28), and to another: Why have you doubted, you of slight faith? (Mt. 14.31), it means that each one has one's own faith.

(De Trin., 13.1.2-13.2.5)

• 25 •

Now let us see what this extended discussion has accomplished, what it has gathered together, and where it has reached. It belongs to all human beings to will to be oneself blessed; yet that faith, by which the heart is cleansed and brought to blessedness, does not belong to all human beings. And so it happens that, through that faith which not all will, one must strive toward that blessedness which no one who exists cannot will. All see within their heart that they will to be blessed; and so great in this respect is the conspiracy of human nature that one may not be deceived in projecting this same will from one's own mind to another's. For we know that everyone wills this.

Many despair, however, of being able to be immortal, although what all will, namely, to be blessed, is not possible otherwise. Still, all will to be immortal, if they could be so. But in not believing that they can be immortal, they do not live so far as for it to be possible. Faith is, therefore, necessary for our reaching blessedness in all the good things of human nature, that is, of soul and of body. Moreover, this same faith holds that this faith is defined in Christ who has risen in the flesh from the dead never to die again and that no one is delivered from the domination of the devil through the forgiveness of sins except through him, and that in the domains of the devil life must necessarily be miserable, unendingly so, and should be called death rather than life. . . .

It has seemed right to us, ascending, as it were, by steps, to seek out both in science and in wisdom in the inner human being some manner of trinity proper to the inner human being just as we previously sought a trinity in the outer human being, so that, with a mind more exercised in these inferior things, we might come to attend, according to our measure, even if this be possible, to that trinity which is God, at least obscurely and through a mirror (1 Co. 13.12).

Say that someone, therefore, has commended to memory the words of this faith in their sounds alone without knowing what they mean, just as those who are ignorant of Greek are accustomed to retaining in memory Greek words, or, likewise, Latin words, or words of any other tongue of which they are ignorant. Considering that those verbal sounds are in one's memory even when not being thought about and that the vision of one's remembrance is formed from them when they are being thought about, and that the will of the one remembering and thinking joins the two together, considering this, does not such a one have in the soul a certain trinity? Yet, in no way should we say that such a one, acting in this manner, acts according to the trinity of the inner human being but rather according to the trinity of the outer human being; because such a one remembers—and when willing, attends to as much as is willed—only what pertains to the sense of the body called hearing and such a one turns round in this kind of thought nothing but images of corporeal things, namely, of sounds. If, however, one retains and recalls what those words mean, then, indeed, one does something belonging to the interior human being; but one should not yet be said or supposed to be living according to the trinity of the interior human being unless one loves what is proclaimed and promised therein (i.e., in the remembered words of this faith).

For one can also retain and think about those things proclaimed and promised such that, judging them to be false, one even tries to refute them. The will, therefore, which joins together those things retained in memory and those things impressed from it upon the vision of thought, indeed completes a certain trinity, since the will itself is the third. But one is not living in accord with this trinity when those things which are thought are found unacceptable, as though they were false. When, however, those things are believed to be true and when those things which are there to be loved are loved, one is already living according to the trinity of the inner human being, for each one lives in accord with what one loves. How, moreover, may things be loved when they are not known but only believed? This question has already been treated in preceding books; and it was found that no one loves that of which one is altogether ignorant. Rather, when unknown things are said to be loved, they are loved from those things which are known.

Now we bring this book to a close in such a way as to call to mind that the just human being lives by faith (Rm. 1.17), a faith which works through love (Ga. 5.6) in such a way that those virtues by which one lives prudently, bravely, temperately, and justly, are all referred to that same faith. For otherwise they could not be true virtues. In this life, however, those virtues are not so powerful that there are not some occasions when the remission of sins of one kind or another is necessary here. And this remission comes to be only through him who has vanquished with his own blood the prince of sinners. From this faith and from such a life whatever notions are in the soul of the faithful human being—when they are held in the memory, and examined in remembrance, and accepted by the will— render a certain trinity of their own kind. But the image of God . . . is not yet in it.

(De Trin., 13.20.25,26)

· 26 ·

Wherefore, since it is written: As long as we are in the body, we are estranged from the lord; for we walk by faith, not by sight (2 Co. 5.6-7), then certainly so long as the just human being lives by faith (Rm. 1.17), even though such a one lives in accord with the inner human being, and even though through this same temporal faith one ascends toward the truth and strains toward eternal things, nevertheless in the holding, the contemplating, and the loving of one's temporal faith there is not yet such a trinity as should now be called the image of God, lest that should seem to be constituted in temporal things which is to be constituted in eternal things.

Surely, when the human mind sees its own faith by which it believes what it does not see, it does not see anything everlasting. For this will not always be, which certainly will not be when that estrangement, by which we are estranged from the lord and so must of necessity walk by faith, with which sight we shall see face to face (1 Co. 13.12), just as now, although we do not see, yet because we believe, we shall deserve to see and we shall rejoice to have been brought to sight through faith. For faith, by which things unseen are believed, will no longer be; rather, there will be sight, by which things are believed and seen. Therefore, even if we then remember this spent mortal life and recall in memory that we once believed what we did not see, that faith will be reckoned among things past and spent, not among things past and present, nor among things present and always remaining. Consequently, even this trinity, which now consists in the memory, sight, and love of this same present and abiding faith, will then be discovered to be spent and past, not enduring. The conclusion here is that, if this trinity is already an image of God, it should not itself be regarded among those things which always are, but rather among those things which are passing away.

Moreover, since the nature of the soul is immortal and since from the first instant of its creation the soul has never ceased to be, far be it that that, than which the soul has nothing better, should not endure with its immortality. Surely what better thing has been created in the soul's nature, than the fact that it has been made after the image of its creator? Therefore, that which it is right to call the image of God is not to be found in the holding, the contemplating, and the loving of faith, which will not always be, but is to be found in that which will always be.

Or shall we investigate this matter somewhat more diligently and abstrusely to see whether this is how the matter stands? For it can be said that this trinity does not perish, even when faith itself will have passed away, since, just as we now hold faith in memory, perceive it in thought, and love it with our will, so also then, when we shall both hold in memory and recall our having once had faith and when we shall join both of these with will as a third, the same trinity will remain. For if, in its passing away, faith has not left in us some trace, as it were, then surely we will not have in our memory anything of it to which we might return—recalling it as past and joining both of these with the will's intending as the third element—both that which was in the memory even when we were not thinking of it and that which is formed from our thinking of it.

But one who says this does not distinguish between this trinity which exists now, when we hold, see, and love the faith present within us, and that trinity which will exist then, when we shall behold in remembrance not faith itself but, as it were, an imaginative vestige of it preserved in our memory and when we shall join these two—namely, that which was in the memory of the one retaining it and that which is impressed from it upon the sight of the one recalling it—with the will as a third.

So that this might be understood, let us take an example from corporeal things. ... Surely, as we ascend from lower to higher things or as we pass from outer things to inner things we discover the first trinity in the body which is seen, in the sight of one who sees, which sight is formed from that body when one sees it, and in the intention of the will which joins the two together. We may constitute a trinity similar to this one, when faith, which now dwells within us, like that body in a place, is so constituted in our memory that the thought of the one recalling it is formed therefrom, just as the sight of the one seeing is formed from that body, and when will is accounted as a third with these other two so that a trinity might be completed. The will, in this case, connects and conjoins the faith constitued in memory and a certain effigy of it impressed upon the sight of remembrance, just as in that trinity of corporeal vision, the intention of the will conjoins the form of the body which is seen and the corresponding formation which comes to be in the sight of the one perceiving.

Let us, then, suppose that that body, which was being perceived, has disappeared and perished and that nowhere has there remained any part of it which one's gaze might return to see. Because the image of that corporeal thing already spent and past remains in the memory, when the gaze of the one recalling it is informed, and the two are joined together by the will as a third, should this be said to be the same trinity which had been when the form of the body fixed in place was being seen? Surely not, but rather a wholly other trinity; for, apart from the fact that the former was from without and the latter was from within, the former was clearly made by the form of the present body and the latter was made by the image of the past body.

So, too, in this matter which we are considering and on which account we have judged that this example should be employed: the faith which is now in our soul, like that body situated in a place, while it is held, looked upon, and loved, effects a certain trinity; but this very trinity will not be, when this faith will no longer be in the soul, as a body in a place. What will, in truth, then be, when we will recall it as having been but as being no longer in us, will be an altogether other trinity. For this trinity is now made by the thing itself, present and affixed to the soul of the one who believes; but that trinity which will then be will be made by the imagination of the thing past left in the memory of the one who recalls it.

Neither, therefore, will that trinity, which does not now exist, be the image of God; nor is this trinity, which will not then exist, the image of God. Rather, the image of the creator, which has been implanted immortally in its immortality, is to be found in the soul, namely, in the rational or intellectual part of human being. For just as the very immortality of the soul is said to be according to a certain measure—for even the soul has a death of its own when it is without the blessed life which should be called the true life of the soul; but the soul is called immortal on account of its never being without life of some sort, even when it is most miserable—so, even though reason or intellect may now be lulled to sleep in it, appearing at one time slight and at another time great, the human soul never exists without being rational and intellectual. And on this account, if the human soul has been made after the image of God according to this, that it can use reason and intellect to understand and to behold God, then surely from the first instant in which that so great and marvelous nature began to be—whether this image be so decayed as to be almost nothing, whether it be obscure and deformed, or whether it be shining and beautiful—it always is.

Finally, the divine scripture laments the disfigurement of the soul's dignity, saying: Although human being walks in the image of God, yet in vain is it disquieted. Human being stores up a treasure and does not know for whom it shall gather those things (Ps. 38.7). Thus it would not attribute vanity to the image of God, unless it saw that it was deformed. Yet in saying: Although human being walks in the image of God, the divine scripture gives sufficient indication that that disfigurement is not so great as to take away its being an image. Wherefore, this sentence can be truly stated beginning with either part, so that just as it is said: Although human being walks in the image of God, yet in vain is it disquieted, so it may be said:

Although human being is disquieted in vain, yet it walks in the image of God. For although human nature is great, it can nevertheless be corrupted, because it is not the highest nature. And although it could be corrupted because it is not the highest nature, yet, because it is capable of the highest nature and can be participant in it, its nature is great.

Let us seek, therefore, in this image of God a certain trinity of its own kind, with the help of him who made us after his own image. For otherwise we cannot investigate these things to our salvation and, in accord with the wisdom which is from him, find something.

(De Trin., 14.2.4-14.4.6)

• 27

This trinity, then, of the mind [i.e., memory-understanding-love] is the image of God, not because the mind remembers itself, understands itself, and loves itself, but rather because it can remember, understand, and love its maker. And when it does this, the mind is made wise. If it does not do this, even if it remembers, understands, and loves itself, the mind is foolish. Let the mind, then, remember, understand, and love its God after whose image it has been made. To say the same thing more briefly, let the mind worship God, who is not made, and who has made the mind capable of God and made possible the mind's participation in God. For this reason it is written: Behold, wisdom is the worship of God *(Ps.* 28.28). And not by its own light but by participation in that supreme light will the mind be wise. And where the eternal light is, there it will blessedly reign. For this wisdom of human being is spoken of in such a way as also to be the wisdom of God. For then it is a true wisdom, since if it is human, it is vain.

(De Trin., 14.12.15)

• 28 •

Concerning the creature too which God has made, we have, insofar as we could, admonished those who demand reason in such matters that they should see the things which are understood, the

invisible things of God, through the things which are made (Rm.
1.20), and most of all through that rational or intellectual creature,
which was made after the image of God. Through that creature, as
if in a mirror, they would discern, insofar as they could, if they
could, in our memory, understanding, and will, the trinity that is
God.

Whoever comes to an enduring insight into these things [memory-
understanding-will] by nature divinely established in one's mind, an
insight into how great a thing dwells in the mind, whence even an
everlasting and unchangeable nature can be recalled, beheld,
desired, whoever remembers it by memory, beholds it through
intelligence, and embraces it in love, truly, such a one discovers the
image of that highest trinity. Human being ought to refer every
living thing to the remembering, the seeing, and the loving of that
supreme trinity so that human being might remember it, contemplate it, and find its delight therein. But lest anyone so compare this
image made by that same trinity and yet changed for the worse by
its own fault that one judges this created trinity to be like that trinity
in every respect, I have admonished that one, as much as seemed
sufficient, rather to consider the great unlikeness in that likeness, of
whatever sort.

Indeed I have taken care, as far as I was able, to give sign of God
the father, and God the son, namely God the begetter who has in
some way in his own word coeternal with himself spoken everything
which he substantially has, spoken his very word, God, who himself
substantially has nothing more and nothing less than what is in him
who begot the word, not deceitfully but truthfully. My aim is not
that all this may be seen now face to face but rather that it may be
seen in an enigma through this likeness, by means of conjectures,
however insignificant, in the memory and the understanding of our
mind, attributing to the memory everything which we know, even if
we are not thinking of it, and attributing to intelligence the
informing of thought in its own particular way.

For we are mostly said to understand when we think about what
we have found to be true; and this we indeed leave again in our
memory. But that is a more abstruse profundity of our memory,
where we first find something in thinking it and where the ultimate
word is begotten which belongs to no tongue—as it were, science
from science, vision from vision, and understanding which appears
in thought from understanding which was already in memory but

which was latent there—although even thought itself, unless it had a certain memory of its own, would not return to those things, which it had left in memory, when it was thinking of other things.

Moreover, concerning the holy spirit, I have shown nothing in this enigma which would appear to be like him except our will, or love [amor], or [decisive] love [dilectio], which is a more prevailing will. For our will, which is ours by nature, has various affectations depending on whether we find the things which adjoin it or which it encounters to be alluring or offensive. What does this mean? Are we going to say that our will, when it is right, does not know what to desire and what to avoid? But if it does know, there is indeed in the will a certain science of its own, which could not be without memory and understanding.

Or should we listen to anyone who says that love does not know what it does when it does not act wrongly? Therefore, just as there is understanding, so too there is love in that principal memory, in which we find prepared and put away that to which we are able to come in thinking; for we also find those two there when, in thinking, we find ourselves both understanding and loving something. And those two were there even when we were not thinking of them. Also, just as there is memory, so there is love in that understanding which is formed in thought. When we say that we have come to know, we speak within us the true word without the language of any nation; for the gaze of thought does not return to anything except by remembering and does not take care to return except by loving. Thus love, which joins together, as a parent and its offspring, the vision constituted in memory and the vision formed by thought about it—love which cannot be without memory and understanding—would not know what it would love rightly unless it had a science proper to desiring.

(De Trin., 15.20.39-15.21.41)

· 29 ·

If, therefore, we seek anything above this nature, and seek in truth, it is God, namely, a nature uncreated but creating. Whether this nature is the trinity is what we must now demonstrate not only to believers, on the authority of the divine scripture, but indeed even to those who would understand, if we are able, by some reason. . . .

For the very God whom we are seeking will, as I hope, come to our assistance lest our labor prove fruitless and so that we might understand how it may be said in the sacred psalm: Let the heart of those who seek the lord rejoice; seek the lord and be confirmed; seek his face always (Ps. 104.3-4). Indeed, it seems that what is always being sought is never found; and how will the heart of those who seek now rejoice rather than be saddened, if they have not been able to find what they are seeking? For it does not say, let the heart of those who find rejoice, but rather, let the heart of those who seek rejoice. And yet Isaiah the prophet testifies that the lord God can be found while he is sought, when he says: Seek the lord; and, as soon as you have found him, call upon him. And when he has drawn close to you, let the impious desert their ways and the iniquitous their thoughts (Is. 55.6, 7).

If, therefore, he who is sought can be found, why is it said: Seek his face always? Or is he perhaps to be sought even when found? Are incomprehensible things to be inquired after such that, lest one regard oneself as having found nothing, one could find out how incomprehensible is that which one was seeking. Why, then, does one seek thus, if one comprehends that what one seeks is incomprehensible, unless because one must not cease so long as one is advancing in the pursuit itself of incomprehensible things, and becoming better and better by seeking so great a good, which is sought so as to be found and found so as to be sought? For it is sought so that it might be found all the more sweetly and is found so that it might be sought all the more avidly.

What is said in the Book of Ecclesiastes may be seen in this light, when wisdom says: Those who eat of me shall hunger and those who drink of me shall yet thirst (Qo. 24.29). For they eat and drink, because they find; and because they hunger and thirst, they yet seek. Faith seeks, understanding finds. On this account, the prophet says: Unless you believe, you shall not understand (Is. 7.9). And again understanding yet seeks him whom it has found, for, as is sung in the sacred psalm: God has looked down upon the sons of human beings so that he might see if there be one who understands or inquires after God (Ps. 13.2). For this reason, therefore, human being ought to be understanding, so that it might inquire after God.

(De Trin., 15.1-15.2.2)

• 30 •

Lord, our God, we believe in you, father, and son, and holy spirit. For the truth would not say: Go, baptize all nations, in the name of the father, and of the son, and of the holy spirit (Mt. 28.19), unless you were a trinity. Nor would you command us, lord God, to baptize in the name of him who is not the lord God. Nor would it be said by the divine voice: Hear, O Israel. The lord your God is one God (Dt. 6.4), unless you were the trinity in such a way as to be the one lord God. And if you were yourself God the father and were yourself the son, your word, Jesus Christ, and your gift, the holy spirit, we would not read in the books of truth: God sent his son (Ga. 4.4; Jn. 3.17); nor would you, O only begotten, say of the holy spirit: Whom the father will send in my name (Jn. 14.26), and: Whom I will send to you from the father (Jn. 15.26).

Directing my intention, so far as I was able, so far as you made me able, in accord with the rule of faith, I have desired to see with the intellect what I have believed; I have argued and labored much. Lord, my God, my one hope, hear me, lest in exhaustion I should not wish to seek you. Rather, may I seek your face ardently, always (Ps. 104.4). Grant to me the strength of seeking you, who have made me find you and who have given me the hope of finding you more and more. Before you are my strength and my weakness; preserve the one and heal the other. Before you are my knowledge and my ignorance. Where you have opened to me, receive me as I enter; and where you have closed to me, open to me as I knock. Let me remember you, let me understand you, let me love you. Increase these in me until you renew me wholly.

I know that it is written: In a multitude of words, you will not escape sin (Pr. 10.19). But if only I would speak in this manner alone, in proclaiming your word and in praising you. Not only would I then escape sin, but I would aquire a good reward, regardless of how much I might say in this manner. For that human being, blessed of you, would not enjoin a sin upon his own true son in the faith, to whom he wrote, saying: Preach the word; be urgent in season and out of season (2 Tm. 4.2). Should we say that that man did not speak much, who not only in season but also out of season was not silent, Lord, concerning your word? But what he said was not "much," because it was only what was necessary.

Deliver me, God, from the multitude of words which I suffer deep within my soul, a soul which is miserable in your sight and is in flight to your mercy. For I do not keep silent in my thoughts, even when my voice is silent. And if, indeed, I thought nothing except what would please you, I would not, of course, ask that you deliver me from this multitude of words. But my thoughts are many—you know of what sort—human thoughts; for they are vain (Ps. 93.11). Grant to me that I may not consent to them. And if they ever delight me, grant that I may nevertheless reject them and not linger in them as one sleeping. Nor may they ever acquire such power with me that something from them would carry over into my works. Rather, under your watch, may at least my opinion and my conscience be safe from them. A certain wise man, when he spoke of you in his book, which is now called by the special name of *Ecclesiasticus,* said: We say many things without reaching the mark, the sum and completion of our words is that he is all things (Si. 15.28). When, therefore, we will have come to you, these many things which we say without reaching the mark shall cease, and you will remain, one, all in all (1 Co. 15.28). And without ceasing we shall say one, praising you as you are; and in you even we shall have become one. Lord, our God, may God the trinity and those who are yours recognize as coming from you whatever I have said in these books; but if in any part from myself, may you and those who are yours forgive me. Amen.

(De Trin., 15.28.51)

Who Loves the Unknown?

The word of God spoken in time has given voice and warrant to the will of all human beings for blessedness. Regardless of the capacity of a few to reach purity and vision apart from a conscious relation to Christ and scripture, Augustine sees it as somehow necessary and fitting that all should follow Christ who is the way to blessedness. He criticizes the Platonists for their proud and rash refusal of divine revelation and grace,[1] and commends the life of faith to all.[2] Regarding the way to God and so to blessedness,

---

1. Cf. *Conf.,* 7.20-21; *De Trin.,* 4.18.24.
2. Cf. *De Trin.,* 13.20.25; 14.1.3.

Augustine comments that "we go to Him not by walking, but by loving" *(Epist.,* 155).

> For if wisdom and truth are not desired with all the powers of mind, in no way can it be found. But if it be sought as it deserves to be, it cannot withdraw or conceal itself from those who singularly love it. ... Ask, and you shall receive; seek, and you shall find; knock, and it shall be opened to you. (Mt. 7.7). Nothing is hidden which shall not be revealed (Mt. 10.26). It is love that asks, love that seeks, love that knocks, love that reveals, and love, too that finally endures in what has been revealed.
>
> *(De mor.,* 1.17.31)

Both negative knowledge of the supreme good and the negative will for blessedness, both the knowledge that one is ignorant of the supreme good and the refusal to embrace fully any good which is known, are inadequate, because for most human beings they are unfeasible. Indeed, Augustine speaks for most others too when he says, "I do not think I can ever possibly hold earthly things in the highest contempt until I will have seen that in comparison with which they become sordid" *(Solil.,* 1.14.24). We are to go to God by loving; but the backwards path of negative loving, the path of denial and withdrawal from all finally inadequate loves, is a path too arduous and abstract for many to follow.

Again we face Augustine's assertion that human being cannot love what it does not know.

> Who loves the unknown? Something can be known without being loved. What I seek to know is whether something can be loved without being known. Because, if this is not possible, no one loves God prior to knowing God ... unless God is loved through faith, the heart cannot be cleansed so as to be fit and well suited to the vision of God.
>
> *(De Trin.,* 8.4.6)

One is able to know not only by seeing for oneself but also by hearing from an authoritative source. The preaching of the word enlightens the minds and inflames the hearts of believers who would otherwise live in darkness and perversity. When the mind of the believer reflects upon and desires blessedness, "surely it does not remember its own blessedness. . . . Rather, it believes what the faith-worthy scriptures of its God tell of the blessedness of paradise" *(De. Trin.,* 14.15.21). Scripture proclaims that compared with which one's loves become sordid; and so the mind is purified and led to its proper love for God. For "even He therefore who is not known, but yet is believed, is loved" *(De Trin.,* 8.4.6). Faith, then, is a form of knowledge in that it enables one to love what is believed.

> We have not seen him but we are to see him; we have not known him but we are to know him. We believe in him whom we have not known. Or is it perhaps that we have known from faith but have not yet known from sight. But in faith we have both seen and known. For if faith does not yet see, why are we said to have been enlightened. There is an enlightening through faith and there is an enlightening through sight. Now, while on pilgrimage, we walk by faith and not by sight (2 Cor. 5.7). Thus our righteousness too is through faith and not through sight. Our righteousness will be perfect when we shall see by actual beholding.
>
> *(Tr. in Joann. ep.,* 4.8)

This brings us to still another of Augustine's trinitarian structures for understanding the life of human being: the holding [*retentio*]—contemplating [*contemplatio*]—and loving [*dilectio*] of faith (cf. *De Trin.,* 14.2.4), which is clearly a modification of the preceding structure of memory, understanding, and will as Augustine himself makes clear when he says of faith that "we hold it in memory, and perceive it in thought, and love it with our will" *(De Trin.,* 14.3.5). It is important throughout this discussion to keep in mind the ambiguity of the word faith *(fides)* for Augustine. He has already distinguished between the act of faith, the faith by which one believes *(fides qua),* and the content of faith, the faith which one believes *(fides quae)* (cf. *De Trin.,* 13.1.1). Consequently, the holding, contemplating, and loving of faith may be understood to refer both to the act of faith, and so to the person, as well as to the content of faith, and so to God. In the former sense, the mind knows itself and loves itself as not knowing and yet believing; and in the latter sense, the mind knows and loves God not as seen but as believed. Thus, knowledge and love of mind and knowledge and love of God begin to converge and to find their proper unity in the experience of faith. In the mystery of faith which encompasses both the divine activity which forms the object of faith and the human act which defines the subject of faith, eternity and time, nature and person, wisdom and science, inner and outer life, spirit and matter begin to touch and commingle.

Faith in both its senses is itself "a thing temporal" *(De Trin.,* 14.1.3). The act of faith is an act of will, an act of the person in the course of lifetime; and the content of faith has to do with actions and events and persons which belong to the temporal, to what has a beginning and an end, particularly "the things temporal which he that is eternal did and suffered as a human being for us, which human being he bore in time and raised to things eternal" *(De Trin.,* 14.1.3). Faith and the word of scripture belong to time and will pass away at the end of time. Faith will yield to vision; and scripture, the memory of the ever-present word, will yield to the very face of God.

> Who but you, our God, has made for us in your divine scripture a firmament of authority stretched above us? ... Above this firmament there are, I believe, other waters, immortal, spared earthly corruption. Let them praise your name, let the multitude of your angels, who dwell above the heavens, praise you. They have no need of looking up to this firmament and of coming to know your word by reading what is written there. For they see your face always, and they read therein without the syllables of time the will of your eternal will. ... Their book is never closed, nor is their scroll ever furled. For you yourself are their text and you are forever. You have placed them in an order above this firmament which you have set over the weakness of lesser peoples. Here below those peoples gaze upwards and come to know your mercy as it announces in time you who are the maker of time.
>
> *(Conf.,* 13.15)

The word of God spoken in time and preserved in scripture is God's compassionate dispensation to human beings, whose lives and livelihoods grow and wither beneath the clouds rather than before the face of God.

> Your scripture is indeed stretched over the peoples of the world even to the end of this present age. Heaven and earth shall both pass away; but your words shall not pass away. For the scroll will be rolled together and the grass over which it was spread will with all its own brilliance wither; but your word endures forever. Your word now presents itself to us in a riddle of clouds and through the mirror of the heavens, not as it is. For, although we are the beloved of your son, what we shall be has not yet dawned upon us.
>
> *(Conf.,* 13.15)

Jesus Christ, his life and his work, is a word spoken to human beings, able to hear and yet not to see in time, a word spoken to persons and so to hearts, accommodated to the temporal and yet full with the eternal. The knowledge human beings have of Jesus is not that of clear sight; rather it is a knowledge filtered through the diffuse clouds of time and reflected in the firmament of scripture, the knowledge one has of what for now can only be spoken and heard, in syllables, and not seen at once, for all time.

> Through the latticed net of flesh he attended to us, caressed us, inflamed us; and we are fast upon his scent. Moreover, when he appears we shall be like him, for we shall see him as he is. It is ours, Lord, to see him as he is; but our moment is not yet come.
>
> *(Conf.,* 13.15)

For now, Augustine is able to look upon God with love only like a confused reflection in a mirror, the mirror of scripture. Memory, understanding, and love of God (or the holding, contemplating, and loving of God) means, for the person in time, faithful memory, understanding, and love of the word spoken in time, that is, the faithful holding, contemplating, and loving of scripture. Correspondingly, in an extended discussion of 1 Corinthians 13.12 in his *De Trinitate,* Augustine has the mirror, the enigma, refer to himself, to the person in time (cf. *De Trin.,* 15.8.14). Memory, understanding, and love of mind or the holding, contemplating, and loving of mind means for the person the memory, understanding, and love of personal conversion, that is, the holding, contemplating, and loving of personal faith. Consequently, Augustine's *Confessions* trace the story of Augustine's conversion, the story of a life which is initially defined by one's own word, one's own loves, a life which becomes questionable in the light of the wisdom of the philosophers who raise the question of nature, a life which is finally defined by God's own word, spoken and received into lifetime.

Thus Augustine closes his *Confessions* as he spent the remainder of his life: holding, and contemplating, and loving the word of God in scripture (cf. *Conf.,* 11.2). The story of Augustine's genesis in his own wilfulness yields faithfully to the story of Genesis and of divine wilfulness. Confused reflection becomes conscious of itself as image and awaits the divine original, the divine origin of all things. Since human being is finally defined by its proper end, God, and finally formed by the full vision of God, Augustine is unable to know himself as he will be. He is able to know himself even as he knows his God, in the reading of scripture. His life, his word, like God's life in time, God's word, is an enigma, a dark saying, which is nevertheless the sole refuge of the life of faith. For now, in time, scripture *is* the divine countenance (cf. *Serm.,* 22.7), and faith *is* the human countenance. Both are dark and hidden in the mystery of the word.

> And still my soul is sad, because it falls back and becomes an abyss, or rather because it realizes that it is still an abyss. My faith, which you have kindled in the night before my steps, my faith speaks into that abyss.
>
> *(Conf.,* 13.14)

Augustine the philosopher and Augustine the exegete and preacher are not to be simply or naively reconciled; and a serious discussion of the precise and complex relationship between reason and revelation in the thought of Augustine extends well beyond the scope and claims of this work. However, it is important and possible at this point in our reflections to suggest in broadest outline one possible interpretation of Augustine's relationship to scripture. We have already seen that, with his conversion, the firmament, the universal whole, comes to mean for Augustine the world of scripture accessible through faith rather than the material world available through prescientific, commonsense experience. Just as for Aristotle and the Platonists the world is seen as radically complete except insofar as one's understanding of it remains incomplete; so for Augustine revelation is radically complete except insofar as one's holding of it (in faith) and beholding of it (in understanding) and love of it remain incomplete. The finite, free soul is thus the one disorderly exception in an order perfectly established. Further, as for classical Greek philosophy the human mind is somehow made for and well-suited to its world, so for Augustine mind is somehow made for and well-suited to scripture. In fact, "It is surely true that as children grow these books grow with them" *(Conf.,* 3.5). Augustine accepts the world of scripture as unquestionably given, as his own proper world, woven into the very fibers of his person from his youth, as surely as the Greek philosophers accept their world, the whole, as unquestionably given. Thus, Augustine does not ask whether or not scripture is true; for he says of spiritual people that they do not "judge on your book, even if something therein is obscure, because we submit our understanding to that book in the certainty that even what is closed to our sight is said rightly and truthfully" *(Conf.,* 13.23).

Rather, Augustine does ask of scripture in each case what it means. Although it is not for human being to judge regardin the truth of scripture, it lies within human being's peculiar capacity and calling to exercise judgment "amidst the signs and sounds of words (which are placed under the authority of your book, as it were flying beneath the firmament) in interpreting, in setting forth, in discussing, in arguing, in blessing and calling upon you" *(Conf.,* 13.23). Augustine's posture toward scripture is that of a philosopher toward the whole, one of insight and understanding. Thus, in recognizing that any single scriptural passage may bear a variety of possible interpretations, he is willing to admit that all such interpretations or insights may be true, even if they were not intended by the scriptural author.

> Each one who reads the holy scriptures strives for that insight which
> the author had in writing the text. What harm can there be, then, if
> a reader should gain an insight which you, the light of all truthful
> minds, show to be a true insight, even if it is an insight different
> from the author's? For the author possessed a true insight in writing
> the text, though not this one.
>
> *(Conf.,* 12.18)

It cannot be assumed, however, that scriptural passages may
support all meanings that might be read in them. Scripture is not
altogether plastic before the reader's mind; and certain readings
of scripture are resisted by and shatter against the passages from
which they are supposedly derived. Clearly, Augustine's polemical
writings would be unintelligible without such an assumption.

Augustine claims that scripture contains all the treasures of
wisdom and knowledge (cf. *Conf.,* 11.2), which he takes to mean
that every truth available to human being finds expression,
whether direct or veiled, in its pages (cf. *Conf.,* 12.26). Whatever
truth human being sees or seeks may be seen in scripture, which
becomes, then, a world, a whole, adequate to and even surpassing
human inquiry.

> A spring, issuing from a small space, flows over into greater spaces
> with more streams, and is thus more abundant, than any of those
> rivers which, reaching far and wide, originate from that spring. It is
> the same with the writing of the steward of your word. That writing
> was to provide for the many who would preach upon it. From a
> narrow measure of speech it overflows into streams of pure truth.
> From these streams, as they wind and branch out into many more
> words, each person draws what truth it can discover therein—this
> person, one truth; that person, another.
>
> *(Conf.,* 12.27)

In the classical tradition, the movement from insight or
contemplation, which are speechless, to speech is a movement
from the eternal to the temporal, in which the truths of vision,
once uttered, become corruptible and questionable even to their
authors. The contemplative, who returns to the cave out of
concern for others, endeavors to address the temporal with the

eternal; but truths beheld lose their compelling warrant and claim once they are spoken. It seems that Augustine finds remedy for this classical dilemma in scripture, the word of God spoken in time; for in the word, truth itself has given an account of itself, eternity has addressed time in utterly privileged words. The word made flesh in Jesus and in the scriptures is definitive and decisive for Augustine; and so, when human being endeavors to speak, to give an account of truth sought or truth discovered, of what it seeks or of what it has seen, it would best and most properly do so through the prism, the imagery, of the scriptures. Thus the life of wisdom and the life of faith become one in the incarnate and revealed word, a word at once eternal and temporal.

Through the holding, and beholding, and loving of faith, which encompasses both the mind that believes and the word that is believed, the mind is purified of its former darkness and perversity and is prepared for its proper love. Faith must lead to understanding. The mind, "by an incorporeal conversion" *(De Trin.,* 14.6.8), is recalled, reminded, of itself and of its God, and of their original and final complicity. Augustine claims that the mind is always present to itself, "in a kind of secret knowledge, which is called memory" *(De Trin.,* 14.6.8), although not always present to its actual gaze, and that the mind is thus available to itself through an immediate intuition, that is, that "the mind's beholding of itself is something pertaining to its nature" *(De Trin.,* 14.6.8). Similarly, Augustine claims that God is always present to the mind and somehow available to its gaze.

> But he is whole everywhere. And, on this account, the mind lives, and moves, and is in him; and so it can remember him.
>
> *(De Trin.,* 14.15.21)

> Indeed, God is not far removed from any one of us, as the apostle says and then adds: In him we live and move and have our being (Ac. 17.27-8). If he were speaking of the body, what he says could be understood with respect to the corporeal world, in which we do in fact bodily live and move and have our being. And then this is to be taken in a higher sense, visible not to the body but to the mind, as said of the mind which is fashioned after the image of God.
>
> *(De. Trin.,* 14.12.16)

Indeed, it is not by virtue of what is highest in human being that it remembers, and understands, and wills itself or that it holds, and beholds, and loves temporal faith. The mind's proper whole, the world for which the mind's gaze is made, is God, rather than the whole of revelation, the world of scripture. This brings us to Augustine's final trinitarian structure for the understanding of human life: the holding, beholding, and loving of the face of God.

> We have undertaken to consider the principal part of the human mind with which it knows or is able to know God, so that we might disclose therein the image of God. For, although the human mind is not of the same nature as God, yet the image of God's nature, which nature has no better, is to be sought and found in us in that part of us which has no better. . . . The mind is God's image precisely in that part in which it is capable of God, able to participate in God. This great good is possible only by virtue of the mind's being the image of God.
>
> *(De Trin.,* 14.8.11)

> This trinity, then, of the mind [i.e., memory-understanding-love] is the image of God not because the mind remembers itself, understands itself, and loves itself, but rather because it can remember, understand, and love its maker. And when it does this, the mind is made wise. If it does not do this, even if it remembers, understands, and loves itself, the mind is foolish. Let the mind, then, remember, understand, and love its God after whose image it has been made. To say the same thing more briefly, let the mind worship God, who is not made, and who has made the mind capable of God and made possible the mind's participation in God. For this reason it is written: Behold, wisdom is the worship of God (Jb. 28.28).
>
> *(De. Trin.,* 14.12.15)

It is not as if the sustained vision of God is available to human being at once or at all in time. A glimpse of the eternal is given to a few; and the promise of the eternal is proclaimed to all. On these grounds Augustine would have each person, through reflection upon scripture and upon creation, as well as through introspection into one's own mind, seek the face of God.

> Therefore, amidst things themselves eternal, incorporeal, changeless, amidst those things in the perfect contemplation of which the

blessed, which is to say eternal, life is promised to us, let us seek after the trinity that is God. For not only does the authority of the divine books declare the existence of God but every authority on every side, the all-encompassing nature of the universe proclaims that it has a preeminent founder, who has also given to us a mind and a natural reason with which to see. . . .

(De Trin., 15.4.6)

Whoever comes to an enduring insight into these three things [memory-understanding-will] by nature divinely established in one's mind, an insight into how great a thing dwells in the mind. . . . Such a one discovers the image of that highest trinity. Human being ought to refer every living thing to the remembering, the seeing, and the loving of that supreme trinity so that human being might remember it, contemplate it, and find its delight therein.

(De Trin., 15.20.39)

Regardless of the temporal inaccessibility of blessedness, the vision of God, Augustine suggests that in the life of wisdom and faith, a life consumed by the holy desire for God's face, the meditation and proclamation of his word, and the worship of his name, the mind "is renewed so as to be no longer old, restored so as to be no longer disfigured, and made blessed so as to be no longer unhappy" *(De Trin.,* 14.14.18).

Those, indeed, who are brought to recollection and thus turned toward the lord and away from that disfigurement in which, through profane desires, they were conformed to this age—those very ones are reformed by him and listen to the words of the apostle: Be not conformed to this age but be made over again in the renewing of your mind (Rm. 12.2) so that that image may begin to be refashioned by him who first fashioned it.

(De Trin., 14.16.22)

Without raising the entire question of grace and free will, we may note that for Augustine it is the creative word of God which first fashions human being after his image and it is the redemptive word of God which renews that image in time. Finally, both nature and person, human being in the beginning and human being in time, are the work of the one word of God "spoken eternally and in whom all things are spoken eternally" *(Conf.,*

11.7). Human being, "from the glory of creation to the glory of justification" *(De Trin.,* 15.8.14), is God's word.

> [He is] your word, by which you have made all things, myself among them. [He is] your only son, through whom you have called a multitude of believers, myself among them, into adoption.
>
> *(Conf.,* 11.2)

Within lifetime, this renewal of mind and conversion of life is never complete; and so human being never knows rest but only desire and hope. The perfection of the image of God requires the full vision of God (cf. *De Trin.,* 14.18.24): "Then we shall be like God, because we shall see him not through a mirror, but as he is (Jn. 3.4), in the apostle Paul's words, 'face to face' (1 Cor. 13.12). *(De Trin.,* 15.11.21). The whole of human being's temporal life is, then, a becoming, a coming to see the face of God (cf. *Tr. in Joann ep.,* 4.5-6).

> Clearly this renewal is not accomplished in the single moment of conversion itself. . . . The apostle has spoken most plainly of this, saying: Even if our outer being is destroyed, our inner being is renewed from day to day (2 Cor. 4.16). . . . When a person is renewed from day to day by growing in the knowledge of God, in righteousness, and in the sanctity of truth, that person transfers its love from things temporal to things eternal, from things visible to things intelligible, from things carnal to things spiritual. Such a person diligently stands fast in restraining and diminishing its desire for the former things and in binding itself to the latter in charity. And all of this is done only to the extent of God's aid; for God himself has stated: Without me you can do nothing (Jn. 15.5).
>
> *(De Trin.,* 14.17.23)

What Augustine describes is a genuine conversion of loves, which Augustine realizes is possible only through revelation and grace. The Greeks cannot conceive of a radical conversion of loves but only of a moderate conversion of motives. For Augustine, as much as for Aristotle, decision rests with perception (cf. *De lib. arb.,* 3.25.76); and what one perceives as compellingly good always appears within a horizon already fixed by earlier decisions.

Augustine's analysis of habit leaves the will as bound as does Aristotle's (cf. *C. Fort.,* 22). Where they differ most significantly is that Augustine knew and affirmed the experience of grace, the sovereign, gratuitous wilfulness of divine freedom, which bends human wills toward salvation or damnation as if they were moist clay, soft and unfired.

> What person has power to touch its own mind with such a sight as would move the will toward faith? Who is able to embrace with the mind what brings no delight? . . . If, therefore, those things delight us which bring us closer to God, this is inspired and brought about by the grace of God. . . . The only conclusion to be drawn is that wills are elected. The will itself, moreover, unless something comes before it which delights and draws the mind, can in no way be moved. To make this happen does not lie within the power of human being.
>
> *(Ad Simpl.,* 1.2.21-22)

Wills, which have every impression of willing themselves in time, are, in fact, willed from eternity. And if wills are elected, then persons too are chosen to be what they apparently make themselves to be. The human word is always an echo of the divine word. Human being, from conception to blessedness (or damnation), is God's gift, a word spoken graciously in time to endure forever. Thus Augustine is prompted to address God:

> I give you thanks for your gifts. Preserve them for me. For thus you will preserve me; and what you have given me will increase and reach completion. And I shall myself be with you; for my very being is your gift.
>
> *(Conf.,* 1.20)

> Let me remember you, let me understand you, let me love you. Increase these in me until you renew me wholly.
>
> *(De Trin.,* 15.28.51)

In the faithful beholding and loving of the divine word, human being contemplates through the obscurities of scripture that original image which human being has never made but, rather, in the light of which it was in the beginning made and will in the end be judged. Human being, like the eye, mirrors and images what it beholds. Thus, in beholding the perfect image, and in listening to the perfect word, human being images that image and echoes that word. When the eyes and ears of faith yield to perfect sight, human being shall be realized and shall be blessed in being who and what it was forever to be. The human word will no longer question nor create. The only remaining human word will be one of pure, responsive joy.

CHAPTER 7

SIGHT

Readings

• 1 •

Accept the sacrifice of my confessions, offered by my tongue which you have prepared and encouraged to confess in your name; make whole all my bones and let them proclaim: Lord, who is like you? (Ps. 35.10). For to confess to you is not to teach you what happens inside us, because a closed heart does not evade your eye, just as human hardness does not keep away your hand. But you soften it whenever you want, from a desire either to pity, or to punish; no one can hide from the heat of you. Let my soul praise you in order to love you. Let it confess to you your acts of compassion, that it may praise you. The whole of your creation never ceases to praise you nor grows silent. Neither does the spirit of every human being cease to turn to you in praise; nor do animals and c rporeal beings, through the mouths of those who contemplate them. Thus may our soul rise up out of our weariness toward you, supporting itself on the things which you have made and then moving on to you who marvelously made them. There lies restoration and true strength.

(Conf., 5.1)

267

• 2 •

We ought, therefore, to love God, the triune unity, father, son and holy spirit, which I would say come to the same thing. For it is with supreme truth that Paul speaks of God: from whom, and in whom are all things (Rm. 11.36). And what does he go on to add? To him be glory (ibid.). This is said with utmost clarity. He does not say "to them be glory"; for God is one. What does this "to him be glory," however, mean except "to him be most excellent, supreme, and widespread fame"? For the finer and more extensive is his fame, the more ardent is he prized and loved. And when this is so, it means simply that the human race is led with sure and steady steps toward the highest and most blessed life.

When the uestion is raised regarding right conduct and life, I do not think that anything more is to be asked than: What is human being's supreme good to which all things must be referred? For it is clear that the supreme good exists—both from reason, as far as reason avails, and from divine authority, which surpasses our reason—and that the supreme good is nothing other than God himself. For what other highest good will there be for human being than that good the clinging to which is most blessed? And that, moreover, is God alone, to whom we are able to cling only by esteem, love, and charity.

(De Mor., 1.14.24)

• 3 •

Let us examine now what the saints will do in their immortal and spiritual bodies when they no longer live carnally but are alive spiritually. To tell the truth, I do not know what that employment, or rather rest and leisure, might be. For I have never observed it with my senses. If, however, I should say that I had observed it with my mind, that is to say, my intelligence, what is our mind, how great is our intelligence in the face of that excellence? For there there is the peace of God which, as the apostle says, surpasses all under-standing (Ph. 4.7). What understanding does he mean if not ours or perhaps the holy angels' also? Certainly not God's. So if the saints will live in the peace of God, they will live in that peace which surpasses all understanding. That it surpasses ours there is no doubt. If it also surpasses the understanding of the angels—and he who says all understanding does not seem to make any exceptions—then we ought to accept that he means to say that neither we nor the angels can ever know the peace of God, by which God himself is pacified, as God knows it. In this way it surpasses all understanding, although doubtless not God's own.

But as we will be made to participate, according to the measure of our own peace, in his peace and will obtain as much of the highest peace in ourselves and with each other and with him as we are able, in the same way the holy angels know God's peace in accordance with the measure of their own. And humankind is far behind the angels, however much they excel in the progress of their mind. We must call to mind how great the man was who said: We know in part and prophesy in part until what is perfect comes; now we see through a mirror darkly but then face to face (1 Co. 13.9, 12). In this way do the angels see now, who are also said to be our angels, because when we have been snatched from the power of darkness and, having received the token of the spirit, are carried to the kingdom of Christ, we begin to belong among those angels with whom we will share the holy and sweet city of God, about which we have written so many books. In this way the angels of God are also ours, in the same way that Christ is both God's and ours. They are God's because they have not left God; and they are ours because we have begun to be their fellow citizens. The lord Jesus said: Take care that you do not despise one of these little ones. For I say to you that their angels in heaven see always the face of my father that is in heaven (Mt. 18.10). Just as these see so will we also see. But we do not yet see. For this reason the apostle said what I quoted above: Now we see through a mirror darkly, but then face to face. That vision is kept for us as the reward for our faith, about which the apostle John said: When he appears we will be similar to him, since we will see him as he is (1 Jn. 3.2). Yet the "face" of God must be understood as his manifestation, not like the appearance of limbs, as we have in our body and call by that name.

So when I am asked what the saints will do in that spiritual body I do not say that I now understand but I say what I believe, in keeping with what I read in the psalms: I believed and for that reason I have spoken (Ps. 116.10). And so I say that they will in their body see God; but whether it will be through their body as now we see the sun through ours, or the moon or the stars or the sea and the

earth and whatever is in them, is no small question. It is hard to say
that the saints will have then the kinds of bodies which cannot open
and shut the eyes at will.

However, it is harder to say that if one closes one's eyes then one
will not see God. For if the prophet Elisha saw, though far away, his
servant accept gifts which Naaman the Syrian, whom the prophet
had cured of the deformities of leprosy, offered him, because the
servant thought that he might do so without his master's seeing it,
how much more easily will the saints in their spiritual bodies see all
things. They will see not only with their eyes shut but also when
they are without their bodies. For then what the apostle spoke of,
the perfect thing, will come. He says: We know in part and we
prophesy in part. When what is perfect shall come what happens in
part shall disappear (1 Co. 13.19 ff.). Then, so that he might
somehow show in a simile how far this life is from what will be in
the future, not just for ordinary people but also for those who are
gifted with special sanctity, he says: When I was a small child, I had
the knowledge of a small child; I spoke like one, thought like one.
When I became a man I left behind the habits of a small child. Now
we see through a glass darkly, but then face to face. Now I know in
part, but then I will know as I am known (1 Co. 13.12). So if in this
life, where the prophecies of remarkable people are, in comparison
with the prophecies of that life, as infants to young people, Elisha
nonetheless saw his servant accepting gifts when he was far away,
then will those saints, when what is perfect comes and the soul is no
longer weighed down by the corruptible body and nothing corruptible impedes it, need eyes to see things which are to be seen, when
Elisha did not need them to see his servant far away? According to
the Septuagint these are the prophet's words to his servant: Did not
my heart go with you when the man descended from his chariot and
met you face to face, and you accepted the money? (2 K. 5.26). The
presbyter Jerome translated it from the Hebrew as follows: Was not
my heart present when the man turned away from his chariot to
meet you? And so the prophet said that he had seen with his heart,
through the miraculous help of God, no doubt. But when God will
exist in all people, then how much more fully will everyone abound
in this gift! However, these corporeal eyes will still have their duty
and will be in their place and the spirit will use them through the
spiritual body. For not even the prophet, although he did not need
them to see things not present, did not dispense with his eyes when
looking at things in his presence. Yet he could have seen these

things with his spirit, even if his eyes had been closed, just as he saw things not present in the place he was. Let us not say, then, that those saints in that life will not see God with closed eyes, since they will see him always with their spirit.

But then the question arises whether they will see him also through the eyes of the body, if they have them open. If in the spiritual body spiritual eyes are capable of seeing only as much as the eyes we have now, there is no doubt that God will not be visible to them. So their power will be far different if they are to see that incorporeal nature which is not contained in space but which is everywhere. Because we say that God is in heaven and on earth—as he himself says through his prophet: I fill the heaven and the earth (Jr. 23.24)—we are not trying to say that one part of him inhabits the heavens and another part the earth. His presence on earth is complete and his presence in heaven is complete, not at different times but simultaneously, which no corporeal nature can do. And so the power of those eyes will be greater, not to see more sharply with the power of vision given to snakes and eagles—for however powerful their vision they can see nothing with their eyes except bodies—but to see incorporeal things in addition. Perhaps that great virtue of sight was given to the eyes of the holy man Job, in his mortal body, at the time when he said to God: Before, I heard you through the hearing of my ears, but now my eyes see you. Therefore I have despised myself and have melted away and considered myself earth and dust (Jb. 42.5 ff.), although nothing prevents us from understanding here the eyes as the eyes of the heart, about which the apostle says: To have the eyes of your heart illumined (Ep. 1.18). But no Christian will doubt that these eyes will see God, when he will be seen, if what God the master said is faithfully accepted: Blessed are the pure in heart for they will see God (Mt. 5.8). But whether he will also be seen with corporeal eyes remains a question.

When it is written: All flesh will see the salvation of God (Lk. 3.6), this can be understood without difficulty to mean: All humankind will see the Christ of God, who has been seen in body and will be seen again in body when he judges the living and the dead. That he is the salvation of God is amply attested to by the scriptures and especially so by the words of the venerable old Simeon who said, when he received the infant Christ in his hands: Now, God you send away your servant in peace, in accordance with your word, since my eyes have seen your salvation (Lk. 2.29). The

words of Job found in the Hebrew manuscripts: In my flesh I shall
see God (Jb. 19.20), without doubt prophesy the resurrection of the
flesh. However, he did not say "through my flesh." If he had said
that, we could understand that he meant, for God, Jesus Christ, who
will be seen through flesh in flesh. Or we can interpret his words "in
my flesh I shall see God" to mean: I will be in my flesh when I see
God. And when the apostle says "face to face" we are not forced to
believe that we will see God through this corporeal face where our
corporeal eyes are, since we will see him with the spirit without end.
If the apostle had not meant the face of the inner self, he would not
have said: With unveiled face we behold as in a mirror the glory of
God and are transformed into his image, from glory unto glory, as if
by the spirit of God (2 Co. 3.18). We understand what the psalmist
sings in the same way: Go to him and be enlightened and your face
will not be ashamed (Ps. 34.6). By faith we approach God, and faith
belongs to the spirit not to the body. But because we do not know
how complete the approaches of the spiritual body will be—as we
are speaking of something we have never experienced—and because
the authority of the scriptures nowhere unequivocally tells us or aids
us in our understanding, it is necessary that we experience what is
spoken of in the Book of Wisdom: Human thoughts are timid and
our foresight uncertain (Ws. 9.14).

The reasoning of philosophers says that things intelligible to the
mind and things perceptible to bodily sense, that is, corporeal
things, are seen in such a way that the mind cannot view the former
through the body nor the latter by itself without the body. If we
could be certain of this, it would be clear that God can in no way be
seen through the eyes of even the spiritual body. But true reason
and prophetic authority mock this reasoning.

Who could be so far from the truth as to dare to say that God has
no knowledge of corporeal things? Then must he have a body
through the eyes of which he can gain knowledge of them?
Furthermore does not the passage we quoted earlier from Elisha
show sufficiently that corporeal things can be discerned by the spirit
without the body? For when his servant accepted the gifts, he did so
with his body. But the prophet saw this action, not through his body,
but through his spirit. So it is agreed that the body is seen by the
spirit; but what if the power of the spiritual body is so great that the
spirit is also seen by the body? For the spirit is God. Furthermore,
human beings see their own lives, which they live in their bodies
and by which their earthly limbs are given life, by an internal sense

and do not know it through their corporeal eyes. But the lives of others, though invisible, they see through their bodies. How do we distinguish the living bodies from the dead, if we do not see the body and its life which we cannot see, except through the body? Lives without bodies we do not see without corporeal eyes.

For this reason it is possible and even strongly credible that we will in the future observe the material forms of the new sky and the new earth in a way that will allow us to see with the clearest vision the presence of God everywhere as he rules all the universe; we will see God through our bodies which we shall wear and which we shall see wherever we turn our eyes, not as we see him now through his creation, as if we were seeing through a glass darkly and only partially, so that we are able to believe more by faith than by the appearance of corporeal things which we see through our corporeal eyes. Just as we do not believe but observe, as soon as we see them, that the human beings who live and move their vital parts, and among whom we exist, are alive, although we are not able to see their life without their bodies but nonetheless are able to see it without any ambiguity through their bodies—just so, wherever we allow those spiritual lights of our bodies, our eyes, to travel we will see even through our bodies, the incorporeal God who rules over everything. So either God will be seen with these eyes in such a way that they have some exceptional quality, similar to the power of the mind, by which they see incorporeal nature but for which it is difficult, if not impossible, to discover evidence in examples or through the testimony of the divine scriptures, or another possibility exists—which is easier to understand—that God will be known to us and visible to us in such a way that he may be seen by our own spirit in ourselves, by each other in each other, in himself, in the new heaven and earth, and in every creature which will exist there. He will be seen through every body in every body, wherever the eyes of the spiritual body reach with their keen vision. Our thought also will be open to all of us. Then indeed there will come to pass what the apostle said: Do not wish to judge anything before the time when the lord comes and enlightens the hidden depths of shadows and makes clear the thoughts of the heart; then will each person have praise from God (1 Co. 4, 5).

What great joy there will be when there is no evil, when no good is hidden, when there is time for praise of God, who will be all in all. For then what will people do other than praise God, when no sloth causes idleness and no need gives rise to labor. I am reminded of the holy song where I read or hear: Blessed are they who dwell in your house. They will praise you for ever and ever (Ps. 84.5). All limbs and entrails of the incorruptible body, which we now see arranged for various necessary uses, will function in praise of God, since there will be no necessity but rather full, certain, secure, and eternal happiness. All those components of the body's harmony, about which I just spoke and which now lay hidden, will no longer be so but will be arranged internally and externally throughout all the body. Along with other things, which will then seem great and wonderful, rational minds will burn with the enjoyment of rational beauty in praise of such a great creator. How such a body will move I dare not boldly define because I cannot imagine. Yet it will have fitting movements and virtues, as well as a fitting appearance. When there is something not fitting, that thing will no longer exist. Wherever the spirit wills, there certainly the body will be immediately; but the spirit shall will nothing which cannot be fitting either to the body or the spirit. Then there will be true glory, when no one will be praised by the error of adulation of the person who praises. There will be true honor, denied to no worthy person and given to no unworthy person. But no unworthy person will strive for it, as no one will be allowed there except the worthy. There will be true peace, since no one will face opposition inside or from another. The reward of virtue will be he who gave it and promised himself because there could be no greater or better reward. What else did he mean when he said through the prophet: I will be their God and they shall be my people? (Lv. 26.12). What else did he mean except to say: I shall be the source of their fullness; I shall be what ever human beings honorably desire—life, health, nourishment, plenty, glory, honor, peace, and all good things? This is also how the words of the apostle are to be rightly understood when he says that God may be all in all (1 Co. 15.28). God himself will be the completion of our desires. Our sight of him will be without end, our love of him without excess, our praise of him weariless. This liturgy, this condition, this movement, will belong in truth to all and will be, like eternal life itself, communal.

Who can think or, harder still, say what other degrees of honor and glory there will be as rewards for the deserving? That there will be rewards cannot be doubted. This blessed state will see in itself one great good: No inferior will envy a superior, just as now the other angels do not envy the archangels. So no one will desire to be other than what each is given, although each is bound in complete harmony to those who are favored, like in the body, where a finger does not want to be an eye, although the structure of the body contains both organs. So one will have a smaller gift than another, but no one will want a greater gift than the one given.

They will not be deprived of the power of free people just because they can no longer delight in sin. Freedom will, in fact, be greater when it is released from the freedom to sin into the unfailing freedom not to sin. For the free will which was given to human beings, when they were first created upright, was the ability not to sin, although they also had the ability to sin. This newest power will, however, be greater than that, for it will not include the power to sin. This will come about through the gift of God, not through natural ability. It is one thing to be God, and another thing to participate in him. By nature God cannot sin. A true participant in God receives from him the ability not to be able to sin. Yet there are different degrees of salvation in the divine gift. At first free will was given to human beings such that they were capable of not sinning. Then, in the newest degree, the capability to sin does not exist. The former leads to the acquiring of merit, the latter to the receiving of merit's reward. But because that nature sinned when it had the capability to do so, it is by a far greater grace that it is freed into a state where the ability to sin does not exist.

Similarly, the first immortality, which Adam lost by sinning, was to be able not to die. The newest will be not to be able to die, just as the first free will was to be able not to sin, while the newest is not to be able to sin. Such will be the unalienable will of piety and righteousness, and, therefore, of happiness. For by sinning we did not keep hold of either piety or happiness, but we did not lose the will to happiness just because we lost happiness. Certainly we cannot deny that God himself has free will although he cannot sin?

There will be, therefore, one inseparable free will in all the citizens of that city, a will freed from all evil and full of every good which enjoys without cease eternal delights, forgetful of guilt, forgetful of punishment. Yet it is not forgetful of its own liberation so that it becomes ungrateful to its liberator. For in as much as it has rational knowledge it remembers its past evils. But inasmuch as it has understanding from experience, they will be forgotten. The most skilled doctors, when it comes to professional knowledge, are familiar with almost all illnesses of the body. But when it comes to the experience of their own body, they are ignorant of all those which they have not suffered. In the same way, there are two kinds of knowledge of evil, one in which it is exposed by mental powers, the other in which it cleaves to the sense of one who has experienced it—in one case, all vice is known through the teaching of wisdom, in the other through the most evil life of a fool. So there are also two ways of forgetting evil: one by which a learned and well-taught person forgets it and the other by which an experienced and jaded person forgets it. The former forgets what has been learned, the latter what has been suffered. By the kind of forgetting I placed second, saints will forget past evil. They will be so empty of it that the evil is even blotted from their senses. But the power of their intellectual knowledge, which will be great, will keep alive not only their own past experience but also the eternal suffering of the damned. If they were ignorant of the fact that they had been miserable how could they, as the psalm says, sing the mercy of God eternally? (Ps. 84.8). Nothing will be more pleasant to the citizens of that state than the song to the glory of the grace of Christ, by whose blood we were freed. There the command will be accomplished: Be still and look, since I am God (Ps. 45.11). This will be the greatest sabbath without an evening to end it, which the lord approved in the first creation of the world, as it is written: And God rested on the seventh day from all the creation which he had made and God blessed the seventh day and sanctified it because, on that day, God rested from his creation which he had begun to make (Gn. 2.2). We ourselves will be the seventh day, when we will be filled and replenished by the blessing and sanctifying of God. Then we will be still and see that he is God; that he is that which we ourselves wanted to be when we went away from him and listened to the tempter's words: You will be as gods (Gn. 3.5), but abandoned the true God through whose doing we might have been gods by participating in him, but not by deserting him. For what have we done without him except to expire in his anger? We will be still eternally, when we have been remade by him and perfected with greater grace and we will see that he is God, by whom we are filled when he is all in all. For our good deeds, when they are understood to be his rather than ours, are credited to us so that we may have the sabbath. If we credit them to ourselves, they will be servile. But it is said of the sabbath: You will not perform any servile work (Dt. 5.14). Therefore he said through the prophet Ezekiel: And I gave to them my sabbaths as a sign between me and them, so that they should know that I am the God who sanctifies them (Ezk. 20.12). This we will know perfectly when we will be perfectly still and will see perfectly that he is God. If the number of the ages is computed as if the ages were days, as they seem to be described in the scriptures, that sabbath will appear clearly to be the seventh age. The first age, like the first day, would be from Adam to the flood; the second from there to Abraham, not counting by equal amount of time but by generations, there being ten in each. From there there are, as Matthew explains, three ages to the coming of Christ, each with fourteen generations: one from Abraham to David, one from David to the migration to Babylon, and a third from Babylon to the carnal birth of Christ. That makes five altogether. The sixth is now taking place and cannot be calculated by numbers of generations, because it is said: It is not yours to know the time which the father has placed in his power (Ac. 1.7). After this, as on the seventh day, God shall rest. We shall be that same seventh day, and God will make us to rest in him, God himself. It would be too much to discuss here each of these ages. But the seventh age shall be our sabbath, which shall be brought to a close not by the approach of evening but by the day of the lord, an eighth and eternal day, as it were, a day made sacred by the resurrection of Christ, a day prefiguring not only the eternal repose of the spirit but of the body as well. On that day we shall take our leisure and we shall see; we shall see and love, love and praise. What shall be in the end shall be without end. For what end awaits us other than to reach the kingdom which has no end?

I seem to have repaid with God's help my debt in writing this huge work. Let those for whom it is too little and those for whom it is too much forgive me. But let those for whom it is just enough give their thanks not to me but with me to God. Amen.

(De civ. Dei, 22.29-30)

• 4 •

We approve far more readily the idea that the life of the wise is social. For from what source would that City of God, about which we how hold in our hands the nineteenth book, either find its beginning, or progress along its course, or reach its proper end, if the life of the saints were not social?

(De civ. Dei, 19.5)

• 5 •

Blessed are they who dwell in your house (Ps. 83.4). If you have a house of your own, you are poor; if you have the house of God, you are rich. In your own house you will fear thieves; in God's house God himself is the wall. Blessed, then, are they who dwell in your house. They possess the heavenly Jerusalem, without distress, without pressure, without diverse and divided boundaries. All possess it; and each singly possesses the whole. Great are those riches. Brother does not crowd brother; for need does not exist there.

What, then, will they do there? For necessity is the mother of all human actions. I have already said this briefly, brothers. Let your soul run through and consider any actions whatsoever; and see if anything but necessity produces them. Consider those remarkable arts which appear so great in coming to the assistance of others, the art of speaking in someone's defense and the remedies of medicine; for in this life they are indeed excellent actions. But take away litigants; and whom is the advocate to help? Take away wounds and diseases; and for whom does the physician care? In addition, all these actions of ours which are needed for and done in daily life emerge from necessity. To plow, to sow, to clear fallow ground, to sail—what other than necessity and need produces all such works? Take away hunger, thirst, nakedness; and who has need of all these things? . . .

Consider those things which I have said are demanded of us. Break your bread with the hungry. But with whom do you break bread, where no one hungers? Take the homeless into your home. But what stranger do you receive, where all dwell in their homeland? Who are the sick whom you visit, where all rejoice in perpetual good health? Whose lawsuits do you resolve, where peace is everlasting? What dead do you bury, where everyone lives forever? None of these honorable works proper to all human beings, therefore, will you perform. You will do none of these good works. . . .

What, then, will you do? You have already said what we shall have: Blessed are they who dwell in your house. Say now what they will do, because I see there no necessities impelling me to act. Behold only what I say and argue: It is necessity that produces. Will there be any such argument as teaches the ignorant or reminds the forgetful? Indeed, will the Gospel be recited in that homeland where the word of God himself shall be contemplated? . . .

For ever and ever they will praise you (Ps. 83.4). This will be our whole occupation, an unceasing Alleluia. It should not seem to you, brothers, that there will be any weariness there; because if you do not endure long in saying only this now, it is necessity that turns you away from that joy. What is unseen brings no great delight now. Yet, if with such eagerness amidst the pressure and fragility of the flesh we praise what we believe, how shall we praise what we shall see? When death has been swallowed up in victory, when this mortal flesh has put on immortality, and this corruptible flesh has put on incorruption no one will say I have stood long (1 Co. 15, 53-54). No one will say, I have fasted long, or I have kept a long vigil. For there our endurance will be great; and the very immortality of our bodies will depend upon the contemplation of God. And if these mere words which I dispense to you keeps our weak flesh standing for so long a time, what will be the effect upon us of that joy? How will it change us? We shall be like him, for we see him as he is (1 Jn. 3.2). Once like him, when will our strength fail us? What will turn us away?

Let us therefore be sure, brothers; we shall never have our fill of the praise of God, or of the love of God. If you would fail to love, you would fail to praise. If, moreover, love will be everlasting, because that beauty will be insatiable, do not fear that you could ever cease praising him whom you will be able always to love. Therefore, blessed are they who dwell in your house; for ever and ever they will praise you. For this life let us sigh.

(En. in Ps., 83.8)

• 6 •

This is the land of the dead. The land of the dead is passing away; and the land of the living is coming. In the land of the dead is labor, grief, fear, tribulation, temptation, groaning, and sighing. Here the false are happy, and the truthful are unhappy, because this happiness is false and this misery is true. Those who acknowledge themselves to be in true misery shall be in true happiness. And yet, because you are miserable now, listen to the lord when he says: Blessed are they that mourn (Mt. 5.5). O blessed mourners! Nothing is so linked to misery than mourning; and nothing is so removed from and contrary to misery than blessedness. You speak of those who mourn, and you call them blessed! Understand, he says, what I say: I call blessed those who mourn. How are they blessed? In hope. How are they mournful? In fact. For they mourn in this death, amidst these tribulations, in this their exile. And because they acknowledge themselves to be in this misery, and because they groan, they are blessed.

When, moreover, our mourning has passed away, we all, with one voice, in one people, in one homeland, will find consolation, thousands upon thousands united with angels playing upon their harps and with choirs of heavenly powers living in one city. Who groans there? Who sighs there? Who labors there? Who is in need there? Who dies there? Who shows mercy there? Who breaks bread with the hungry where all have their fill of the bread of justice? No one says to you, Receive the stranger. For no one there will be a wanderer. No one says to you, Resolve your friends' lawsuits. For they enjoy in everlasting peace the face of God. No one says to you, Visit the sick; for health and immortality remain. No one says to you, Bury the dead; for all will be in eternal life. Works of mercy cease, because misery is not to be found.

And what shall we do there? Shall we perhaps sleep? . . . We shall be awake, we shall not sleep. What shall we do? These works of mercy will not be, because there will be no misery. Will there, perchance, be these works of necessity which are here now: sowing, plowing, cooking, grinding, weaving? None of these; for there will be no necessity. So there will be no works of mercy, because misery is passing away. And where there will be neither necessity nor misery, there will not be the works of necessity and of mercy. What will be there? What business shall we have? What activity? Or if no activity, what rest? Shall we sit, grow torpid, and do nothing? If our love will cool, so will our activity. That love, therefore, resting in the face of God, for whom we now only long and sigh, how will that love not inflame us, when we have come to him? He, yet unseen, for whom we sigh so, how will he illumine us, when we have come to him? How will he change us? What will he make of us? What, then, shall we do, brothers? Let the psalm tell us: Blessed are they who dwell in your house. Why? For ever and ever they will praise you (Ps. 83.4). This will be our activity, the praise of God. You love, and you praise. You will cease to praise, if you cease to love. You will not, however, cease to love, because the one whom you see is such that he never surprises you with weariness. He both satisfies you and does not. What I am saying is wonderful.

(En. in Ps., 85.24)

• 7 •

In this wandering, we are worn away. Our dwelling will be our sole joy. Labor and groaning will perish. Speeches pass away. Praises take their place. There will be the dwelling of the joyous. No longer will there be the groans of longing, but, instead, the gladness of enjoyment. He for whom we sigh will be present. We shall be like him, for we shall see him as he is (1 Jn. 3.2). There it will be our whole task to praise and to enjoy the presence of God. And what else shall we seek, where he alone suffices, through whom all things have been made? We shall be dwelt in and we shall dwell. All things shall be subjected to him, so that God may be all in all (1 Co. 15.28).

Blessed, therefore, are they who dwell in your house. Why blessed? In having gold, silver, a large household, or numerous offspring? Why blessed? Blessed are they who dwell in your house; for ever and ever they will praise you (Ps. 83.4). They are blessed in that one tireless occupation. Let us, then, long for this one thing, brothers, when we have come to this point. Let us make ready to rejoice in God, to praise God.

The good works, which somehow conduct us there, will not be there. . . . In that place there will be no works of mercy; for there will be no misery. You will find no one in need, no one naked. No one will come to you thirsty. There will be no wanderers, no sick for you to visit, no dead for you to bury, no litigants for you to pacify. What will you do? Perhaps, to meet the necessities of our bodies, shall we clear fallow ground, shall we plow, shall we do business, shall we make journeys? In that place there will be great rest; for all those works demanded by necessity shall be taken away. With necessity dead, the works of necessity will perish too.

What will be there? As far as is possible, a human tongue has told us: As though the dwelling of all who rejoice is in you (Ps. 86.7). . . . There is nothing to compare with that joy. . . . There is a joy which neither eye has seen, nor ear heard, nor has it entered into the human heart (1 Co. 2.9).

Let us ready ourselves for no ordinary joy. What we find here is somehow like it, but is not that joy. So we must not ready ourselves to enjoy there such joys as now delight us. Otherwise our continence will be only greed. There are, after all, people who, invited to a splendid feast where many costly dishes are to be set forth, meanwhile keep their fast. If you should ask the reason for their not eating, they would explain that they are fasting. Fasting is a great work, a Christian work. But do not be hasty in your praise. Ask why they fast. It is a matter of the belly, not of religion. Why do they fast? Lest cheap fare pre-occupy their belly leaving no room for delicacies. Therefore, in fasting, they work for the gullet's sake. Fasting is, indeed, a great thing. It wars against belly and gullet. But sometimes it campaigns for them.

Therefore, my brothers, if you suppose that we shall have anything of that sort in that fatherland to which the heavenly trumpet urges us on and, for that reason, abstain from present delights, so as to receive such things there all the more plentifully, you are no different from those who fast for greater feasting and are continent with a view toward grander incontinence. Do not do that. Make yourselves ready for something ineffable. Purify your heart of all your earthly and secular affections. And we shall see something the sight of which will make us blessed. This alone will satisfy us.

What then? Shall we not eat? Indeed, we shall eat. And he will be our food, who will refresh us and never fail. ... As though the dwelling of all who rejoice is in you. We have already been told how we shall be made joyful. Blessed are they who dwell in your house; for ever and ever they will praise you. Let us somehow praise the lord, as much as we can, mixing groans with our praises; for in praising him we long for him without yet having him. But when we have held fast to him, all our sorrows will be taken from us, and nothing will remain but praise, unmixed and everlasting.

(En. in Ps., 86.9)

Nothing Will Remain But Praise

The central focus of all of our reflections has been, from one perspective or another, Augustine's understanding of human blessedness. This continuous preoccupation from his earliest dialogues to his last polemics unifies his myriad concerns and questions. In his conception of human blessedness his reflections upon God and human being converge and find their fullness of meaning.

Blessedness is finally made available to human being not as the culmination of its own capacities and virtues but rather as the culminating grace of "the one God, the giver of felicity" *(De civ. Dei,* 4.25). Blessedness is not the prerogative of those few, graced with wealth, leisure, intelligence, a good upbringing, and beautiful offspring, as the Greeks would have it. Such blessedness as these serve to provide is fleeting, imperfect, and prideful, according to Augustine, who explains:

> They wanted somehow to construct for themselves their own blessed life which they suppose is something to be done for oneself rather than done for one, even though there is no other giver of blessedness than God. No one makes human being blessed except he who made human being. . . . To the good, whose very goodness is his gift, God will give himself so that they might be blessed.
>
> *(Epist.,* 155)

Blessedness, the vision of God, belongs to the pure in heart, those whose righteousness is perfect; and "in the twinkling of an eye . . . that greatness of perfect righteousness will be given as a reward to those who have obeyed the commandments" *(C. duas ep. Pel.,* 3.23). Consequently, regardless of gifted birth and gifted status, Augustine would caution us "lest anyone believe that blessedness and the beloved God may be reached so long as one's neighbor is held in contempt" *(De mor.,* 1.26.51). And whereas sickness, care, poverty, or grave misfortune of any sort were recognized by Aristotle as genuine impediments to blessedness, Augustine cites with assurance the words of Paul: "I know for certain that neither death, nor life, nor angels, nor virtue, nor things present, nor things to come, nor height, nor depth, nor any other creature will be able to separate us from the love of God, which is in Christ Jesus our lord" (Rm. 8.38-39) (cf. *De mor.,* 1.11.18-19). Clearly, what distinguishes Augustine from Aristotle most decisively on this point is Augustine's belief in a revelation which makes clear promise of personal immortality and blessedness.

Aristotle, as we have seen, understands human blessedness to reside in the well performance of human being's own proper work or activity, defined formally as the activity of human being's highest power with respect to its worthiest object.[1] Aristotle and Augustine concur that human being's highest and most proper work belongs to mind's contemplative capacity, the mind's capacity for pure beholding. Aristotle sees the worthiest object of pure beholding to be the first being, with which there can be no fellowship, from which there is no response to our devotion; for this God is "too remote" *(polu choristhentos)* [2] from human being. Augustine, however, believes the worthiest object of contemplation to be the God who has spoken to human being through his son, and with whom there is the promise of eternal fellowship. According to Aristotle, each thing has its own proper good which it seeks and to which it refers the whole of its life. According to Augustine, human being's own proper good is God.

> Seek your own good, O soul. For one thing is good for one creature, and another thing for another creature. And all creatures have a certain good of their own which works to the completeness and perfection of their nature. What is required for the perfection of each imperfect thing varies from thing to thing. Seek your own good. No one is good except the one God (Mt. 19.17). The highest good, this is your good.
>
> *(En. in Ps.,* 102.7)

Human blessedness, then, consists in the full vision of the face of God, the holding, beholding, and loving of the divine trinity.

> This, he says, is eternal life, that they should know you, the true God, and Jesus Christ, whom you have sent (1 Jn. 17.3). Eternal life, then, is the very knowledge of truth.
>
> *(De mor.,* 1.25.47)

At the end of time, Augustine explains:

> God shall rest on the seventh day. We shall be that same seventh

---

1. Cf. Aristotle, *Nicomachean Ethics,* 1.7; 10.4.
2. Cf. Aristotle, *Nicomachean Ethics,* 8.7.

day and God will make us to rest in him, God himself. . . . The
seventh age shall be our sabbath, which shall be brought to a close
not by the approach of evening but by the day of the lord, an eighth
and eternal day, as it were, a day made sacred by the resurrection of
Christ, a day prefiguring not only the eternal repose of the spirit but
of the body as well. On that day we shall take our leisure and we
shall see; we shall see and love, love, and praise. What shall be in
the end shall be without end.

(De civ. Dei, 22.30)

Aristotle does not consider contemplation to belong to the *polis,*
while Augustine sees the vision of God as belonging only to the
city, not the earthly city but the heavenly city, the city of God, not
in its earthly sojourn but in its eternal repose.

Human blessedness understood as life in the City of God, in
contrast to the Greek understanding of blessedness as solitary,
apersonal contemplation, is both personal and communal. Augustine's claim that heavenly felicity "shall lack no good" *(De civ.
Dei,* 22.30) is followed by the assertion that "All the members and
organs of the incorruptible body . . . shall aid in the praises of
God" *(De civ. Dei,* 22.30). The resurrection of the body clearly
provides the foundation for the personal character of Christian
blessedness; for one's uniqueness is rooted in the uniqueness of
one's corporeal life. It is the altogether immaterial and therefore
unindividuated character of the agent intellect in Aristotle that
may be seen to account for the impersonal character of contemplation as well as for the absence of personal consciousness
after death. Blessedness, as Augustine understands it, involves joy,
delight, love, praise, memory, and gratitude as well as simply
vision. And blessedness is essentially communal, the celebration
of a city, of a delivered people.

I will be their God, and they shall be my people (Lv. 26.12). What
else did God mean in speaking thus through his prophet except to
say: I shall be the source of their fullness; I shall be whatever
human being honorably desires—life, health, nourishment, plenty,
glory, honor, peace, and all good things? This is also how the words
of the apostle are to be rightly understood when he says: that God
may be all in all (1 Cor. 15.28). God himself will be the completion

of our desires. Our sight of him will be without end, our love of him
without excess, our praise of him weariless. This liturgy, this
condition, this movement, will belong in truth to all and will be, like
eternal life itself, communal.

(De civ. Dei, 22.30)

It is this shared presence of God—beheld, loved, enjoyed, and
praised by all without weariness and without end—that is the bond
of the one true city, the city of God. In contrast with this, it seems
to be the distance and inaccessibility of God that for Aristotle
render impossible both fellowship with God and contemplative
fellowship among human beings. In Christian blessedness the love
of God is itself a bond of human community.

Our greatest reward is that we might enjoy him perfectly and that
all of us who enjoy him might even mutually enjoy one another in
him.

(De doct. chr., 1.32.35)

The inseparability of the two commandments of love, the unity of
love for God and love for one's neighbor, finds its perfect
expression in the fellowship of the communion of saints.

This brings us to Augustine's final understanding of the human
person, and so of human speech. The person is the mind's word;
the person is itself speech, which finally means neither creation
nor inquiry nor judgment nor faith but praise. Regarding the life
of the blessed in the city of God, Augustine asks:

What shall we do? . . . What will be there? What business shall we
have? What activity? . . . This will be our activity, the praise of God.

(En. in Ps., 85.23)

There it will be our whole task to praise and to enjoy the presence of
God . . . all our sorrows will be taken from us, and nothing will
remain but praise, unmixed and everlasting.

(En. in Ps., 86.8)

There, Alleluia will be our food, Alleluia our drink; Alleluia shall be
the activity of the peaceful. Our whole joy shall be Alleluia, which is

to say, the praise of God. For whose praises are without ceasing unless one whose delight is weariless?

(Serm., 252.9)

The vision of the blessed, then, is neither impersonal nor speechless, but is, rather, filled with speech precisely because of its personal and communal character.

In the eternal moment of vision and praise, when human being sees God as he is, the mind shall be perfectly renewed and made again after the image of God.

> Perhaps then our thoughts will not be inconstant, no longer passing from one thing to another. Rather, in a single moment's glance we shall see every knowledge. Yet, when even this will have come to pass, if indeed it does, the creature, once formable, will be formed so that nothing will be lacking to that form which it was to attain.
>
> *(De Trin., 15.16.26)*

The human mind, completed and shaped by the sight and knowledge of God who is pure form is sheer possibility, which recalls Aristotle's understanding of human being. Human life is finally a word of praise spoken by the mind, a word altogether faithful to and formed by the mind's full vision of its maker, "having nothing of itself, being wholly of that knowledge from which it is born" *(De Trin., 15.12.22)*. This final word is the mind's true word, the mind's true life, in which person and nature are perfectly one.

> The word that is true comes into being when that which I have said we cast about with inconstancy [i.e., that whereby we think first one thing, then another] attains to what we know and is formed by what we know, taking on wholly its likeness. ... Indeed, when our thinking attains to what we know and is therein formed, then our word is true.
>
> *(De Trin., 15.15.25-15.16.25)*

This word is at the same time God's word spoken both into time and immortally, although Augustine necessarily distinguishes the word that is the creature of God from the word that is the son of God, explaining that the human word is the word of a divine image "not born of God, but made by God" *(De Trin.,* 15.11.20), called out of nothingness by the creative word, called out of sin by the redemptive word, and perfected in the image of God by the eternal word.

> If to anyone the tumult of the flesh should grow silent, if the images of earth and sea and air grow silent, if the heavens grow silent, if the soul too would become silent and pass beyond itself by not thinking of itself, if all dreams and imagined visions should grow silent, every tongue, every sign, and whatever undergoes change, if all this would become wholly silent to someone—for if anyone would hear them, they say all these things: We have not made ourselves but he who dwells eternally made us—all this said, if there should now be silence ... and if he alone should speak, not through them but through himself, so that we would hear his word, not through a tongue of flesh, nor through the voice of an angel, not through the sound of thunder, nor through the riddle of a likeness, but so that we would hear himself whom we love in these things. If he alone should speak so that we would hear himself without them ... and if this would be continued without interruption, and if other visions of a far different kind would be taken away, and if this one vision should so seize and consume and steal away the see-er in inward joys so that life might be forever like that moment of understanding for which we sighed,[3] would this not be: Enter into the joy of the lord? (Mt. 25.21).
>
> *(Conf.,* 9.10)

Human speech, the life of human being, is finally, originally, and forever, a silence into which the word of God sounds and finds resonance.

---

3. This reference is to Augustine's and Monica's vision at Ostia.

CONCLUSION

There can be no question here of bringing this commentary to a conclusion. In fact, there is no conclusion to be drawn from the questions which we have raised as if together they related a fable which, once told, becomes transparent to a moral.

The question which Augustine raised in the activity of thinking and speaking was the question which he thereby became to himself, the question of human becoming and of human being, the question of person and of nature. This question, revealed and lived in the human word, is no clever riddle, composed by a mythical beast and dissolved by legendary wit. Still less is it a textual or linguistic question of a sort and scale to be dealt with by expertise and distance. The activity of the word, human-being-at-work, is closer to a circle than to a line, closer to a dance than to a march, closer to madness than to competence. Augustine's own thinking gives to us an image of this circle, this dance, this madness. The question, the inquiring word, which he first turns inward, back upon himself, becomes as large as life and larger still. To live is to question, to seek; and this lived quest strains against every limit. I suspect that Augustine loses us or that we lose Augustine as we endeavor to mind this quest with him, in his words. This particular loss seems inevitable and of slight consequence if we have meanwhile noticed the reach and the reality of the human word, the human question, which we have known with him. In reading Augustine with an open mind we find ourselves questioned and questioning. And so it should be when minds converse.

What must seem immediately questionable is Augustine's lived conviction that words, and thus lives, may be true or false. In fact, he once imagined the contrary, that words could strive no further than to be seemly and persuasive and that lives could at most be successful. As an ambitious rhetorician, he lived accordingly.

He asks us to imagine his shock in reading Cicero and in hearing Ambrose, when he reached the human age of discretion and came to discern the truthful word and the truthful life. At this point his words seem, to many, to become altogether undisciplined and arbitrary. What he would call the work of grace seems merely gratuitous. Augustine speaks in the service of an irrational doctrine, or so it must seem apart from the caprice or grace which moves him. Still, without avowing a single one of his doctrines, we may recognize the humanity of his questioning, the brilliant drivenness of his insights into the recesses of our deepest desires. By comparison, it is contemporary philosophy which is embarrassingly parochial and arbitrary.

Contemporary philosophy appears to bear the same relationship to thinking as does classical ballet to dancing. The mind, like the body, is rigorously, even torturously, trained to perform quite extraordinary operations utterly removed from instinct. And it is instinct, desire, passion clinging to thought like tendon and muscle to bone which we find in the thinking of Augustine.

Coleridge once wrote that a true teacher is one who excites power; and by this measure Augustine remains a true teacher. It is both possible and perhaps even more honest to participate in the power of Augustine's thinking, or rather in the power to which Augustine's thinking directs us, than to know that power under the same name as he. At its center, Augustine's thinking is a quest, an inquiry, and a seeking which is so unavoidably human that it cannot be said to prejudice the human. It is as real, or as unreal, as are we.

Questionable, too, is the humility of Augustine's thinking. It must seem so to an age which is characterized by nothing so much as its arrogance. This characteristically modern and Western pride, a cosmic pride dissembled or disavowed to no avail by all but the boldest thinkers, does not lie in the boundlessness of thinking and willing. Augustine gives himself to the same infinite restlessness. Rather, our pride lies in our claim that the endlessly elusive object of all human thinking and willing is, in fact, the product, the unwitting projection, of that very thinking and willing.

Nietzsche's Zarathustra speaks sheer secular prophecy when he calls upon the sun to give an account of itself:

> You great star, what would your happiness be had you not those for whom you shine?

Within the classical vision it is the sun which most perfectly images the good, the source of all being and knowing. Human being draws its light and life from this source as the eye draws upon the sun to illumine and empower its own activity. Nietzsche heralds a reversal, a fundamental upheaval in this vision. It is the sun which is needy and which is required to offer some account of itself. It is the sun which would be nothing without human vision. Rather than ask what human being would be without the gods, Nietzsche would have us ask what the gods would be without human being. In Augustinian terms Nietzsche's claim here is that divine being is made in the image of human being, all traditional delusions to the contrary. There is no god that is not an idol, no god that is not a graven image of human being. Idolatry is prohibited now no longer by piety but by lucidity. It is not human being that is nothing without God but God that is nothing without human being. God cannot look upon the face of human being and live.

Nevertheless, it remains a quite hypothetical question to ask what the gods or God would be without human being. It is a question of little consequence. For, even if an answer were available, of what conceivable interest could it be to us? Like so much of the modern critique of premodern religious and philosophical thinking, the intention of such a question is to dismiss and to ridicule that earlier vision. However, no amount of sheer dismissal and ridicule counts for refutation. We are always left with the necessity of asking what human being would be or is with or without divine being.

We surely need not accept Augustine's conviction that when human being ceases to serve the divine it is driven to serve the bestial. We may prefer to ask, with Camus, whether one can become a saint without God. Is there a secular image of human perfection, of human fullness of life, of human right-and-well-being which might inform our strivings and our judgments? Can we speak of human nature without God? Can we ask what it means to be or to become human without addressing this inquiry to God?

We seem able to know only what we have made; and what we have made, of ourselves or of our world, is cast always adrift upon a sea of what we have never made. We claim vast power; and, to be sure, the forces in which we meddle are vast. However, to possess power is not only to be able to summon it forth but to call it home as well. The truest sign of power lies not in troubling the seas but in calming them. The weakest child may turn a forest into an inferno; but only fools would call that true power. We may yet show ourselves capable of bringing about a last day, but can we bring about a first day? Our power is derivative. We mediate forces which we did not and cannot call forth from nothing. We are not primarily creators but knowers; and to knowers a degree of humility is essential. Here too Augustine is a true teacher.

Perhaps the most central and enduring question with which Augustine leaves us is this: If the human word is not essentially creative, what may it disclose? Above all, Augustine would have us see that the human word may serve to disclose the divine word—the creative word spoken in the beginning of time and the redemptive word spoken once for all time. All proper human speech is prophecy in which the eternal word sounds forth through the always temporal, always personal, human word. If, however, the human word misses its calling as prophecy and aspires to speak on its own behalf, it then engages in sheer mimicry. And, Augustine warns, the wages of such mimicry are death, a second and final death. Human speech gone awry and called to account possesses no more than the near-nothingness of a lie. To lie, to dissemble, to live hypothetically, is a peculiarly spiritual temptation; and to be caught forever in one's lie, to be forever what one is manifestly not, is a curse reserved for fallen spirit. Within the obscurity of time, to speak a lie may be as concrete, as substantial, as to speak a truth; but nothing is so abstract, so empty, so resourceless as a lie, once revealed.

To avoid this utter despoilment, Augustine would have us see the firmament of the world and the firmament of the Bible as foundations firmly laid, as perfect words already spoken, as texts upon which human speech, human life, is to be a homily. The human word is appropriately exegetical, self-effacing, and wishing to be nothing if not repetitive. Nothing is more central to the vision of Augustine than that human being must understand itself to be an image, a metaphor, a way of saying something else. Nothing is further from this vision than to claim that the human word is self-assertive, a blind command flung with naive futility nowhere. Confronted with such extremes, we find ourselves questioned and called upon to situate our own understandings.

For myself, to speak of the human word as an image of the divine word reaches beyond my experience and to speak of the human word as an image of itself falls short of my experience. I find myself bordered, defined by words which are too big and words which are too small. I simply do not know whether human questioning, human thinking shall in every or any instance truly disclose the reality of a living, self-disclosing God and the divinely analogous character of human reality. But with such imaginative prospects before me it seems quite obvious that what *I* may or may not understand at this moment is of little consequence. I do not honestly know where human thinking not shy of instinct, desire, and passion may lead; but I am as sure as I need be that human thinking embarrassed of instinct, desire, and passion leads nowhere. Somehow the risk of saying too much seems more worthy than the risk of saying too little. And, with Augustine as a companion, we need not gravely fear the latter.

BIBLIOGRAPHICAL GUIDE

This Guide is at best suggestive of the exhausting range of resources, primary and secondary, available for further Augustinian study. My own rather modest yet demanding recommendation for an initial serious study of the mind and the heart of Augustine would be to read *The Confessions, The City of God,* and *The Trinity,* in the translations of Warner, Dods, and McKenna, respectively, together with Peter Brown's *Augustine of Hippo.* And, when this has been completed, to read them all again.

PRIMARY WORKS

Latin Editions

CSEL   *Corpus Scriptorum Ecclesiasticorum Latinorum* (Vienna)

PL   *Patrologiae cursus completus. Series Latina,* ed. J. B. Migne (Paris)

The PL lists over 400 titles in its index of Augustine's complete works, while only a fraction (approximately 70 titles) of his works are available in English.

English Editions

ACW	*Ancient Christian Writers* (Westminster, Md.)
CUA	Catholic University of America, Patristic Studies (Washington)
E	*The Works of Aurelius Augustinus* (Edinburgh)
FC	*The Fathers of the Church* (Washington)
LCC	*Library of Christian Classics* (Philadelphia)
NPN	*A Select Library of Nicene and Post-Nicene Fathers* (New York)

Partial List of Augustine's Works

(Date)	(Title)	(Editions, vol. no.)
380	*De pulchro et apto* (On the Beautiful and the Fitting)	not extant
386	*Contra Academicos* (Against the Academics)	CSEL, 63; PL, 32; ACW, 12; FC, 5
386	*De beata vita* (On the Blessed Life)	CSEL, 63; PL, 32; CUA, 72; FC, 5
386	*De ordine* (On Order)	CSEL, 63; PL, 32; FC, 5
386-387	*Soliloquia* (Soliloquies)	PL, 32; FC, 5; FC, 5; LCC, 6
387	*De immortalitate animae* (On the Immortality of the Soul)	PL, 32; CUA, 90; FC, 4
387-389	*De musica* (On Music)	PL, 32; FC, 4

387-388	*De quanitate animae* (On the Greatness of the Soul)	PL, 32; ACW, 9; FC, 4
388-396	*De libero arbitrio* (On the Freedom of the Will)	CSEL, 74; PL, 32; ACW, 22; FC, 59
388-390	*De moribus ecclesiae catholicae, de moribus Manichaeorum* (On the Ways of the Catholic Church and of the Manichaeans)	PL, 32; E, 5; FC, 56; NPN, 4
388-389	*De Genesi contra Manichaeos* (On Genesis against the Manichaeans)	PL, 34
389-396	*Ad Simplicianum de diversis quaestionibus* (To Simplician, On Various Questions)	PL, 40; LCC, 6
389	*De magistro* (On the Teacher)	PL, 32; ACW, 9; FC, 59; LCC, 6
390	*De vera religione* (On True Religion)	PL, 34; LCC, 6
391-392	*De utilitate credendi* (On the Usefulness of Believing)	CSEL, 25, 1; PL, 42; FC, 4; LCC, 6; NPN, 3
391-392	*De duabus animabus* (On the Two Souls)	CSEL, 25, 1,; PL, 42; NPN, 4
392	*Acta contra Fortunatum Manichaeum* (Against Fortunatus the Manichaean)	CSEL, 25, 1; PL, 42; NPN, 4
392-420	*Ennarationes in Psalmos* (Expositions on the Psalms)	CSEL, 37; PL, 36; ACW, 29, 30; NPN, 8

393	*De fide et symbolo* (On Faith and the Creed)	CSEL, 41; PL, 40; E, 9; FC, 27; LCC, 6; NPN, 3
393	*De Genesi ad litteram opus imperfectum* (Unfinished Commentary on Genesis)	PL, 34
394	*De sermone Domini in monte* (On the Lord's Sermon on the Mount)	PL, 34; ACW, 5; E, 8; FC, 11; NPN, 6
394	*Expositio quarundam propositionum ex epistola ad Romanos* (Exposition of 84 Propositions Concerning the Epistle to the Romans)	CSEL, 84; PL, 35
395	*Expositio epistolae ad Galatas* (Exposition of the Epistle to the Galatians)	CSEL, 84; PL, 34
395	*Epistolae ad Romanos inchoata expositio* (Unfinished Exposition of the Epistle to the Romans)	CSEL, 84; PL, 35
396	*De agone christiana* (On the Christian Struggle)	CSEL, 41; PL, 40; FC, 2
396	*De doctrina christiana* (On Christian Instruction)	PL, 34; E, 9; CUA, 23; FC, 2; NPN, 2
397-400	*Confessiones* (Confessions)	CSEL, 33; PL, 32; E, 14; FC, 21; LCC, 7; NPN, 1
397-398	*Contra Faustum Manichaeum* (Against Faustus the Manichaean)	CSEL, 25, 1; PL, 42; E, 5; NPN, 4
397-400	*Quaestiones evangeliorum* (Questions of the Gospels)	PL, 35

399	*De natura boni* (On the Nature of the Good)	CSEL, 25, 2; PL, 42; CUA, 88; LCC, 6; NPN, 4
399	*Ad catechumenos de symbolo* (To the Catechumens, on the Creed)	PL, 40; FC, 27; NPN 3
399-400	*De catechizandis rudibus* (On Catechizing the Unlearned)	PL, 40; ACW, 2; CUA, 8; E, 9; NPN, 3
399-419	*De Trinitate* (On the Trinity)	PL, 42; E, 7; FC, 45; LCC, 8; NPN, 3
400	*De fide rerum quae non videntur* (On Faith in Things Unseen)	PL, 40; CUA, 84; FC, 4; NPN, 3
400	*De consensu evangelistarum* (On the Harmony of the Evangelists)	CSEL, 43; PL, 34; E, 8; NPN, 6
400-401	*De baptismo contra Donatistas* (On Baptism, Against the Donatists)	CSEL, 51; PL, 43; E, 3; NPN, 4
400-401	*De opere monachorum* (On the Work of Monks)	CSEL, 41; PL, 40; FC, 16; NPN, 3
401	*De bono conjugali* (On the Good of Marriage)	CSEL, 41; PL, 40; FC, 27; NPN, 3
401	*De sancta virginitate* (On Holy Virginity)	CSEL, 41; PL, 40; FC, 27; NPN, 3
401-405	*Contra litteras Petiliani* (Against the Writings of Petilianus)	CSEL, 52; PL, 43; E, 3; NPN, 4

401-414	*De Genesi ad litteram* (Literal Commentary on Genesis)	CSEL, 28, 1; PL, 34
406-411	*De divinatione daemonum* (On the Divination of Demons)	CSEL, 41; PL, 40; FC, 27
407-416	*Tractatus in epistolam Joannis ad Parthos* (Tracts on the First Epistle of John)	PL, 35; LCC, 8; NPN, 7
407-417	*Tractatus in Joannis evangelium* (Tracts on the Gospel of John)	PL, 35; E, 10, 11; NPN, 7
408-412	*De utilitate jejunii* (On the Usefulness of Fasting)	PL, 40; CUA, 85; FC, 16
410	*De urbis excidio* (On the Destruction of the City)	PL, 40; CUA, 89
411-412	*De peccatorum meritis et remissione* (On the Wages and the Remission of Sins)	CSEL, 60; PL, 44; E, 4; NPN, 5
412	*De Spiritu et littera* (On the Spirit and the Letter)	CSEL, 60; PL, 44; E, 4; LCC, 8; NPN, 5
412	*De continentia* (On Continence)	CSEL, 41; PL, 40; FC, 16; NPN, 3
413	*De fide et operibus* (On Faith and Works)	CSEL, 41; PL, 40; CUA, 47; FC, 27
413-427	*De civitate Dei* (On the City of God)	CSEL, 40; PL, 41; E, 12; FC, 8, 14, 24; NPN, 2
414	*De bono viduitatis* (On the Good of Widowhood)	CSEL, 41; PL, 40; FC, 16; NPN, 3

415	*De natura et gratia* (On Nature and Grace)	CSEL, 60, PL, 44; E, 4; NPN, 5
415-416	*De perfectione justitiae hominis* (On the Perfection of Human Righteousness)	CSEL, 42; PL, 44; E, 4; NPN, 5
417	*De gestis Pelagii* (On the Proceedings of Pelagius)	CSEL, 42; PL, 44; E, 4; NPN, 5
417	*De patientia* (On Patience)	CSEL, 41; PL, 40; FC, 16; NPN, 3
418	*De gratia Christi et de peccato originali* (On the Grace of Christ and Original Sin)	CSEL, 42; PL, 44; E, 12; NPN, 5
419-421	*De nuptiis et concupiscentia* (On Marriage and Concupiscence)	CSEL, 42; PL, 44; E, 12
419-421	*De anima et eius origine* (On the Soul and Its Origin)	CSEL, 60; PL, 44; E, 12; NPN, 5
419-421	*De coniugiis adulterinis* (On Adulterous Marriages)	CSEL, 41; PL, 40; FC, 27
420	*Contra mendacium* (Against Lying)	CSEL, 41; PL, 40; FC, 16; NPN, 3
420-421	*Contra duas epistolas Pelagianorum* (Against Two Pelagian Letters)	CSEL, 60, PL, 44; E, 15; NPN, 5
421	*Contra Julianum* (Against Julian)	PL, 44; FC, 35
421-423	*Echiridion ad Laurentium* (The Enchiridion)	PL, 40; ACW, 3; E, 9; FC, 2; LCC, 7; NPN, 3

421-424	*De cura pro mortuis gerenda* (On the Care to be Taken for the Dead)	CSEL, 41; PL, 40; FC, 27; NPN, 3
422-425	*De viii Dulcitii quaestionibus* (On the Eight Questions of Dulcitius)	PL, 40; FC, 16
426-427	*De gratia et libero arbitrio* (On Grace and Free Will)	PL, 44; E, 15; FC, 59; NPN, 5
426-427	*De correptione et gratia* (On Rebuke and Grace)	PL, 44; E, 15; FC, 2; NPN, 5
426-427	*Retractiones* (Retractions)	CSEL, 36; PL, 32; FC, 60
428-429	*De haeresibus ad Quodvultdeum* (To Quodvultdeum, on Heresies)	PL, 42; CUA, 90
428-429	*De praedestinatione sanctorum* (On the Predestination of the Saints)	PL, 44; E, 15; NPN, 5
428-429	*De dono perseverantiae* (On the Gift of Perseverance)	PL, 45; CUA, 91; E, 15; NPN, 5
429-430	*Tractatus adversus Judaeos* (Answer to the Jews)	PL, 42; FC, 27
386-429	*Epistolas* (Letters)	CSEL, 35, 44, 57, 58; PL, 33; E, 6, 13, FC, 12, 18, 20, 30, 32; NPN, 1
	Sermones (Sermons)	PL, 38, 39; ACW, 15; FC, 38; NPN, 6

SECONDARY WORKS

General Studies

Adam, Karl. *Die geistige Entwicklung des hl. Augustinus.* Darmstadt: Gentner, 1956.

Battenhouse, R. W. *A Companion to the Study of St. Augustine.* New York: Oxford University Press, 1955.

Bonner, Gerald. *St. Augustine of Hippo: Life and Controversies.* Philadelphia: Westminster, 1963.

Bourke, V. J. *Augustine's Quest for Wisdom: Life and Philosophy of the Bishop of Hippo.* Milwaukee: Bruce, 1945.

Brown, Peter. *Augustine of Hippo, A Biography.* Berkeley: University of California Press, 1967.

———. *Religion and Society in the Age of Saint Augustine.* London: Faber and Faber, 1972.

Burnaby, John. *Amor Dei: A Study of the Religion of St. Augustine.* London: Hodder and Staughton, 1938.

Dorner, August. *Augustinus. Sein theologisches System und seine religions-philosophische Anschauung.* Berlin: Wilhelm Hertz, 1873.

Gilson, Etienne. *The Christian Philosophy of St. Augustine.* New York: Random House, 1960.

Jaspers, Karl. *Plato and Augustine.* New York: Harcourt, Brace & World, 1962.

Markus, R. A., ed. *Augustine: A Collection of Critical Essays.* New York: Doubleday, 1972.

Marrou, Henri Irénée. *St. Augustine and His Influence Through the Ages.* London: Longmans, 1957.

———. *Saint Augustin et la fin de la culture antique.* Paris: Boccard, 1938. "Retractio," 1946.

Roy, Oliver (Jean-Baptiste) du. "Augustine." *New Catholic Encyclopedia,* I, 1041-1058.

TeSelle, Eugene. *Augustine the Theologian.* New York: Herder and Herder, 1970.

Van der Meer, F. *Augustine the Bishop.* Translated by Brian Battershaw and G. R. Lamb. London and New York: Sheed and Ward, 1961.

West, Rebecca. *St. Augustine.* New York: Nelson, 1938.

Special Studies

Alfaric, Prosper. *L'Evolution intellectuelle de saint Augustine. I. Du manichéisme au néoplatonisme.* Paris: E. Nourry, 1918.

Arendt, Hannah. *Der Liebesbegriff bei Augustinus. Versuch einer philosophischen Interpretation.* Berlin, 1929.

Arnou, René. "Le thème néoplatonicien de la contemplation créatrice chez Origène et chez saint Augustin." *Gregorianum,* XIII (1932), 124-136.

Ball, Joseph. "Libre arbitre et liberté dans saint Augustin." *Année théologique augustinienne,* VI (1945), 368-382.

———. "Les développements de la doctrine de la liberté chez saint Augustin." *Année théologique augustinienne,* VII (1946), 400-430.

Berlinger, Rudolf. *Augustins dialogische Metaphysik.* Frankfurt: Klostermann, 1962.

Boyer, Charles. *Essais sur la doctrine de saint Augustin.* Paris: Beauchesne, 1932.

———. *L'Idee de vérité dans la philosophie de s. Augustin.* Paris: Beauchesne, 1940.

Brunhemer, Anne. "The Art of Augustine's Confession." *Thought,* XXXVII (1962), 109-128.

Burrell, David. "Reading *The Confessions* of Augustine: An Exercise in Theological Understanding." *Journal of Religion,* L (1970), 327-351.

Cayré, Fulbert. *La contemplation augustinienne. Principes de spiritualité et de théologie.* Paris: Desclée de Brouwer, 1927.

———. "Le mysticisme de la sagesse dans les Confessions et le De Trinitate de s. Augustin." *Année Théologique Augustinienne,* XIII (1953), 347-363.

———. *Les sources de l'amour divin. La divine présence d'après saint Augustin.* Paris: Desclée de Brouwer, 1933.

Chevalier, Irénée. *S. Augustin et la pensée grecque. Les relations trinitaires.* Fribourg en Suisse: Collectanea Friburgensia, 1940.

Courcelle, Pierre. *Recherches sur les 'Confessions' de saint Augustin.* Paris: Boccard, 1950.

———."Source chrétienne et allusions païennes de l'épisode du 'Tolle, lege.' " *Revue d'histoire et de philosophie religieuse,* XXXII (1952), 171-200.

Dodds, E. R. "Augustine's Confessions: A Study of Spiritual Maladjustment." *Hibbert Journal,* 26 (1927-28), 459-473.

Fortin, Ernest. *Christianisme et culture philosophique au cinquième siècle. La querelle de l'âme humaine en Occident.* Paris: Etudes Augustiniennes, 1959.

——. "Saint Augustin et la doctrine néoplatonicienne de l'âme." *AM,* III, 371-380.

Guitton, Jean. *Le temps et l'éternité chez Plotin et saint Augustin.* Paris: Boivin, 1933.

Hassel, David J. "Conversion-Theory and *Scientia* in the *De Trinitate.*" *RA,* II (1962), 282-401.

Henry, Paul. *La vision d'Ostie. Sa place dans la vie et l'oeuvre de S. Augustin.* Paris: J. Vrin, 1938.

——. *Saint Augustine on Personality.* New York: Macmillan, 1960.

Holte, Ragnar. *Beatitude et Sagesse: S. Augustin et le problème de la fin de l'homme dans la philosophie ancienne.* Paris: Etudes Augustiniennes, 1962.

Jonas, Hans. *Augustin und das paulinische Freiheitsproblem.* Göttingen: Vandenhoeck & Ruprecht, 1965.

Körner, Franz. "Deus in homine videt. Das Subjekt des menschlichen Erkennens nach der Lehre Augustins." *Philosophisches Jahrbuch,* LXIV (1956), 166-217.

——. *Das Sein und der Mensch. Die existentiellen Seinsentdeckung des jungen Augustin. Grundlagen zur Erbellung seiner Ontologie.* Freiburg and Munich: Karl Alber, 1959.

Löhrer, Magnus. "Glaube und Heilsgeschichte in 'De Trinitate' Augustins." *Freiburger Zeitschrift für Philosophie und Theologie,* IV (1957), 385-419.

Lorenz, Rudolph. "Fruitio Dei bei Augustin." *Zeitschrift für Kirchengeschichte,* LXII (1950), 75-132.

Maréchal, Joseph. "La vision de Dieu au sommet de la contemplation d'après saint Augustin." *Nouvelle revue théologique,* LVII (1930), 89-109, 191-204.

Maritain, Jacques. "De la sagesse augustinienne." *Revue de Philosophie* (1930), 715-741.

Markus, R. A. " 'Imago' and 'Similitudo' in Augustine." *Revue des études augustiniennes,* XI (1964), 125-143.

O'Connell, Robert J. *St. Augustine's Confessions: The Odyssey of Soul.* Cambridge: Harvard University Press, 1969.

——. *St. Augustine's Early Theory of Man, A.D. 386-391.* Cambridge: Harvard University Press, 1968.

O'Meara, John J. *The Charter of Christendom: The Significance of the City of God.* New York: Macmillan, 1961.

———. *The Young Augustine: The Growth of St. Augustine's Mind up to His Conversion*. London: Longmans, Green, 1954.

O'Toole, Christopher J. *The Philosophy of Creation in the Writings of St. Augustine*. Washington: Catholic University Press of America, 1944.

Roy, Olivier (Jean-Baptiste) du. "L'expérience de l'amour et l'intelligence de la foi trinitaire selon saint Augustin." *RA*, II (1962), 414-445.

———. *L'Intelligence de la foi en la Trinité selon saint Augustin. Genèse de sa théologie trinitaire jusqu'en 391*. Paris: Etudes Augustiniennes, 1966.

Schindler, Alfred. *Wort und Analogie in Augustine Trinitätslehre*. Hermeneutische Untersuchungen zur Theologie, IV. Tübingen: J. C. B. Mohr, 1965.

Schmaus, Michael. "Die Denkform Augustins in seinem Werk *de Trinitate*." Sitzungsberichte de bayerischen Akademie der Wissenschaften, Philosophische-historische Klasse, 1962, no. 6.

———. *Die psychologische Trinitätslehre des hl. Augustinus*. Münsterische Beiträge zur Theologie, XI. Münster: Aschendorff, 1927.

Schneider, Rudolph. *Seele und Sein. Ontologie bei Augustin und Aristoteles*. Stuttgart: Kohlhammer, 1957.

Sullivan, John Edward. *The Image of God: The Doctrine of Saint Augustine and Its Influence*. Dubuque: Priory Press, 1963.

Tremblay, R. "La théorie psychologique de la Trinité chez s. Augustin." *Etudes et Recherches* (Ottawa), VIII (1952), 83-109.

———. "Les processions du verbe et de l'amour humains chez s. Augustin." *Revue de l'Université d'Ottawa* 24 (1954) 93-117.

Verbeke, Gérard. "Connaissance de soi et connaissance de Dieu chez s. Augustin." *Augustinian* (Heverlee-Leuven), IV (1954), 495-515.

Versfeld, Marthinus. *A Guide to the City of God*. London: Sheed and Ward, 1958.

INDEX TO CITATIONS FROM AUGUSTINE'S WORKS

307

INDEX

313